A Critique of Politeness Theories

Gino Eelen

IPrA Research Center
University of Antwerp (UIA)

Routledge
Taylor & Francis Group

LONDON AND NEW YORK

First published 2001 by St. Jerome Publishing

Published 2014 by Routledge
2 Park Square, Milton Park, Abingdon, Oxon OX14 4RN
711 Third Avenue, New York, NY 10017, USA

Routledge is an imprint of the Taylor & Francis Group, an informa business

Notices
Knowledge and best practice in this field are constantly changing. As new research and experience broaden our understanding, changes in research methods, professional practices, or medical treatment may become necessary.

Practitioners and researchers must always rely on their own experience and knowledge in evaluating and using any information, methods, compounds, or experiments described herein. In using such information or methods they should be mindful of their own safety and the safety of others, including parties for whom they have a professional responsibility.

To the fullest extent of the law, neither the Publisher nor the authors, contributors, or editors, assume any liability for any injury and/or damage to persons or property as a matter of products liability, negligence or otherwise, or from any use or operation of any methods, products, instructions, or ideas contained in the material herein.

ISBN 13: 978-1-900650-40-3 (pbk)

Cover design by
Steve Fieldhouse, Oldham, UK

Typeset by
Delta Typesetters, Cairo, Egypt

British Library Cataloguing in Publication Data
A catalogue record of this book is available from the British Library

Library of Congress Cataloguing in Publication Data
Eelen, Gino.
   A critique of politeness theories / Gino Eelen.
      p. cm. -- (Encounters, ISSN 1471-0277)
   Includes bibliographical references and index.
      ISBN 1-900650-41-X (hardback : alk. paper) -- ISBN 1-900650-40-1 (pbk.
:   )
      1. Courtesy. 2. Sociolinguistics. I. Title. II. Encounters
(Manchester, England)
      BJ1533.C9 E45 2001
      177'.1—dc21
                              2001000426

Encounters

A new series on language and diversity
Edited by Jan Blommaert & Chris Bulcaen

Diversity has come to be recognized as one of the central concerns in our thinking about society, culture and politics. At the same time, it has proved one of the most difficult issues to deal with on the basis of established theories and methods, particularly in the social sciences. Studying diversity not only challenges widespread views of who we are and what we do in social life; it also challenges the theories, models and methods by means of which we proceed in studying diversity. Diversity exposes the boundaries and limitations of our theoretical models, in the same way it exposes our social and political organizations.

Encounters sets out to explore diversity *in* language, diversity *through* language and diversity *about* language. Diversity *in* language covers topics such as intercultural, gender, class or age-based variations in language and linguistic behaviour. Diversity *through* language refers to the way in which language and linguistic behaviour can contribute to the construction or negotiation of such sociocultural and political differences. And diversity *about* language has to do with the various ways in which language and diversity are being perceived, conceptualized and treated, in professional as well as in lay knowledge – thus including the reflexive and critical study of scientific approaches alongside the study of language politics and language ideologies. In all this, mixedness, creolization, crossover phenomena and heterogeneity are privileged areas of study. The series title, *Encounters*, is intended to encourage a relatively neutral but interested stance towards diversity, moving away from the all too obvious 'cultures-collide' perspective that is dominant within the social sciences.

The target public of *Encounters* includes scholars and advanced students of linguistics, communication studies, anthropology, cultural studies, sociology, as well as students and scholars in neighbouring disciplines such as translation studies, gender studies, gay and lesbian studies, postcolonial studies.

Jan Blommaert is former Research Director of the IPrA Research Centre of the University of Antwerp and currently Professor of African linguistics at the University of Ghent. His publications include *Debating Diversity* (co-author, 1998), the *Handbook of Pragmatics* (co-editor, 1995-2003), *The Pragmatics of Intercultural and International Communication* (co-editor, 1991), and *Language Ideological Debates* (editor, 1999).

Chris Bulcaen studied African Philology and History (University of Ghent) and Cultural Studies (University of Lancaster), and has worked for the IPrA Research Centre in Antwerp, where he mainly did ethnographic and discourse-analytic research in the field of social work and immigration. He currently works for the Department of English at the University of Ghent and is co-editor of the *Handbook of Pragmatics* (1994-2003).

Contents

Acknowledgements

Any scientific work is always the result of a long process of contemplation, organization and discussion, and synthesizes ideas formed and matured through conversations with people, publications and other sources of information, many not even directly concerned with the topic at hand. So the list of people who have directly or indirectly contributed to the ideas outlined in this publication is very long, and only a few can be mentioned here. With this in mind, I would like to extend my special thanks to Jef Verschueren, whose support has made possible most of the research on which this book is based, and to Jan Blommaert for his invaluable feedback and much appreciated encouragement throughout all stages of its conception. Also many thanks to Manfred Kienpointner, Shigeko Okamoto and Robert Arundale for their insightful remarks and trying questions, and to Chris Bulcaen for helping to give the book its final structure. The Belgian National Science Foundation (FWO) and the University of Antwerp provided financial backing for most of the analytical endeavour, while my wife Katia provided the necessary moral and emotional support.

Introduction

Politeness

Politeness is a commonsense term with a considerable history, going back to at least the sixteenth century (see, for example Burke 1993; Ehlich 1992; Elias 1978[1939]). Although it is easily and seemingly transparently glossed as the *"quality of being polite"*, which in turn refers to *"having or showing that one has good manners and consideration for other people"* (*Oxford Advanced Learner's Dictionary*), associated terms such as 'civility', 'courtesy', 'good manners', or translations such as French *courtoisie*, German *Höflichkeit*, Italian *cortesia* and *urbanità* or Dutch *beschaafdheid*, *beleefdheid* and *hoffelijkheid*, point up various associative connections: to 'civil society', 'civilization', life at court and in the city, or the general quality of having 'life-experience' (Dutch *be-leefd-heid*). Thus, historically a number of different factors seem to be involved in determining politeness: aspects of social hierarchy (the court) and social status (life in the city), but also a more general notion of 'proper behavioural conduct'. Its meaning is therefore not as straightforwardly clear and simple as may seem at first sight, as during its long historical life, it has gathered a complex of interconnecting associative meanings.

But politeness is also a well-established scholarly concept, basic to 'politeness theory' – one of the more popular branches of contemporary pragmatics, and a widely used tool in studies of intercultural communication. Dufon et al.'s (1994) bibliography of politeness-related publications comprises 51 pages in small print – with an explicit denial of any claim for exhaustiveness – and a great many have appeared since its publication. But the popularity politeness has enjoyed as a research topic in the last quarter of a century is not always matched by theoretical or conceptual clarity. The notion has received a myriad of different definitions and interpretations, ranging from a general principle of language use governing all interpersonal aspects of interaction, to the use of specific linguistic forms and formulae. As a result, it is not always easy to determine the status of any new piece of research in terms of its precise place within the field, or in terms of the relationship of its empirical data and claims *vis-à-vis* those of other researchers. Obviously, empirical analyses based on disparate theoretical approaches are not automatically or even necessarily compatible. In order to compare research results meaningfully, as well as to gain a coherent view of the field, one needs at least a clear insight into the relative positions of the results of different studies.

Although a number of excellent overviews of the field have been published, such as Fraser (1990), Kasper (1990, 1996), or the introductory chapters to the many special issues of journals or other edited volumes on the subject (for example, Watts et al. 1992), they constitute in essence topographical efforts to chart the terrain. Glossing the basic tenets of different theoretical approaches, they are usually more focused on the distinctive features of one theory versus another rather than on mutual similarities. What seems to be missing is an examination of how the different perspectives are mutually related by theoretical similarities and points of overlap, as well as a look beneath the surface, going beyond the features of the terrain to look at the underlying assumptions from which these topographical features arise. The present analysis attempts to show how both objectives can be attained simultaneously. By unearthing the epistemological and ontological foundations on which politeness theory is built, a geological instead of a topographical effort reveals a single theoretical substratum underlying all of the theoretical perspectives, a common ideology that unites even the most disparate conceptualizations into a coherent whole.

The exercise undertaken here follows Figeroa's (1994) metatheoretical investigation of sociolinguistics, where she examines three leading paradigms (Hymes, Labov and Gumperz) in terms of their underlying presuppositions regarding the nature of language. Her leading question – 'what sort of linguistics is sociolinguistics'– is answered by looking at the paradigms' fundamental, and often implicit, ideas and notions about the basic characteristics, constituents, internal structural relationships, functions etc., of language. Although it does not lie within her aim and scope, Figeroa remarks that a similar analysis could be made regarding the nature of society and culture. The leading question would then be 'what sort of anthropology/sociology is sociolinguistics?', and its answer would involve basic ideas and presuppositions about the structure of society, how it comes into being, how it is maintained, how it relates to individual human beings, etc. The present analysis of politeness will to some extent explore both of these avenues, by examining current conceptualizations of politeness in terms of their social and linguistic presuppositions. The emphasis will largely be on the social, however, and linguistic aspects will be considered mostly for their contribution to the social worldview.

But the present analysis is also different from Figeroa's. Besides questions about language and society, it also explores how their relationship is implicitly conceptualized, while still other questions will concern elements of scientific epistemology and methodology. A further difference lies in the fact that the analysis does not aim to be exhaustive about any of these issues. The search for presuppositions is strictly relative to the investigative aims of a more in-depth comparative overview of the field, and the formulation of a critique. And that critique will then be used as the starting point for the development of an alternative approach to the study of politeness.

So although definitely an investigation of politeness theory, the conceptualizations of politeness themselves will be of lesser interest here than the sociolinguistic presuppositions on which they are built. The latter will be examined by looking at the implications of specific conceptual choices and constructions for the conceptualization of language and social reality. But as the notion of 'presuppositions' already indicates, such an analysis not only involves the researchers' explicit theoretical claims and constructions, but also any implicit information that can be derived from those claims as well as from the 'ordinary language' used by researchers in 'non-critical' passages – passages without definitions, claims or conclusions, but where, for example, incidental comments are made, examples are discussed, or matters are explicated through the use of metaphors, intuitive notions or commonsense language. The analysis will thus examine the scientific texts *as a whole*, not only those parts that indulge in explicit theorizing, nor even only those that are concerned with politeness. Moreover, the focus of the analysis will be on the scientific texts *as texts*, as discourses on language and society. In this sense, instead of real-world politeness examples, the empirical data for the investigation are the scientific texts themselves, which will be examined for the implicit clues they contain regarding the nature of social reality.

Scope and motivation

Although politeness has received various amounts of attention from all areas of linguistics throughout the twentieth century (Held 1992), the present study will only cover politeness research as it is carried out within the field of contemporary sociolinguistics and linguistic pragmatics – in a broad definition, as outlined in Verschueren et al. (1995, 1996). Furthermore, for practical reasons, the investigation will be restricted to the Anglo-Saxon research tradition. Together, these restrictions entail that the period under examination covers roughly the last quarter of the twentieth century, beginning with Lakoff's (1973) discussion of politeness in terms of Grice's theory of linguistic cooperation. Although this imposes some limitations on the scope of the analysis, it still covers a vast amount of literature. And, as will be argued in the Chapter 1, at least a number of non-Anglo-Saxon works are based on theories incorporated here, so their approaches are equally relevant to the conclusions of the present analysis.

The commonsense definition of politeness in terms of 'proper behaviour' points out that politeness is not confined to language, but can also include non-verbal, non-linguistic behaviour. Most people will be familiar with examples of politeness such as holding the door open for someone, greeting someone with a wave of the hand or a nod and so on. Politeness may manifest itself in any form of behaviour, and even in the absence of behaviour: on many social occasions, not returning a greeting or simply remaining silent may be interpreted as impoliteness, whereas in a library or church, talking aloud may be regarded as impolite and politeness involves refraining from speech. Other non-linguistic behavioural options such as bodily proximity, gazing behaviour and so on may all be interpreted in terms of (im)politeness. Staring at a stranger for too long, or peering extensively into someone else's home through a window, may quickly elicit hostile reactions. So the scope of politeness stretches well beyond purely verbal choices, and includes the whole spectrum of behaviour, as is clearly illustrated by another stock example of politeness: table manners, which include guidelines for verbal as well as non-verbal behaviour. This broad scope will be retained in the present analysis, which will refer to examples of verbal as well as non-verbal behaviour. Most of the theoretical claims, however, will be focused on linguistic behaviour. This is mainly a reflection of a similar preoccupation in the majority of existing theories and should not be interpreted as a restriction in scope. Claims about linguistic practices can easily be extrapolated to the non-linguistic domain, as the important thing for politeness is not so much the verbal or non-verbal nature of the behaviour in question, but rather how it is evaluated. These evaluations can be applied to both forms without implying any major changes in the underlying notion of politeness.

But the aims of the analysis also reach beyond the field of politeness proper. One of the interesting aspects of politeness is the fact that it is situated at the intersection of language and social reality. The commonsense notion of politeness relates language to aspects of social structure (life at the court and in the city) as well as behavioural codes and ethics ('proper' behaviour). As such, its study can be of value for understanding how society and ethics are connected to language and to behaviour in general, and provide a deeper insight into how society is established and maintained through interaction. This pivotal position of politeness as a link between language and social reality is also found in current theorizing, where politeness as a form of language use is invariably coupled with social relationships and social roles, and through these to the large-scale social phenomena of society and culture. So besides politeness itself, the present study also aims to contribute to our understanding of social reality and its connection to language and interaction.

True to its metatheoretical perspective, a second, broader aim of the analysis is to make a contribution to theory formation in pragmatics. As a critique of politeness theory, it aims to contribute to the tradition of critical reflexive metatheoretical research within the social sciences. Besides Figeroa's research, the analysis will also refer to work by Williams (1992). Both writers focus on the scientific tradition of sociolinguistics, examining its underlying fundamental presuppositions about language and society respectively. Other examples of critical reflexive research include Taylor & Cameron (1987), who criticize what they call the 'rules and units approach' in the majority of work on the analysis of conversation, where research is focused on the identification of all kinds of 'interactional units' which are then explained by reference to 'interactional rules'. Methodology is also the focus of Blommaert (1997), who examines the notion of 'evidence' in pragmatics – what is taken to count as 'data' in the practice of 'doing' pragmatics – examined in the interactional context of a workshop. In other areas, the notion of intentionality has been the focus of much reflection, as evidenced by, for example Du Bois (1987), Duranti (1988) or Rosaldo (1982), while the Gricean notion of cooperation has been questioned by, for example Sarangi & Slembrouck (1992). Situating the present analysis within this reflexive critical tradition implies that its aim will not so much be to investigate the social reality of politeness as it occurs and lives among ordinary speakers, but also and primarily the *scientific* social reality of politeness: the way scientists have handled the notion in their theoretical endeavours, as well as how it is related to other areas of scientific thinking.

Besides the negative aspects of a critique, the analysis also aims to make a more positive contribution to theory formation, by the proposal of an alternative framework that provides an answer to the issues raised by the critique. This alternative approach is fundamentally different from any of the existing perspectives because it is based on a different sociolinguistic ideology, which allows it to explore theoretical avenues that have up to now been left unexplored. It relies on an alternative view of the language-social reality interface that incorporates an element largely ignored by current theorizing: the individual. Instead of a two-sided relationship with language on one side and social reality on the other, it argues for a triple distinction, where language functions as the mediating factor between social and individual reality. In this way, the analysis makes the case for an integrated view of social reality, where aspects of linguistics, social theory and psychology combine into one coherent whole.

From the observation that politeness is a commonsense as well as a scientific notion, the analysis sets out to explore the relationship between these two notions, both on a general theoretical level as well as on the more concrete level of how existing frameworks integrate it into their conceptualizations. It is shown how this trivial but crucial epistemological distinction is insufficiently accounted for by the theories. This disregard leads to a number of common conceptual characteristics, each of which introduces certain problematic elements into the theoretical models, and all of which cooperate to form a coherent outlook on social and linguistic reality. This worldview and its associated problematic aspects are then used as input for the development of the alternative approach. Apart from individual reality, this alternative view introduces a number of additional elements that fall outside the theoretical grasp of traditional conceptualizations. A focus on the evaluative aspects of politeness leads to a contemplation of the notion of argumentativity, which in combination with a greater emphasis on variability results in a more dynamic view of social and individual reality, allowing the incorporation of historicity and social evolution. Finally, all of these elements together lead to a radical reinterpretation of the nature and role of normativity, both in politeness and in social reality in general.

Overview of the book

This book is divided into six chapters. Chapter 1 introduces the nine theories that will be the object of investigation, explains the logic behind the selection process, and argues for the general representativeness of the selected frameworks for the entire field of politeness research. Chapters 2 to 5 form the actual core of the analysis. Each focuses on one general aspect of politeness theorizing that leads to the identification of a number of mutually interrelated paradigmatic presuppositions that are each examined in detail for their origins and theoretical consequences. In Chapter 2, the distinction between 'commonsense' and 'scientific' notions of politeness is discussed, and each of the nine perspectives is tested for its epistemological position on the issue. Chapter 3 queries the theories' positions on three further distinctions: between politeness and impoliteness, between speaker and hearer and between language production and reception. The analysis reveals a distinct and consistent conceptual bias towards one side of each of the distinctions, causing the other side to disappear from view. In Chapter 4, normativity is identified as a crucial aspect of politeness. After an examination of its constituent dimensions and a review of its various manifestations in politeness theory, it is argued that it is mostly handled in a fundamentally inadequate way. As the last of the analytical chapters, Chapter 5 shows how the various conceptual choices discussed in previous chapters influence the frameworks' implicit views on society and the individual. The distinctive Parsonian flavour of their common social worldview combines with a rather meagre and bleak picture of individual reality. On the basis of Bourdieu's sociological thinking, in combination with insights from discursive psychology, a possible alternative conceptualization of politeness is sketched, one that presents a more balanced picture of social and individual reality and is able to cope adequately with many if not all of the issues and problems raised in previous chapters. Finally, the concluding chapter summarizes the main arguments and findings, discusses a few additional aspects of the alternative view on politeness, and explores possible routes for further analysis.

Chapter 1: Theories of politeness

Within the Anglo-Saxon scientific tradition, politeness research is carried out from the perspective of linguistic pragmatics and sociolinguistics. All theories considered here agree they belong to either of these linguistic subfields, the consensus deriving from the fact that politeness has to do with language, and more specifically language *use* – which warrants its classification within pragmatics – and that it is a phenomenon which connects language with the social world – which warrants the 'socio-' prefix. So although the pragmatic and sociolinguistic perspectives can to a greater or lesser degree be distinguished from one another depending on their exact definition and delimitation, for the present discussion they unite the field of politeness theory, in that politeness is invariably seen as a phenomenon connected with (the relationship between) language and social reality.

Beyond this general level, however, agreement is much harder to find, as each theory more or less has its own (private) definition of politeness. In fact, the vast majority of publications on politeness contribute to some extent to theory formation on the subject. In order to reduce this mass of theoretical claims and innovations to manageable proportions, a selection has to be made. And it appears, in the light of the search for underlying linguistic and social ideologies, not all theoretical claims are equally important. On this basis, many theoretical amendments and innovations to existing theories can be excluded because the changes they propose do not touch the linguistic or social presuppositions of the existing theory on which they are based. Likewise, theories that are based on the same presuppositions as other theories can be left out. In such cases only the oldest or most widely known framework is retained. On the other hand, a theory that perhaps only tackles a small aspect of politeness but does so by introducing elements that significantly distinguish its social worldview from that of other (more encompassing) frameworks is retained in the final selection. So neither size nor renown were used as criteria in their own right, and therefore the term 'theory' must be taken in rather a broad sense, as it may refer to more or less elaborated models of politeness; that is to say, not all theories are equally well-developed, nor elaborated to the greatest possible detail.

In the end, this method has led to a selection of nine theories which form the basis of this study, and which are introduced in the following sections. Their main outlines will be sketched and their distinguishing features highlighted. No in-depth discussion is provided at this point, as each theory will be the subject of further – and closer – scrutiny at various points throughout the remainder of the presentation.

1.1 Theories of politeness: an overview

1.1.1 Robin T. Lakoff

Robin Lakoff could well be called the mother of modern politeness theory, for she was one of the first to examine it from a decidedly pragmatic perspective.[1] She defines politeness as *"[…] a system of interpersonal relations designed to facilitate interaction by minimizing the potential for conflict and confrontation inherent in all human interchange"* (Lakoff 1990:34).

With roots in Generative Semantics (Lakoff 1989b), Lakoff used politeness to point out certain weaknesses of traditional linguistic theory, and did this by connecting politeness with Grice's Cooperative Principle (CP). Grice's theory rests on the assumption that people are intrinsically cooperative and aim to be as informative as possible in communication, with informativeness referring to a maximally efficient information transfer. These assumptions are captured by the CP and its associated maxims of Quantity, Quality, Relation and Manner, which function as rules of linguistic behaviour governing linguistic production and interpretation. When they are followed (which according to Grice is the default situation), maximally informative communication or clarity is reached. However, they can also be flouted, in which case special interpretive processes are triggered. In this way, people can come to mean more than they literally say, and be understood as such. In short, the CP and its maxims aim to explain how it is that people can understand each other beyond the literal words that are spoken. However, in normal informal conversation, the CP and its maxims are almost never strictly followed, and in order to account for this, Lakoff proposed a 'politeness rule', on a par with the Gricean 'clarity rule' and complementing it:

> […] if one seeks to communicate a message directly, if one's principal aim in speaking is communication, one will attempt to be clear, so that there is no mistaking one's intention. If the speaker's principal aim is to navigate somehow or other among the respective statuses of the participants in the discourse indicating where each stands in the

---

[1] Relevant publications: Lakoff 1973, 1977, 1979, 1984, 1989a, 1989b, 1990, 1995; Lakoff & Tannen 1979.

> speaker's estimate, his aim will be less the achievement of clarity
> than an expression of politeness, as its opposite. (Lakoff 1973:296)

Thus, whereas the CP is geared to the 'information content' of communication, the politeness rule attends to social issues. If hearers notice that speakers do not seem to be following the Gricean maxims to the fullest, they search for a plausible explanation in the politeness rule: if speakers are not maximally clear, then maybe they are trying to avoid giving offence. In all, three such politeness rules are envisaged: 'Don't impose' (rule 1), 'Give options' (rule 2) and 'Make A feel good, be friendly' (rule 3, 'A' being 'Alter') (Lakoff 1973:298). Although these rules are all to some extent always present in any interaction, different cultures tend to emphasize one or other of them. Thus, definitions of politeness – of how to be polite – differ interculturally. Depending on which of the rules is most important, cultures can be said to adhere to a strategy of Distance (rule 1), Deference (rule 2), or Camaraderie (rule 3) (Lakoff 1990:35). Distance is characterized as a strategy of impersonality, Deference as hesitancy, and Camaraderie as informality. Roughly, European cultures tend to emphasize Distancing strategies, Asian cultures tend to be Deferential, and modern American culture tends towards Camaraderie.

1.1.2 Penelope Brown and Stephen C. Levinson

Although not the first, Brown & Levinson's theory is certainly the most influential – witness the innumerable reactions, applications, critiques, modifications and revisions their 1978/1987 publication has triggered, and still does (a few of the more recent examples are Bilbow 1995, Macauley 1995, O'Driscoll 1996, Kerbrat-Orecchioni 1997, Lee-Wong 1998).[2] The names Brown & Levinson have become almost synonymous with the word 'politeness' itself, or as one researcher puts it, *"it is impossible to talk about it without referring to Brown & Levinson's theory"* (Kerbrat-Orecchioni 1997:11).

Like Lakoff, Brown & Levinson see politeness in terms of conflict avoidance, but their explanatory toolbox differs substantially from Lakoff's. The central themes are 'rationality' and 'face', which are both claimed to be universal features, i.e. possessed by all speakers and hearers – personified in a universal Model Person. Rationality is a means-ends reasoning or logic, while face consists of two opposing 'wants': negative face, or the want that one's actions be unimpeded by others, and

---

[2] Relevant publications: Brown & Levinson 1978, 1987; Brown 1990.

positive face, or the want that one's wants be desirable to (at least some) others. The theory claims that most speech acts inherently threaten either the hearer's or the speaker's face-wants, and that politeness is involved in redressing those face-threats. On this basis, three main strategies for performing speech acts are distinguished: positive politeness (the expression of solidarity, attending to the hearer's positive face-wants), negative politeness (the expression of restraint, attending to the hearer's negative face-wants) and off-record politeness (the avoidance of unequivocal impositions, for example hinting instead of making a direct request).

Brown & Levinson also relate their theory with the Gricean framework, in that politeness strategies are seen as 'rational deviations' from the Gricean CP. But politeness has a totally different status from the CP: whereas the CP is presumptive – it is the 'unmarked', 'socially neutral' strategy, the natural presupposition underlying all communication – politeness needs to be communicated. It can never be simply presumed to be operative, it must be signalled by the speaker. Politeness principles are "principled reasons for deviation" from the CP when communication is about to threaten face (Brown & Levinson 1987:5).

The amount and kind of politeness that is applied to a certain speech act is determined by the 'weightiness' of the latter, which is calculated by speakers from three social variables: P (the perceived power difference between hearer and speaker), D (the perceived social distance between them) and R (the cultural ranking of the speech act – how 'threatening' or 'dangerous' it is perceived to be within a specific culture). This calculation is explicated in the following formula, where x denotes a speech act, S the speaker, and H the hearer:

$$Wx = D(S,H) + P(H,S) + Rx$$

On the basis of the outcome of the calculation, speakers select a specific strategy according to which they structure their communicative contributions. When speakers find themselves in a situation where a face-threatening act (FTA) may have to be performed (for example, they want the salt but cannot reach it, and so may have to make a request), their calculations lead to the decision-tree shown in Figure 1, resulting in five possible communicative choices (italicized in Figure 1).

Once a decision has been made, the speaker selects the appropriate linguistic means by which to accomplish the chosen strategy. Different linguistic means are associated with specific strategic choices, thus for a request, a straight imperative is a bald-on-record strategy ('Give me the salt'), prefacing the request with a compliment constitutes a positive po-

Figure 1. Brown & Levinson (1987) communicative choices

liteness strategy ('What a lovely dress you're wearing tonight ...'), using conventional indirectness constitutes a negative politeness strategy ('Could you pass the salt?'), hinting qualifies as an off-record strategy ('These fries could use some more salt'), while quietly shovelling down a tasteless dinner would be an appropriate way of not doing the FTA.

Contrary to what this example may lead us to believe, for Brown & Levinson politeness encompasses much more than table manners and etiquette, its social significance reaching far beyond the level of decorum. Politeness is fundamental to the very structure of social life and society, in that it constitutes the 'expression of social relationships' (ibid. 1987:2) and provides a verbal way to relieve the interpersonal tension arising from communicative intentions that conflict with social needs and statuses. In this way politeness is part and parcel of the construction and maintenance of social relationships and addresses the social need for the control of potential aggression within society. Because of this fundamentally social functionality, Brown & Levinson claim their theory to be universally valid, which is captured by their concept of a universal speaker/hearer or Model Person. In the light of the social significance of politeness, the Model Person can be seen as the embodiment of universally valid human social characteristics and principles of social reasoning. This does not necessarily imply an assumption of cultural universalism, however. Their framework describes:

> [...] the bare bones of a notion of face which (we argue) is universal, but which in any particular society we would expect to be the subject of much cultural elaboration. (ibid.:13)

This cultural elaboration is expected on the level of what kinds of speech acts threaten face, what kinds of social relationships will engender face-protective strategies, what kinds of politeness styles are (dis)preferred, etc. The core theoretical notions of the existence of positive and negative face, the principle of face-threat, the operation of rationality and so on are expected to be cross-culturally constant and thus universally valid.

1.1.3 Geoffrey Leech

Leech's theory of politeness situates politeness within a framework of 'interpersonal rhetoric.'[3] The point of departure is his broader distinction between semantics (as the domain of grammar, the linguistic system, the code) and pragmatics (as the domain of rhetoric, i.e. the implementation of the code). Semantics is concerned with a sentence's abstract logical meaning or sense, while pragmatics is concerned with the relationship between the sense of a sentence and its pragmatic force, i.e. its communicative meaning *"[...] for speakers and hearers in given utterance situations"* (Leech 1980:2). Whereas semantics is rule-governed, pragmatics is principle-governed, the difference between these two being that rules are descriptive, absolute, of the 'either/or' type and involve discrete values, while principles are normative, relative in their application, can conflict with co-existing principles and refer to continuous rather than discrete values. Semantic sense and pragmatic force are distinct but not separate phenomena, because force includes sense. The possible pragmatic force of an utterance depends on and includes its semantic sense.

Leech applies these distinctions to the familiar question of indirect meanings – why 'Can you pass the salt?' is not so much (taken as) a question about someone's ability, but rather (as) a request for action (the imperative 'pass the salt'). Leech argues that:

> [...] the direct and indirect interpretations of such utterances are re-spectively their semantic and pragmatic interpretations, and [...] the relation between the two, in the case of directives, requires the formulation of a 'Tact maxim' in addition to the maxims of Grice's Cooperative Principle. The determinations of pragmatic force, in this analysis, requires the placing of an utterance in relation to scales of politeness, authority, etc. in a multidimensional 'pragmatic space'. (ibid.:7–8)

Thus the mapping of the (semantic) sense to the (pragmatic) force of an utterance requires an 'interpersonal rhetoric', in the form of an 'informal logic', as outlined by the Gricean maxims, but expanded through the addition of a Tact maxim. In later work (Leech 1983), the Tact maxim is

---

[3] Publications used: Leech 1977, 1980, 1981, 1983.

seen as only one of a number of maxims subsumed under a separate Politeness Principle (PP), and the list of principles of interpersonal rhetoric is said to include at least one more principle (the Irony Principle or IP).

Leech's distinction between semantics and pragmatics interfaces with the Hallidayan functional distinction between the ideational (language functioning as a means of conveying and interpreting experience in the world), the interpersonal (language functioning as an expression of one's attitudes and of one's relationship with the hearer) and the textual functions of language (language functioning as a means of constructing a text, i.e. a spoken or written instantiation of language) (ibid.:56). Semantics – and thus grammar – covers the ideational function, *"[…] which conveys ideas to the hearer through a sense-sound mapping"* (ibid.:57), while pragmatics involves both the interpersonal and the textual functions. Thus, every utterance involves all three functions, and as such is simultaneously an interpersonal transaction (which Leech calls 'discourse'), an ideational transaction ('message-transmission'), and a textual transaction ('text'). These are ordered in relation to one another, in that the whole utterance may be described as 'discourse' by means of 'message' by means of 'text' (ibid.:59). In attempting to convey a certain illocutionary force to the hearer, the speaker must encode this force into a message which conveys the intended force. The principles of interpersonal rhetoric are active in this encoding process (as well as in the hearer's decoding from message to force). This message itself must then be encoded as a text, *"[…] which is a linguistic transaction in actual physical form (either auditory or visual)"* (ibid.:60). It is here that the principles of textual rhetoric are operative *"[…] which help to determine the stylistic form of the text in terms of segmentation, ordering, etc"* (ibid.:60). Thus, interpersonal and textual rhetoric are both involved in the encoding and decoding of the utterance, but they differ in that textual rhetoric is involved in shaping the utterance as a 'well-behaved text' in terms of purely 'language-internal' aspects such as syntactic clarity and processibility, etc., while interpersonal rhetoric is involved in ensuring that the utterance is 'well-behaved' in contextual or interpersonal terms, for example that it accords with situational politeness demands, that it is cooperative, etc. The whole theoretical schema can be represented as in Figure 2. The different styles of arrows refer to the fact that grammar involves constitutive rules (absolute, descriptive, etc.), whereas pragmatics (interpersonal and textual rhetoric) involves regulative principles (normative, relative, etc.).

Politeness (the PP) is thus on a par with the Gricean CP. The two are related in that when the latter is breached, this can be explained by

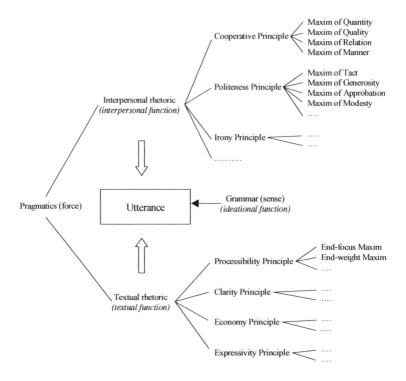

Figure 2. Leech (1983) Theoretical schema

Adapted from Leech (1983:16,58)

reference to the former. For example, when the maxim of Quantity is
flouted, this may trigger additional interpretive processes in the hearer,
leading him or her to infer that this is done in order to uphold the PP, i.e.
out of politeness considerations. Although this is highly reminiscent of
Lakoff's theory, Leech's definition of politeness differs from Lakoff's, in
that his Politeness Principle is paraphrased as 'Minimize the expression
of impolite beliefs' – and its (less important) counterpart 'Maximize the
expression of polite beliefs'. (Im)politeness is thereby defined in terms of
(un)favourableness: impolite beliefs are beliefs that are in some way un-
favourable to the hearer, while polite beliefs are beliefs that are favourable.

As can further be seen from the above schema, there are at least four
politeness maxims, but Leech mentions two more, bringing the total to
six. These are Tact, Generosity, Approbation, Modesty, Agreement and
Sympathy. Tact concerns minimizing cost and maximizing benefit to the
hearer. Generosity tells people to minimize their own benefit, while
maximizing that of the hearer. Approbation involves minimizing dispraise

and maximizing praise of the hearer. Modesty concerns minimizing self-praise and maximizing self-dispraise. Agreement is about minimizing disagreement and maximizing agreement between Self and Other. Finally Sympathy warns to minimize antipathy and maximize sympathy between Self and Other.

The kind and amount of politeness that is called for depends on the situation, which can be competitive (where the illocutionary goal competes with the social goal, e.g. ordering or asking), convivial (where the illocutionary goal coincides with the social goal, e.g. offering, thanking), collaborative (where the illocutionary goal is indifferent to the social goal, e.g. asserting, announcing) or conflictive (where the illocutionary goal conflicts with the social goal, e.g. threatening, accusing). In the latter two situations, politeness is either irrelevant – in a collaborative situation – or simply out of the question – in a conflictive situation. Politeness is therefore most relevant in competitive and convivial situations. In the former, politeness will be mostly negative – for example to avoid discord or giving offence – while in the latter it will be positive, as convivial situations are of themselves already intrinsically favourable to the hearer. Furthermore, a number of scales are involved in determining the amount and kind of politeness: cost-benefit, optionality, indirectness, authority and social distance. While cost-benefit, authority and social distance are reminiscent of Brown & Levinson's R, P and D variables respectively, optionality refers to the degree of choice the speaker leaves the hearer (much as in Lakoff's rule 2: 'Give Options'), and indirectness indexes the inferential workload imposed on the hearer.

The maxims, situations and scales all interact to lay out a fine maze of communicative choices and interpretive processes for speaker and hearer. In general, Leech's concept of politeness is concerned with conflict-avoidance, which is attested by the specifications of the maxims, as well as by his claim that politeness is geared to establishing comity.

1.1.4 Yueguo Gu

Gu's theory is based on the Chinese concept of politeness.[4] Although arguably not one of the major theories of politeness, it is incorporated here because it introduces an aspect that is not found in other frameworks: it explicitly connects politeness with moral societal norms. Basically, Gu's theory is based on Leech's, but with a revision of the status of the

---

[4] Publications considered : Gu 1990, 1993, 1994.

Politeness Principle and its associated maxims. Leech claims that the PP is a regulative principle and explicitly denies any moral or ethical nature for it. Like Lakoff's rules, Leech's PP is supposed to be descriptive, not prescriptive. Gu on the contrary, when describing the Chinese concept of *limao* (politeness), stresses the fact that it is essentially morally prescriptive in nature, and that the rules or maxims which it subsumes are moral, socially sanctionable precepts. Likewise, when discussing Brown & Levinson's theory, Gu argues that in the Chinese context, the notion of face is not to be seen in terms of psychological wants, but rather in terms of societal norms. Politeness is not just instrumental, it is above all normative. Face is threatened not when people's individual wants are not met, but rather when they fail to live up to social standards, i.e. when they fail to fulfil society's wants.

For Chinese, the PP is thus regarded as *"[…] a sanctioned belief that an individual's behaviour ought to live up to the expectations of respectfulness, modesty, attitudinal warmth and refinement"* (Gu 1990:245). In Gu (1990), four maxims are discussed: Self-denigration, Address, Tact and Generosity. The Self-denigration maxim admonishes the speaker to 'denigrate Self and elevate Other'. The Address maxim reads 'address your interlocutor with an appropriate address term', where appropriateness indexes the hearer's social status, role and the speaker–hearer relationship. The Tact and Generosity maxims closely resemble Leech's, with the exception that they involve specific speech acts (impositives and commissives respectively), and that they operate differently on the 'motivational' as opposed to the 'conversational' level. In the latter distinction, the motivational level refers to what could be called the 'operational' side of an impositive or commissive, i.e. the 'real' cost or benefit to the hearer – for example, the difference between asking for directions and asking for money, or asking for $5 instead of $5000, and the difference between offering someone a ride or offering a car, or offering $5 or $5000. The conversational level, on the other hand, refers to the verbal treatment of impositives and commissives. For impositives this means maximizing the benefit received (genre 'you would do me a tremendous favour if you could…'), while for commissives this means minimizing the cost to Self (genre 'no problem, I'm going in that direction anyway' upon offering someone a lift).

Finally, politeness also involves a Balance Principle, which prescribes the reciprocation of politeness or of the cost/benefit resulting from impositives and commissives – paying back a debt incurred as a result of a request, or performing a counter-offer, a counter-invitation, etc.

1.1.5 Sachiko Ide

Ide's theory is based on research into the Japanese concept of politeness.[5] She sees politeness as basically involved in maintaining smooth communication. She criticizes other theories – notably those of Brown & Levinson, Leech and Lakoff – for being overly concerned with strategic interaction, i.e. interaction in which the speaker employs a verbal strategy in order to attain some individual, personal goal. As this kind of politeness allows the speaker a considerably active choice, she labels it 'Volition' and contrasts it with 'Discernment', which she claims is a second and separate component of politeness especially prominent in Japanese. Discernment is not volitional, it does not depend on the speaker's free will but consists in socially obligatory verbal (grammatical) choices.

Ide's development of Discernment is based on the (Japanese) use of honorific forms, for which Brown & Levinson's theory is said to be unable to provide an adequate explanatory account. Moreover, in Gricean theories, politeness complements the Gricean CP by drawing the speaker–hearer social relationship into the interaction – the Gricean maxims are flouted for politeness reasons, i.e. in order to signal something about the speaker–hearer relationship. So in this sense purely Gricean speech – fully according to the Gricean maxims – is socially neutral: it is pure information-transmission without any relation to the speaker–hearer relationship. In Japanese, however, this would not be possible. There are no socially neutral forms, and the speaker must always choose between honorific or non-honorific forms, and as such always (and necessarily) conveys information about the speaker–hearer relationship, even in making the most banal, factual statements. *"This use of an honorific verb form is the socio-pragmatic equivalent of grammatical concord, and may thus be termed socio-pragmatic concord"* (Ide 1989:227). The use of honorific forms is said to be absolute, because it is not relative to the speaker's free will and because it directly indexes socio-structural characteristics of speaker and hearer. This absolute use of honorifics is then coupled with a view of politeness as determined by social conventions, which is expressed by the Japanese term *wakimae*. *"To behave according to wakimae is to show verbally one's sense of place or role in a given situation according to social conventions"* (ibid.:230). Four such conventional rules are identified: 'be polite to a person of a higher social position'; 'be polite to a person with power'; 'be polite to an older person' and 'be polite in a formal

---

[5] Publications: Ide 1982, 1989, 1993; Ide et al. 1986, 1992; Hill et al. 1986.

setting determined by the factors of participants, occasions or topics'.

Thus in Japanese and other languages with a strongly developed honorific system, politeness rules are akin to grammatical rules. They are part of the language itself, and depend on the socio-structural characteristics of speaker and hearer as well as on characteristics of the situation, which must be faithfully reflected in the speaker's linguistic choices:

> The speakers of honorific languages are bound to make choices among linguistic forms of honorifics or plain forms. Since the choices cover such parts of speech as copulas, verbs, nouns, adjectives, and adverbs, the discernment aspect of linguistic politeness is a matter of constant concern in the use of language. Since there is no neutral form, the speaker of an honorific language has to be sensitive to levels of formality in verbalizing actions or things, just as a native speaker of English, for example, must be sensitive to the countable and noncountable property of things because of a grammatical distinction of property of the singular and plural in English. (ibid.:231)

In other words, Japanese politeness is not simply about the way in which the speaker strategically chooses to treat the hearer, it is an inalienable part of the language through which socio-structural concordance is achieved.

1.1.6 Shoshana Blum-Kulka

Blum-Kulka examines politeness in the Israeli-Jewish context.[6] She borrows elements from various other theories, but reinterprets them in a culture-relativistic way. 'Cultural norms' or 'cultural scripts' are terms of central importance in her approach. Although she endorses the existence of face-wants, she stresses that these are culturally determined and that their specific form(ulation) can thus never pretend to be universal (as they are in Brown & Levinson). Like Ide, she acknowledges the differentiation between strategic and obligatory linguistic choices, but argues that its scope and depth differ from culture to culture, capturing the obligatory choices under the label 'cultural conventions'. In Blum-Kulka's view, Discernment merely refers to that part of politeness which is strongly conventionalized, and languages with a high incidence of Discernment

---

[6] Publications: Blum-Kulka 1982, 1985, 1987, 1989, 1990, 1992; Blum-Kulka & House 1989a, 1989b; Blum-Kulka & Olshtain 1984; Blum-Kulka & Sheffer 1993; Blum-Kulka & Weizman 1998.

strategies are simply more strictly conventionalized in terms of politeness than languages with a high incidence of Volition strategies. Even the content of the term 'politeness' itself (i.e. the phenomena to which it refers) is said to differ cross-culturally. In short, in her view politeness is about appropriate social behaviour as determined by cultural expectations or cultural norms.

Her theoretical position is that:

> [...] systems of politeness manifest a culturally filtered interpretation of the interaction between four essential parameters: social motivations, expressive modes, social differentials and social meanings. Cultural notions interfere in determining the distinctive features of each of the four parameters and as a result, significantly effect the social understanding of 'politeness' across societies in the world. (Blum-Kulka 1992:270)

Social motivations refer to the reasons why people are polite, i.e. to the functionality of politeness; expressive modes to the different linguistic forms that are used for politeness; social differentials to the parameters of situational assessment that play a role in politeness (such as Brown & Levinson's P, D and R factors); and social meanings to the politeness value of specific linguistic expressions in specific situational contexts. Culture sets the values of all of these parameters through conventional rules, which take the form of cultural scripts that people rely on in order to determine the appropriateness of a specific verbal strategy in a specific context. Apart from speech acts (requests, offers, etc.), Blum-Kulka also argues for the importance of the more general notion of speech events in determining politeness. Speech events refer to the kind of interaction in which speech acts occur, such as 'family dinner conversations', 'business negotiations', 'formal speeches', etc.

1.1.7 Bruce Fraser and William Nolen

Fraser & Nolen present what they label the 'conversational-contract view' of politeness.[7] They state that each participant, upon entering a given conversation, brings to that encounter a set of rights and obligations that determine what the participants can expect from each other. This interpersonal 'contract' is not static but can be revised in the course of time (by renegotiation), or because of a change in the context (for example, before

---

[7] Publications: Fraser 1980, 1990; Fraser & Nolen 1981.

and after the chairman of a meeting says 'the meeting is closed'). The rights and obligations of each participant – the terms of the contract – are established on various dimensions: conventional, institutional, situational and historical. Conventional terms are very general in nature, usually apply to all forms of interaction, and are exemplified by, for example, turn-taking rules, rules about loudness/softness of speaking, and so on. Institutional terms concern rights and duties imposed by social institutions, for example, rights of speaking in court, silence in church, and so on. Situational terms involve factors such as the mutual assessment of the relative role, status and power of speaker and hearer, so for example a child cannot authorize a parent to do something. Finally, the historical dimension refers to the fact that the social contract crucially depends on previous interactions between specific speakers and hearers, i.e. the contractual terms negotiated during previous interactions determine the starting position for each new interaction. These different dimensions vary in negotiability: whereas conventional rights and obligations are seldom negotiable, this is more often the case for those that arise from previous encounters or the immediate situation.

Politeness, then, is a matter of remaining within the then-current terms and conditions of the conversational contract (CC), while impoliteness consists of violating them. Staying within the terms of the CC is said to be the 'norm', and is related to the notion of 'rationality'. It is what every rational participant usually does by default. As 'normal' interaction proceeds within the terms of the CC, politeness mostly passes by unnoticed, while impoliteness is marked. People only notice when someone is impolite. So politeness is not involved with any form of strategic interaction, nor with making the hearer 'feel good', but *"[...] simply involves getting on with the task at hand in light of the terms and conditions of the CC"* (Fraser 1990:233). Neither is politeness seen as an intrinsic characteristic of certain linguistic forms or verbal choices: *"Sentences are not ipso facto polite, nor are languages more or less polite. It is only speakers who are polite [...]"* (ibid.:233). Although it is acknowledged that certain verbal choices, such as 'Sir' or 'please' can, by virtue of their intrinsic meaning, convey information about hearer-status, these are captured under the notion of 'deference'. They are not intrinsically polite, but merely forms of status-giving, whose politeness depends on how they relate to the terms of the CC that are in effect at any specific moment. Finally, it is stressed that politeness is totally in the hands of the hearer. No matter how (im)polite a speaker may attempt to be, whether or not he or she will be heard as being (im)polite ultimately depends on the hearer's judgement.

1.1.8 Horst Arndt and Richard Janney

Arndt & Janney react against what they label the 'appropriacy-based' approach to politeness, where politeness is a matter of using the right words in the right contexts as determined by conventional rules of appropriateness.[8] Most of the foregoing theories would qualify for inclusion in this category. Arndt & Janney denounce the emphasis laid by other theories on linguistic forms, social conventions or situational variables, because this emphasis causes the theories to lose sight of the speakers and hearers involved in communication. Arndt & Janney's own framework is said to be interpersonal, because it focuses on *people* as the locus and determining factor of politeness.

At the heart of their alternative approach is 'emotive communication': *"[...] the communication of transitory attitudes, feelings and other affective states"* (Arndt & Janney 1985a:282). Emotive communication is distinguished from emotional communication, in that the latter is the spontaneous, uncontrolled expression of emotion, while the former refers to *"[...] the conscious, strategic modification of affective signals to influence others' behavior"*, [i.e. emotional expression] *"[...] regulated by social sanctions, norms of interaction, and 'civilized' expectations that enable people to control their natural impulses"* (Arndt & Janney 1991:529). Emotive communication, which involves not only speech but also para- and non-linguistic signals, further has three dimensions: confidence, positive-negative affect and intensity. Thus, through their verbal, vocal and kinesic choices – grouped under the label 'cross-modal emotive cues' – speakers signal information about their confidence in what they say, about their affect towards the speaker and about their emotional involvement. High confidence can be signalled, for example by verbal directness, a falling intonation and a direct bodily posture, while low confidence is signalled by verbal indirectness, a questioning intonation and an averted bodily posture. Affect cues can be positive (positively value-laden verbal choices, warm tone of voice, smile) or negative (negatively value-laden language, harsh voice, angry look). And involvement can be signalled as being high (by high referential intensity – for example, saying 'I demand' rather than 'I expect' – , positive articulatory force – i.e. prominent pitch differences – and a full gaze) or low (low referential intensity, a flat tone of voice and an averted gaze).

---

[8] Publications: Arndt & Janney 1979, 1980, 1981a, 1981b, 1983, 1985a, 1985b, 1987, 1991; Janney & Arndt 1992, 1993.

Within this model, politeness refers to that part of emotive communication where the speaker behaves in an interpersonally supportive way. In fact, in Arndt & Janney's view 'interpersonal supportiveness' replaces the notion of politeness entirely. When a speaker is polite, he or she is not so much conforming to social expectations, but rather avoiding interpersonal conflict by conveying his or her message in an interpersonally supportive way:

> The key idea is that there are supportive and nonsupportive ways of expressing positive and negative feelings; the effective speaker generally attempts to minimize his partner's emotional uncertainty in all cases by being as supportive as possible. (Arndt & Janney 1985a:283)

Although they criticize most other frameworks, they do borrow Brown & Levinson's definition of face as 'wants for autonomy and social approval' and claim that interpersonal supportiveness consists of the protection of 'interpersonal face' (which more or less coincides with Brown & Levinson's 'positive face'):

> A supportive speaker smoothes over uncomfortable situations, or keeps situations from becoming interpersonally uncomfortable, by constantly acknowledging his partner's intrinsic worth as a person. He does this by verbally, vocally and kinesically confirming his partner's claim to a positive self-image; he attempts to minimize personal territorial transgressions and maximize signs of interpersonal approval. (ibid.:294)

In more detail, in terms of emotive cues, interpersonal supportiveness stipulates that:

> [...] positive messages have to be accompanied by displays of confidence and involvement in order to avoid creating the impression that they are not positive enough (i.e. covert threats to face); and negative messages have to be accompanied by displays of lack of confidence and uninvolvement in order to avoid creating the impression that they are too negative (i.e. overt threats to face). (ibid.:294)

All in all, the intersection of the distinctions between positive and negative messages and between supportiveness and non-supportiveness with the notion of face gives rise to four different strategies for face-work, which can be pictured as in Figure 3, and of which only interpersonally supportive strategies are said to constitute politeness, as they are the only ones that acknowledge the hearer's interpersonal face needs.

Figure 3. Arndt & Janney (1985a) Strategies of face-work

Emotive strategies	Hearer's face needs	
	Personal (need for autonomy)	Interpersonal (need for social acceptance)
Supportive positive	acknowledges	acknowledges
Non-supportive positive	acknowledges	threatens
Supportive negative	threatens	acknowledges
Non-supportive negative	threatens	threatens

So Arndt & Janney's framework resembles that of Brown & Levinson, albeit with a somewhat narrower definition of politeness. Its most distinguishing characteristics, however, are first that it conceptualizes politeness as embedded in a broader aspect of communication (emotive communication), and second, the fact that politeness is not linked to sociological variables but rather to human emotion.

In later work, Arndt & Janney elaborate their theory by adding to it the notion of 'social politeness', while interpersonal politeness is captured under the label 'tact'. Tact is a somewhat expanded notion of supportiveness, in that it is not only linked to positive but also to negative face – although this was arguably already the case in their earlier version – witness their reference to 'minimizing territorial transgressions' (Arndt & Janney 1985a:294, quoted above). Social politeness, on the other hand, comprises highly conventionalized language usages and refers to *"[…] standardised strategies for getting gracefully into, and back out of, recurring social situations"* (Arndt & Janney 1992:23), for example, strategies for initiating, maintaining and terminating conversation. Social politeness is of an entirely different nature from tact, and is likened to traffic rules, where a set of conventionalized rules and *"[…] socially appropriate communicative forms, norms, routines, rituals, etc."* (ibid.:24) smooth the flow of interaction. Whereas tact has a 'conciliative' function, social politeness is said to be 'regulative' in nature.

1.1.9 Richard Watts

The theoretical role of emotive communication as a broader context in which politeness is to be situated in Arndt & Janney's framework is assumed by the notion of 'politic behavior' in Watts' theory.[9] Politic behaviour is defined as *"[…] socioculturally determined behavior directed towards the goal of establishing and/or maintaining in a state of*

---

[9] Publications: Watts 1989a, 1989b, 1991, 1992a, 1992b.

equilibrium the personal relationships between the individuals of a social group" (Watts 1989a:135), where 'equilibrium' does not refer to social equality but rather to the maintenance of a social status quo. Politeness is seen as a special case of politic behaviour.

An important aspect of the theoretical background of Watts' framework is Bernstein's (1971) distinction between restricted and elaborated codes and their respective association with closed and open communication systems. Social groups with closed communication systems (or simply 'closed groups') are those in which the interests of the group – the 'we' – supersede those of the individual – the 'I' – whereas in 'open groups', the interests of the 'I' supersede those of the 'we'. This distinction is related to Ide's distinction between Volition and Discernment, in that Watts regards cultures in which Discernment plays a dominant role (such as Japanese culture) as essentially closed communication systems, while Volition-oriented societies are more open. Volition strategies involve a conscious choice by the speaker and as such foreground the individual more than the group, while the opposite is true of Discernment, in which the individual conforms to his or her social role within the group. The identification of cultures with open or closed systems is not absolute, however, as Watts talks of "social groups in a Volition culture with closed communication systems" (Watts 1989a:133). Both open and closed groups can occur within a culture, so that the notions of a Volition versus a Discernment culture seem to refer to the relative importance of open versus closed communication systems or groups.

Politeness enters the picture in that it is associated with open groups:

> Since, following Brown & Levinson (1978, 1987), we may take politeness strategies to be forms of rational behavior, they will tend to occur in speech events in which the interests of the individual, the 'I', rather than those of the group, the 'we', are at a premium. In Bernstein's terms we might classify such strategies as 'elaborated speech variants' used as 'defensive strategies to decrease potential vulnerability of self and to increase the vulnerability of others'. (ibid.:133)

So the Bernsteinian distinction between elaborated and restricted codes fits into the picture in that politeness and Volition can be seen as elaborated codes because they foreground the individual more than the group. On the other hand:

> [...] verbal interaction in speech events in social groups with a closed communication system [...] is ideally directed towards the establish-

ment and maintenance of interpersonal relationships and in-group
identity (ibid.:134)

which is captured by the notion of politic behaviour. So Watts differs from
Ide in that he associates politeness with Volition only, while Discernment
is associated with politic behaviour. Again, however, the distinctive association with open and closed groups is not absolute, but rather a matter of
'more or less', as the notion of 'speech event' also plays a role in determining the relative importance of politic behaviour and politeness. Politic
behaviour occurs in both open and closed groups. It is a universal form of
behaviour permeating all verbal interaction because any interaction always involves relational work. Politeness in contrast occurs in open groups
or speech events only and is a subset of politic behaviour. More specifically, it consists of that part of politic behaviour which is explicitly marked
and conventionalized, i.e. conventionally interpretable as 'polite'. It includes highly ritualized formulaic behaviour, indirect speech strategies
and conventionalized linguistic strategies for maintaining and saving
face – the latter indicating that Watts also aims to encompass Brown &
Levinson's framework. Politic behaviour on the other hand:

> [...] will include all this as well as highly codified honorific language
> usage based on socially-agreed upon rules of politeness [...] and ut-
> terances which would not fall into any of these general categories and
> are thus neither marked nor unmarked with respect to a parameter of
> politeness. (ibid.:136)

So the differentiation between politeness and politic behaviour does not
really imply a fundamental difference in the strict sense of the word, as
politeness is also essentially (a form of) politic behaviour. In its full definition, Watts' notion of politeness can thus be characterized as:

> [...] an explicitly marked, conventionally interpretable subset of po-
> litic verbal behavior responsible for the smooth functioning of
> socio-communicative interaction and the consequent production of
> well-formed discourse within open social groups characterized by elabo-
> rated speech codes. (ibid.:136)

Moreover, because politic behaviour is also involved in achieving smooth
communication and well-formed discourse, and can be seen as behaviour
"[...] which is conventionally appropriate to the ongoing social activity"
(Watts 1991:92), the only real difference between politeness and politic

behaviour seems to be that the former is marked and the latter unmarked with regard to 'conventions of politeness'. But as politic behaviour is said to also include codified honorific language which is "based on socially agreed upon rules of politeness" (1989a:136, quoted above), the true nature of the distinction ceases to be all that clear.

In Watts' framework, much of what the other theories regard as politeness is construed as politic behaviour, which is the unmarked form of conventionally appropriate behaviour and from which politeness is a marked deviation. But politeness is not the only possible deviation:

> Two forms of marked behavior may now be posited, one leading to communicative breakdowns and the other to an enhancement of ego's standing with respect to alter, i.e. to 'making other people have a better opinion' of oneself. The first type of behavior is 'non-politic', the second, I contend, 'polite'. (Watts 1992a:51)

Thus while non-politic behaviour is a negative deviation from politic behaviour, politeness constitutes a positive deviation, consisting as it does of behaviour that is 'more than merely politic', 'more than merely appropriate'. It is conscious strategic behaviour which aims to positively influence the hearer's opinion of the speaker.

Thus politeness is not connected to specific linguistic forms, as its differentiation from politic behaviour hinges on conventional notions of appropriateness for specific behaviour in specific speech events or groups. Only the relationship of behaviour to appropriateness conventions determines politeness, not the specific linguistic forms involved. Linguistic forms are never 'intrinsically polite', so for example terms of address may be politic (if they are applied merely appropriately), or polite (if they are used 'more than merely appropriately'). Finally, it can also be noted that because politeness is basically a form of politic behaviour, both notions must be considered together for a full understanding of Watts' notion of politeness.

1.2   A preliminary round-up

Although in the remainder of this study the nine theories set out above will be the object of more in-depth comparison, a few preliminary comparative remarks can already be made at this point. The issues introduced here will be taken up again in a later stage of the discussion, where they will be examined in more detail.

Kasper's (1990) overview of politeness theorizing distinguishes two

main trends in the conceptualization of politeness: politeness as strategic conflict-avoidance and politeness as social indexing. These notions
provide an excellent point of reference for a first comparison of the theoretical perspectives, as they surface in some form or other in all of them.
Conflict-avoidance is most clear in Brown & Levinson, as it is the very
starting point for their model. They locate the basic social role of politeness in its ability to function as a way of controlling potential aggression
between interactional parties (Brown & Levinson 1987:1). But in light of
their emphasis on the fact that face-threat is inherent to many speech acts,
it may even be argued that their notion of politeness is not only about the
avoidance of *potential* conflict, but about the defusing of conflict that is
intrinsic to the very act of communicating. Explicit acknowledgement of
conflict-avoidance can also be found in Lakoff (see above, section 1.1.1),
Arndt & Janney (Janney & Arndt 1992:23), and Gu (1990:239), and is
implicitly present in most of the other accounts. Ide connects politeness
with smooth communication, i.e. communication "without friction" (Ide
1989:225, 230), Leech with avoiding "disruption" and "maintaining the
social equilibrium and friendly relations" (Leech 1983:17, 82), while Watts'
politic behaviour is also involved in maintaining the interpersonal equilibrium, and Blum-Kulka mentions the maintenance of "interpersonal
harmony" (Blum-Kulka 1992:277). In Fraser & Nolen, finally, politeness
means abiding by the rules/terms of the relationship, and this emphasis on
politeness as doing what is socially appropriate – which incidentally can
also be found in any of the other frameworks – implies that not doing so
would entail interpersonal conflict.

Equally, the notion of politeness as social indexing is universal to some
extent in the theories discussed here. It is of course most prominent in
Ide's notion of Discernment as 'socio-pragmatic concord' which states
that a person's linguistic politeness behaviour is dictated by his or her
social position and his or her social relationship with the hearer, meaning
this behaviour effectively functions as a social indexing mechanism.
Through the notion of Discernment that same idea also finds its way into
Watts' notion of politic behaviour, but it can equally be found in any of
the other frameworks, in the idea that what is socially appropriate depends on the speaker's social position (*in relation to* the hearer). Politeness
is invariably connected with social or socio-structural parameters that determine what is (im)polite for a certain speaker *vis-à-vis* a certain hearer
in a certain situation. Brown & Levinson's P and D factors are the most
explicit example, but it is implicitly present in the very idea of politeness
as 'appropriateness'. In applying politeness, the speaker acts in a socially

appropriate way, i.e. a way that suits his or her social situation (in respect of the hearer and situation). In this sense, politeness is also almost directly dependent on the social characteristics of the interactants, and thus is a reflection of their respective social positions.

Besides these two universal connections, in the sense of connecting *all* the theories, a number of smaller groups can be discerned. For example, Lakoff, Leech and Gu could be labelled Gricean accounts, as they all in some way or other involve Grice's notion of the CP and its maxims. Arguably Brown & Levinson also belong to this category, as they generally accept the Gricean CP (Brown & Levinson 1987:4) and the idea that politeness constitutes a motivated deviation from its maxims, although their model as such does not involve the notion of 'maxims'. Ide and Gu both use the notion of societal (moral) norms, thereby explicitly acknowledging the ethical foundations of politeness. Especially Blum-Kulka, but also Watts, Ide, Gu, Lakoff and Arndt & Janney conceptualize politeness in an explicitly culture-specific framework. They adopt a culture-relativistic perspective, where notions and rules of politeness are seen as being variable across different cultures. This idea is also present in Fraser & Nolen, albeit less explicitly, since "subculture" is mentioned as a constraining factor on the general terms of the CC (Fraser 1990:232). Brown & Levinson on the contrary adopt an explicitly universalistic perspective, claiming that their model of politeness can explain politeness across different cultures, although their R parameter does refer to the ranking of a speech act in terms of face-threat within a particular culture, and they also acknowledge the possibility that the specifics of face-wants and face-threats are *"[…] subject to cultural specifications of many sorts"* (Brown & Levinson 1987:13). Leech adopts more or less the same position, locating his approach within general pragmatics, *"[…] the study of language in total abstraction from situation"* (Leech 1983:11), while acknowledging that the general, abstract notion of the PP is also subject to local conditions of language use and can thus be expected to *"[…] operate variably in different cultures or language communities"* (ibid.:10).

Finally, although all the frameworks incorporate the idea that politeness is in some way or other strategic (in the sense of 'a means to get things done'), as already illustrated regarding the notion of politeness as a strategy for conflict-avoidance, this strategic nature appears in different guises. It may range from politeness as a cunning device by which the speaker manipulates the hearer to get him or her to comply with a request (e.g. Brown & Levinson), to politeness as a way in which the speaker shows his or her consideration for the hearer by breaking negative news in a friendly, humane fashion (Arndt & Janney's notion of Tact as interpersonal supportiveness), to the more or less unconscious, automatic application of the rules of a language (Ide's Discernment). So strategically, politeness spans the full range from deliberate, conscious linguistic choices to the unconscious application of rules or scripts, as well as from the unmarked (politeness as the normal, usual, unnoticed way of interacting) to the explicitly marked (e.g. Watts' notion of politeness as 'more than merely politic').

1.3 Politeness beyond the core theories

It is clear that the nine theories used for the present analysis constitute only a small part of the vast field of politeness research. Numerous other studies have made contributions to the field that go beyond the straightforward application of one of the theories under discussion here. Nevertheless, the nine theories do seem to be representative of the field, in the sense that they form a core of research around which the field is built. This is certainly true for Lakoff, Brown & Levinson and Leech, who together can be considered the founding fathers of modern politeness research, and whose theories figure (or are at least mentioned) in a great many if not most of the publications on the subject. The other six theories then represent a more recent outer ring around this older core, subsuming the major trends and elaborations that have appeared since.

Other contributions can be roughly divided into two broad categories: studies that propose more or less independent frameworks, and studies that propose amendments to existing theories. This is not always a straightforward either/or classification, and neither can the two categories be clearly or rigidly distinguished. It would be more accurate to say that a continuum exists between total acceptance of an existing theory and completely novel models with their own concepts and terminologies. The following paragraphs will discuss a selection of both categories of work, briefly sketching their main characteristics and indicating how they relate to the core theories.

A few frameworks approach politeness from totally different angles than the core theories, which sets them apart as truly independent frameworks. William R. Kelley (1987) interprets politeness in a semiotic framework based on Jakobson, Hymes and Silverstein. His view is centred around the form-function problem – how different formal forms may have the same functional effect. Within a particular pragmatic function, formal variants are said to be related to each other through 'deference scales', which classify variants as more or less deferential depending on their metapragmatic entailments in respect of the speaker–hearer relationship. The use of these variants is governed by three systems of rules or norms: respect, tact and etiquette. The respect system involves group-related norms for mapping forms onto situational contexts. Within this system, politeness consists in the maintenance of a respectfully neutral form-function relation to the speaker–hearer relationship. The tact system refers to a speaker's attempt to attain a particular effect on the hearer while remaining within the normative confines of respect. Finally, the etiquette system consists of explicit behavioural rules that capture native ideologies of appropriate formal functions, and is said to exist because speakers have only partial knowledge of the respect and tact systems. For the present study, two elements of Kelley's approach are of importance. As in many of the core theories, politeness is ultimately a matter of social group-related norms (the respect system), and this system of norms is an absolute system in the sense that it is a complex of which ordinary speakers have only limited knowledge.

The same notion of an absolute system of politeness is found in the work of Konrad Werkhofer (1992), who approaches politeness from an economic angle. Like money, politeness is seen as a socially constituted symbolic medium, based on social values that are derived from the notions of social order and social identity. These notions determine the rights and duties associated with social relationships, which in turn determine appropriate behaviour. As a socially and historically constituted medium, the politeness system has a power of its own, motivating and structuring behaviour independently of the individual actor's wishes and choices, and due to its complexity, no individual can ever achieve complete mastery of it. Although rights and duties are not necessarily equally distributed and can to a certain extent be negotiated, their equal distribution is said to constitute an ideal case which often informs evaluations of politeness. Owing to its emphasis on a partially negotiable independent system of rights and duties relevant to the speaker–hearer relationship, Werkhofer's framework closely resembles Fraser & Nolen's social contract view, with the addition of the historical dimension and the functional involvement of politeness with the maintenance of social order.

Konrad Ehlich (1992) also emphasizes the historical dimension and distinguishes between 'concepts that exist in society' and 'scientific conceptualizations' of politeness. He points out that politeness consists of a qualification of a speaker-act by a hearer or third party, based on a socially agreed standard of behaviour. This standard is not innate but needs to be learned, its internalization proceeding through the conceptualization of a Generalized Other, constructed from the different actual Others with which the individual comes into contact, and who apply the social standard in their evaluations. In addition to elaborating on the way in which social norms are reproduced in society, Ehlich expands the notion by identifying a historical trend where politeness norms have evolved from the direct expression of socio-structural relationships to a transcendental generalized moral standard in its own right. But because the basis of his theory is still a system of socially shared norms of behaviour, Ehlich's approach can for the purpose of this analysis be subsumed under the core theories.

A few frameworks emphasize the aspect of politeness as an action. Asa Kasher (1986:109) explains politeness through a single 'rationality principle': "Given a desired end, one is to choose that action which most effectively and at least cost attains that end, other things being equal". The notion of cost is intended to complement the Gricean notion of effectiveness in terms of informativeness. The more effective an act is, the more it may cost in terms of politeness. The rationality principle aims to capture the points of equilibrium between effectiveness and cost. In this sense, the rationality principle functions as a 'super-maxim', balancing the Conversational and Politeness maxims, and so Kasher's approach can be likened to Leech's and the other Gricean frameworks.

Dagmar Neuendorff (1987) uses the perspective of action-theory and its distinction between 'action' and 'action-type' to tackle the paradox of politeness being simultaneously universal and temporally and culturally variable. As an action (*eine Handlung*), politeness is said to answer to social rules and conventions, and is thus relative to culture, while as an action-type, politeness is a universal. But since the action-type characteristics of politeness are then linked to Brown & Levinson's face-work interpretation, while the action-related social rules and conventions are linked to the Gricean maxims, Neuendorff's framework can for this study be regarded as a combination of the Gricean theories with Brown & Levinson's approach.

A number of other studies are more explicitly based on one or more of the core theories, but elaborate and expand them to a greater or lesser degree by introducing alternative concepts. A. J. Meier (1995), for example, proposes an alternative to Brown & Levinson's framework with an approach based on the notion of Repair Work, which refers to the effort a speaker puts forth after having acted inappropriately. Inappropriateness is measured against behavioural standards relative to the speech community and the situational context, and is no longer connected to specific linguistic forms or speech acts. In Meier's view, politeness is not a secondary act applied to a primary act (as in the *mitigation of* a directive), but can very well itself be a primary act.

The separation of politeness from speech acts and linguistic forms is retained by Roger D. Sell (1992), who accepts Brown & Levinson's notions of positive and negative face but rejects their view that politeness comes into operation only when a face-threat is imminent. Rather, politeness is seen as a constant behavioural consideration which is involved in all interaction all the time, so that it is perfectly possible to perform a non-face-threatening act impolitely. Although like Brown & Levinson, Sell regards politeness as strategic, he acknowledges that speakers may achieve their interactional goals through impoliteness as well as through politeness. As in most other frameworks, (im)politeness is defined in terms of a society's conventions.

Arin Bayraktaroglu (1991) also endorses much of Brown & Levinson's theory but expands it to cover the dynamics of politeness over longer conversational stretches. In order to do this, Bayraktaroglu proposes the notion of a face-boosting act (FBA – the opposite of an FTA) and introduces the Goffmanian notion of 'interactional disequilibrium', which refers to a situation in which one of the interactants has suffered damage to his or her face. On this basis, the notion of an ideal balance or equilibrium is developed, referring to the state of established face-values for both speakers obtaining at any specific moment in the interaction. Disruptions of the equilibrium result in an interactional imbalance which must be remedied by subsequent actions. (Im)politeness results from specific sequences of FTAs and FBAs.

A mix of elements of more than one of the core theories, with the addition of a few specific distinctions, is exemplified in Henk Haverkate's (1988) notion of politeness. In his view, cultural norms and values determine regulative rules that operate on the metacommunicative as well as on the communicative level, the former being involved with general conversational maxims such as 'don't interrupt' that are geared to the preservation of sociability, while the latter is concerned with rules for speech act realization. Speech acts can be inherently polite, impolite or nonimpolite. Polite speech acts such as thanking do not need any further politeness strategies, while for impolite speech acts such as threatening, politeness is largely irrelevant. Only nonimpolite speech acts such as assertives or directives may need mitigation in order to protect the hearer's face.

A vast number of other works present various mixes of elements from the core theories with expansions, elaborations and more or less profound amendments. A case in point is Held (1989, 1992, 1994), who combines elements from all of the core theories except Gu, resulting in a very broad and rather eclectic concept of politeness as interactional 'work' ("Beziehungsarbeit" – Held 1994:107) involving notions such as maxims, strategies, supportiveness, norms, cognitive scripts, conventions, values, rationality, interactional roles with rights and duties, equilibrium, face, conflict-avoidance, etc., which are all said to be relative to cultures and other groups, as well as to the interactional context. In addition, Held introduces the notion of 'maximization', to contrast with the traditional theoretical emphasis on 'minimization' strategies – such as in the notion of politeness as a form of mitigation. Although Held does acknowledge the importance of the conflict-avoidance function, her notion is broader in that it sees politeness as being involved with mutually creating or maintaining good interactional relations.

Kerbrat-Orecchioni (1992, 1997) stays within a more limited theoretical fishing ground, as she modifies Brown & Levinson's framework and combines it with aspects of Leech's theory. However, the amendments she proposes are more profound than those introduced by Held. She redesigns the notion of face, differentiating between negative/positive *face* and negative/positive *politeness*, so that it becomes possible to speak of, for example, 'negative politeness towards the hearer's negative face-wants'. And she proposes two additions: the notion of a 'face-enhancing act' (FEA, similar to Bayraktaroglu's FBA), and the distinction between hearer-oriented and speaker-oriented acts. The resulting system of three axes (speaker/hearer orientation, positive/negative face and positive/negative politeness) is claimed to be a universal framework that can be adapted to cover culture-specific notions of politeness. Culture plays a role in the form of 'ethnolects' – complexes of culture-specific conceptualizations of interpersonal relationships, conflict-handling norms, etc. – which determine culture-specific systems of politeness rules or sets of instructions about behaviour with which speakers must comply. As with the other frameworks discussed here, although these modifications certainly have a number of important operational consequences for identifying and explaining politeness in speech, they do not as such alter the epistemological and/or ontological bases of the Brown & Levinsonian framework, in that the resulting approach remains faithful to the notion of politeness as face-work and the whole ontological model implied by it.

Whereas Held integrates a large number of theories, and Kerbrat-Orecchioni proposes many and relatively radical amendments, O'Driscoll (1996) occupies the other extreme, in concentrating on the revision of only one aspect of only one theory: the notion of 'face' in Brown & Levinson's theory in the light of its intercultural applicability. In short, O'Driscoll proposes a scalar notion of face-wants to replace Brown & Levinson's dualistic one, while the notion of face-wants itself is broadened into wants of association versus dissociation. As cultures may differ in where on this scale they place their normative ideal, O'Driscoll claims this revised framework can account for a wider range of cross-cultural data.

True to its roots in sociolinguistics, the cultural angle is also popular in politeness research, with innumerable studies into various culture-specific, cross-cultural or intercultural settings. A prominent example is Sifianou (1992a, 1992b, 1993), whose notion of politeness results from cross-cultural research into English and Greek notions of politeness. She combines elements of Brown & Levinson, Ide, Lakoff, Arndt & Janney and Fraser & Nolen, and mixes these with a number of insights from Goffman (1956), such as his differentiation between 'deference' (showing appreciation of others) and 'demeanour' (an individual's claim to certain qualities) and between 'substance' and 'ceremonial' rules (where the former are based on moral and ethical values, and the latter refer to conventionalized means of communication). The same Goffmanian distinctions are found in Srivastava & Pandit (1988) who examine politeness in Hindi, but here they are combined with Lakoff's theory. Lakoff also features in Matsumoto's (1988, 1989) investigation of politeness in Japanese, which concludes that Japanese could fit in with Lakoff's Deference strategy, on condition that it be reformulated in a culture-specific way as 'Leave it to someone higher'. Van de Walle (1993), who examines politeness in classical Sanskrit, proposes a reassessment of the import of Brown & Levinson's P, D and R variables and the replacement of their one-dimensional hierarchy of strategies by a two-dimensional one featuring clarity/vagueness vs. (in)formality. Both revisions are then combined with Fraser & Nolen's emphasis on politeness as social appropriateness.

As already noted, Brown & Levinson's framework has been an especially popular object for theoretical amendments. Both Chen (1991) and Mao (1994) examine politeness in Chinese, questioning the Brown & Levinsonian notion of face. Some studies focus on even smaller amendments, such as that by Rhodes (1989), who concludes from his analysis of Ojibwa data that, contrary to Brown & Levinson's assumptions, positive politeness strategies can also be conventionalized; or Chilton (1990), whose analysis of political texts merely indicates the need to extend their framework to incorporate multiple audiences. Finally, some studies also use empirical data to arbitrate between different theoretical perspectives. An example is Chen (1993), whose contrastive study of politeness in American English and Chinese concludes that Brown & Levinson's theory can account for the American English data but not for Chinese, while Gu's framework is adequate for the Chinese data but not for American English. On the other hand, Leech's perspective is said to be able to account for both of them adequately.

All of these examples, and with them most of the field of politeness research, can be placed on a continuum with at one end a primary preoccupation with theoretical matters, and at the other a primary empirical concern. The further one moves to the latter side, the less attention is devoted to theoretical thinking, and at its extreme end one finds studies that merely apply one of the theories to empirical data, such as Adegbija (1989) on Nigerian English, Yoruba and Ogori, or Berk-Seligson (1988) on courtroom interaction (both based on Brown & Levinson). Other empirically inclined studies use a combination of bits and pieces of different theories, such as Koike (1989) on Brazilian Portuguese, who proposes some insights into why certain verb tenses are polite, and others are not, and uses notions from Brown & Levinson, Lakoff, Leech and Fraser & Nolen. Garcia (1993) on requests in Peruvian Spanish mentions Brown & Levinson and Blum-Kulka. El-Sayed (1989) on Arabic refers to Lakoff and Fraser & Nolen. And so on. The theoretical aspect of such investigations often seems inspired by practical *ad hoc* considerations, as it is general practice simply to enumerate a number of isolated aspects of various theories with which one agrees, and subsequently discuss empirical data by reference to any theory or part thereof that can provide a convenient explanation.

1.4 Summary

Besides briefly sketching their main positions and highlighting their distinctive aspects, this general introduction to the nine theoretical perspectives on which the analysis will be focused also already revealed a few common characteristics, such as the idea that politeness is involved in social indexing and functions as a strategic means of conflict-avoidance. These characteristics are retained in most other works on politeness, not only in purely empirically oriented research explicitly relying on one or more of the core theories, but also in more 'independent' frameworks that offer seemingly 'alternative' approaches to politeness. The overall claim of the present chapter is therefore that the nine core theories are representative for a large part, if not most, of current scientific thinking about politeness.

Chapter 2: First- and second-order politeness: epistemological concerns

In their introduction to a collection of papers on politeness, Watts et al. (1992a:3) argue for the need to make a clear distinction between first-order politeness (henceforth politeness1) and second-order politeness (henceforth politeness2), with the former referring to the commonsense notion of politeness, and the latter to its scientific conceptualization. Politeness1 is a socio-psychological concept, referring to *"the various ways in which polite behaviour is talked about by members of sociocultural groups"* (ibid.:3), whereas politeness2 is a linguistic, scientific concept, *"a more technical notion which can only have a value within an overall theory of social interaction"* (ibid.:4). Both concepts should be carefully distinguished, something the authors claim is not sufficiently done in current theorizing.

The distinction is indeed a relevant one, and of greater importance than might appear at first sight. By distinguishing between speakers' assessments of their own linguistic behaviour – the speaker's perspective – and scientists' assessments of that behaviour – the scientific perspective – it touches on methodological and epistemological issues regarding the study of linguistic behaviour which are seldom, if ever, thoroughly discussed in politeness research. It foregrounds the relationship between what people actually (say they) do and the various ways of theoretically capturing that behaviour – between the practice and the science of linguistic behaviour. In this sense it provides a direct pathway into the often hazy depths of sociolinguistic theorizing about language and social reality, and as such constitutes a good starting point for a more in-depth comparative study of the different theoretical perspectives. This chapter will therefore examine more closely the distinction between politeness1 and politeness2, and the way in which it is dealt with by current theories.

2.1 Politeness1 vs. Politeness2

Contrary to how it may seem at first sight – as in Kasper's statement that *"[f]irst order politeness phenomena constitute the input to politeness theories" (Kasper 1996:2)* – the distinction is neither a simple nor a straightforward one, and this may well be one of the main reasons why so many researchers fail to be consistent about it or to assess its implications thoroughly. As Watts et al. (1992a) point out, the distinction makes explicit the danger of unquestioningly using politeness1 concepts in scientific analysis. For if that is allowed to happen, the theory ends up with *"[…] a lay concept which has been elevated to the status of a second order concept"*, causing the analysis to *"[…] constantly vacillate between the way in which politeness is understood as a commonsense term that we all use and think we understand in everyday social interaction and a more technical notion that can only have value within an overall theory of social interaction"* (ibid.:4). According to the authors, this unhappy situation can only be avoided if *"[…] the theoretical second order concept is clearly defined and given some other name"* (ibid.:4), and so far, it is claimed, this has only been done by Watts and Arndt & Janney. Presumably, the latter statement is a reference to the notions of politic behaviour (Watts) and emotive communication (Arndt & Janney).

The danger identified by Watts et al. is real. For if the distinction is not properly made and politeness1 and politeness2 are simply equated, the epistemological status of the theoretical analysis becomes blurred. The concepts it uses then pertain simultaneously to the commonsense world of everyday interaction and to the world of scientific theorizing, and the distinction between these activities is lost, which causes the analysis to (possibly randomly) oscillate between both epistemological perspectives. As we will see later on, this is a major problem in much current theorizing.

However, the issue is more encompassing than Watts et al. envision. The danger they identify – the unquestioning incorporation of politeness1 concepts into scientific theory – occurs at the input stage of the theoretical process, where the move is one from politeness1 to politeness2, from the everyday world to the world of scientific theorizing. But there is also a point where the opposite move occurs, where the analysis moves from the world of scientific concepts back to the world of everyday reality. This move occurs at the output stage of the analytical process: any sociolinguistic analysis will always claim to say something relevant about everyday reality, and the products of theorizing (its politeness2 concepts) will need to be applied to that reality. Everyday reality is not only the input for the analysis, but also its target. There the danger lies in unquestioningly transferring our politeness2 concepts back into everyday reality, into the realm of politeness1. At that point too we need to examine closely the status of our politeness2 concepts in relation to politeness1 reality, lest a similar confusion between the scientific and everyday worlds results. So the problem occurs twice, because the politeness1–politeness2 relationship runs in two directions. Therefore, politeness2 concepts should not just be different from politeness1 concepts, or given different names, but rather the relationship between both notions should be carefully monitored *throughout the entire analytical process* – not only at the input stage.

As we will see, this is not done very often, if at all, by current politeness theories. The overall result is confusion at the conceptual level, creating a tension between the fluid, contingent reality of social interaction on the one hand, and the scientific aims of conceptual rigour and predictive theorizing on the other. But before going into that, and even before examining how the different theories handle the epistemological pitfalls of the politeness1-politeness2 distinction, let us first examine the distinction itself somewhat more closely, by attempting to determine the characteristics of both of its sides in more detail.

2.1.1 Politeness1

At first glance, there seem to be two possible sides to politeness as an everyday concept: an action-related and a conceptual side. The action-related side refers to the way politeness actually manifests itself in communicative behaviour, that is, politeness as an aspect of communicative interaction. The conceptual side, on the other hand, refers to commonsense ideologies of politeness: to the way politeness is used as a concept, to opinions about what politeness is all about. Whereas the former refers to lay assessments *of* (one's own or other speakers') politeness in action, and is thus concerned with what goes on when people *use* politeness, the latter refers to lay assessments *about* politeness from a more detached standpoint: it is concerned with the way people *talk about* and provide accounts of politeness. From Watts et al.'s definition, although succinct, it is clear that they aim for the second aspect: politeness as a lay *concept*. They do not explicitly state whether the first aspect is to be incorporated under politeness1 or not, but implicitly it can be assumed that this is not what they intend: they introduce the distinction in order to foreground the relationship between commonsense and scientific *concepts*. But nor can it belong to politeness2, so it must fall outside the scope of the distinction altogether. Watts et al.'s distinction is a strictly theoretical one, a distinction between different concepts, and this does not include the practice that is being conceptualized. The latter seems rather to fit into their theoretical scheme in the role of *explanandum*, making a third category of politeness: let us call it politeness-in-action. It does not belong to theory, it is *data*, that which should be explained by theory. This would lead to a picture where on the one hand you have data (people using politeness, politeness-in-action), and on the other, two kinds of concepts: a lay concept (what those people say/think they do when they use politeness, politeness1) and a scientific one (what scientists say/think those people do when they use politeness, politeness2), each on a different level of abstraction. Clear as it may seem, this still leaves a few crucial problems unaccounted for.

First, it seems that politeness-in-action and politeness1 will be very closely related in actual practice. In the field of study of concepts and concept formation, an important distinction is that between spontaneous and scientific concepts. Vygotsky characterizes these as:

> [...] two different forms of reasoning. In the case of scientific thinking, the primary role is played by *initial verbal definition*, which being applied systematically, gradually comes down to concrete phenomena. The development of spontaneous concepts knows no systematicity and goes from the phenomena upward toward generalizations. (Vygotsky 1968:148, original emphasis)

Scientific concepts are exact and pre-defined. They are abstract concepts, detached from everyday reality. In terms of their acquisition, they start off *as concepts*, in an abstract definitional form, and are only later on gradually 'filled up' with empirical content, a process which typically involves the explanatory efforts of a teacher. Spontaneous concepts, on the other hand, evolve in the opposite direction: they belong to the world of everyday reality and experience, so their initial acquisitional form is empirical. They follow a bottom-up path of development, from practice (experience) to generalizing conceptualization, they are known in action before they are known consciously and conceptually. By the time they reach the state of definitional conceptualization, their empirical content is already completely assimilated. As examples Vygotsky uses 'Archimedean law' versus 'brother' (ibid.:158). Whereas the former initially has no repercussions in personal experience, the latter is deeply rooted within it. Politeness1 as an everyday concept clearly belongs to Vygotsky's category of 'spontaneous concepts', as it originates in the realm of personal experience. Since such concepts are *post hoc* abstractions from personal experience, how a person thinks and feels about, or conceptualizes politeness will be very closely connected with that person's personal experiences in concrete social interaction, the latter providing the empirical building blocks for its construction.

Of course, adults and especially parents play a strong guiding role in politeness1 (see, for example, Blum-Kulka 1990; Demuth 1986; Clancy 1986; Gleason et al. 1984; Snow et al. 1990; Yahya-Othman 1994): on the one hand, they provide explications of how and why to be polite, issue directives such as 'Be polite, say "thank you"', or forbid things on the grounds that they are 'impolite'; on the other hand, they implicitly elaborate the concept by instructing the child on how he or she should behave in general. In this regard, politeness1 differs from a concept such as 'brother', the learning of which does not involve such directives, but proceeds through hearing it being used referentially. Its content is built from the referents for which it is used in everyday situations and speech. But although politeness1 does not have any physical referents such as 'brother', it is still denotative in that it involves directives for, and thus references to, action. Just as the 'brother' concept initially consists of the *people* referred to as 'brother' (and only later acquires its more general and abstract classificatory meaning), 'politeness' initially consists of the specific *acts* referred to as 'polite'. This can clearly be seen from, for example,. Blum-Kulka's (1992) study of everyday concepts of politeness in Israel, where the informant Maayan, age 7, defines politeness by saying that *"[...] it is polite to say 'thank you', and 'please' but also 'it was good' after a meal, and 'to hug my Mommy'"* *(ibid.:260)*. Initially, the concept of politeness *is* the actions, the concept is defined by summing up the actions that can be subsumed under it.

On the other hand, everyday concepts can also be seen as Vygotskian signs, as "psychological tools" (Wertsch 1985:77-81), and as such they are forms of mediation between consciousness and the external world. Since politeness1 is a concept concerned specifically with social interaction, its mediating position will be between consciousness and the social world. But mediation of course works in two directions. Concepts influence one's interpretation of the world, passively shaping it through providing it with order, but they also actively shape that world since they will influence concrete action taken in and on that world. Thus, how a person thinks and feels about politeness will also influence when and how he or she will behave politely. As a consequence, when concepts such as politeness1 are seen as psychological tools or signs that affect our perception as well as our action, they cease to be (static) objects, but should in fact be regarded more as practices.

This means that the distinction between politeness-in-action and politeness1 is an artificial one at best, and that, if it is made at all, it should at least be treated with caution. Due to the mediating nature of Vygotskian signs/concepts, politeness-in-action is not only a function of concepts of politeness1, but politeness1 will also be a function of politeness-in-action. Thus a view arises in which not only action is influenced by cognition, but also cognition by action. Since politeness-in-action and politeness1 are inherently and dynamically interrelated, both should be covered by the term politeness1. So the term will be used to refer to speakers speaking politely (the practice of politeness in everyday interaction), as well as to their spontaneous conceptualizations. As the notion is thus deeply rooted in the *practice* of everyday interaction, the whole complex sub-sumed under politeness1 can be termed the 'practice of politeness', or 'politeness-as-practice'.

Now that this 'action-centredness' is established as a fundamental characteristic of politeness1 in general, the preliminary dual distinction be-tween the action-related and conceptual sides of politeness1 made at the beginning of this section becomes obsolete. Instead, a three-way subdi-vision presents itself, as three different kinds of politeness-as-practice can be distinguished, which can be labelled *expressive, classificatory* and *metapragmatic*. Expressive politeness1 refers to politeness encoded in speech, to instances where the speaker aims at 'polite' behaviour: the use of honorifics or terms of address in general, conventional formulaic ex-pressions ('thank you', 'excuse me', ...), different request formats, apologies, etc. ..., i.e. the usual objects of investigation in most politeness research. Classificatory politeness1 refers to politeness used as a categorizational tool: it covers hearers' judgements (in actual interaction) of other people's interactional behaviour as 'polite' or 'impolite'. Finally, metapragmatic politeness1 covers instances of talk about politeness as a concept, about what people perceive politeness to be all about. Although these labels cover different interactional practices related to polite-ness1, they are of course closely interrelated. Even so, looking at them separately can reveal other fundamental characteristics of politeness1.

Evaluativity

As becomes clear from classificatory politeness1, and as we also learn from existing investigations into the nature of commonsense notions of politeness (e.g. Blum-Kulka 1992; Ide et al. 1992), politeness1 has a notably *evaluative* character: the notions of politeness and impolite-ness are used to characterize (other) people's behaviour, and to do so judgementally. In this sense politeness involves what could be called an 'evaluative moment'.

Generally speaking, politeness comprises a positive, and impoliteness a negative evaluation. The noun 'politeness' is associated with 'civilized' forms of behaviour (Blum-Kulka 1992:258), as well as with 'tolerance', 'good manners', and 'being nice to people' (ibid.:257), while the adjec-tive 'polite' strongly correlates with adjectives such as 'appropriate', 'friendly', or 'respectful', and generally leads to 'pleasant' interactions (Ide et al. 1992:290). As Ehlich (1992:75) puts it, 'polite' actions are *"posi-tively marked"*. Some exceptions to this have been noted however, and should be examined more closely. Culpeper (1996) for example discusses what he terms 'mock impoliteness', or 'banter', and defines it as *"[...] impoliteness that remains on the surface, since it is understood that it is not intended to cause offence."* (ibid.:352). Included are interactional practices such as ritual insults ('sounding' amongst black adolescents in the USA (Labov 1972), but also occurring in other cultures). It would thus be a form of impoliteness which is not evaluated negatively.

However, I would argue that banter is not a form of politeness1 at all. For one thing, it is not a case of classificatory politeness1, since the speaker's behaviour is obviously not evaluated by the hearer as genuinely impolite or rude. If it were, it would no longer qualify as 'banter' but would rather become 'insult'. By the same token, it cannot be expressive politeness1 either (where the speaker aims at being impolite), since one of the characteristics of banter is exactly that the 'insults' used are not sincere. Since it is neither intended nor perceived as impoliteness, banter does not seem to qualify as politeness1; it is only a form of (im)politeness according to the scientist's classification. Note how the scientific interpretation thus involves a separation between politeness1 and politeness2.

Another exception would be when people affirm and positively associate with their own 'impoliteness'. However, this would only seem to occur in situations in which the definition of (im)politeness is foreign to the evaluator, for example when politeness is equated with formality or etiquette when the evaluator strongly believes in the value of informal behaviour, or in reaction to someone else's actual criticism of impoliteness. In the latter case, the qualification of (im)politeness emerges from a real Other, while in the former it emerges from a hypothetical Other – who believes in the value and politeness of formal behaviour and would thus consider informal behaviour 'impolite'. In both cases the evaluator him- or herself would not spontaneously qualify his or her own behaviour as 'impolite', so again these examples do not really qualify as instances of politeness1.

Thus I would argue that when interactional behaviour is classified as 'impoliteness', this always involves a negative evaluation. The reverse is not true, however. The evaluative term 'polite' can have negative implications. Apart from the prevailing positive orientation, Blum-Kulka's (1992) Israeli informants also characterize politeness as *"[...] something external, hypocritical, unnatural"* (ibid.:257). This negative qualification is associated with the view of politeness as an outward mask, an insincere performance delivered for the sake of displaying good manners, or even worse, the possibility of manipulative use of politeness (saying one thing while meaning or trying to achieve something completely different). In this case, the qualification of behaviour as 'polite' would be sincere and negative at the same time: the hearer would indeed consider the speaker to have behaved politely, but the fact that he or she did would be evaluated negatively, (for example, if the hearer preferred sincerity in the speaker's expression of opinion). Another possible case of politeness implying a negative evaluation would occur when, as in Bourdieu's (1991:40) discussion of *soigné*, the term would be used to mean 'petty and mean-spirited', or 'petit-bourgeois'. So, although polite(ness) and impolite(ness) are generally each other's opposites, they are not equal in evaluative scope: where impolite(ness) always implies a negative qualification, polite(ness) can be positive as well as negative. But whichever is the case, there will be no doubt that they are always evaluative in nature.

Argumentativity
Evaluativity shows that classificatory politeness1 should not be regarded as a neutral or objective categorization of behaviour, but is intimately connected with (social) values. It is a principle of social judgement, and, as Bourdieu notes, such *"[...] practical classifications are always subordinated to practical functions and oriented towards the production of social effects"* (1991:220, original emphasis). As a classificatory tool, politeness1 is always geared to some social effect, it tries to accomplish some social aim; it is not categorization *for the sake of categorization*, as has long been the purported aim of scientific classification. In science, the aim of classification is the taxonomy itself, whereas in practical classifications this is not the case. In the ideal scientific classification, the objects of study should organize themselves, as it were, into a taxonomy. A biological classification of animals based on their (structural) characteristics is scientifically acceptable, whereas a classification based on social evaluation that serves some social (e.g. political) end is not, such as the distinction of human beings into 'Untermenschen' and 'Übermenschen'. The scientific taxonomy and the characteristics used to construct it are expected to be socially neutral or objective. In practical classifications however, such as in calling someone (im)polite, one is involved in immediate social action: one draws a social distinction based on value, one subjects the other's behaviour to (social) evaluation, one approves or condemns. In the sense that it is always aimed at some social effect, classificatory politeness1 can be said to be inherently *argumentative*.[1] It

---

[1] Throughout the discussion, the term 'argumentative' will be used in a loosely descriptive sense, referring to various forms of 'involvedness' or 'interestedness'.

always and only occurs in situations that involve social stakes, situations in which there is something to lose or gain.

A simple example involving the use of Terms of Address (ToA) – traditionally one of the central topics in politeness research – can illustrate how argumentativity is also prominent in expressive politeness1. When a child addresses or refers to its father as 'daddy', 'dad', 'father' or 'sir', these terms are not merely free substitutes for each other. Neither are they substitutes for 'male (biological) parent', which would be a plausible candidate for a scientifically acceptable, socially neutral, objective referential term. What is more, if the child were to address its father as 'male biological parent', that term too would lose its socially neutral character and become a value-laden social evaluation. This is the case because no matter by what term a child addresses its father, it is *de facto* always *relating* to him, so that anything the child says will automatically take on social value and have a social effect. In short, politeness1 is always an instance of everyday social life, and as a social practice it will always be geared towards, or at least have, some social effect.

An apparent exception to this claim could be situations involving metapragmatic politeness1, as they occur for example in interviews with informants in sociolinguistic investigations into politeness. There we have situations in which there appears to be nothing to lose or gain, while informants are definitely involved in talk about their (commonsense) conceptualization of politeness. In fact, in taking the information produced in such interviews at face value, as statements of fact and not as argumentative statements, such studies *presuppose* that the informants talk freely and objectively (i.e. non-argumentatively) about their conceptions of politeness, and thus that there is nothing for them to lose or gain in the situation.

There are three caveats to this presupposition, however. First, in everyday interaction such instances of people talking about their conception of politeness will mostly occur in situations which are argumentative, as for example when prompted by an actual assessment of actual behaviour. Second, as argued above, informants' conceptions about politeness are

---

An act or notion can thus be said to be argumentative in that, for example, it is geared towards some social effect or other strategic goal (such as behavioural control); or when social stakes such as one's status or identity are involved (as in processes of social assimilation vs dissimilation, social distinction, etc.); or when it assumes a morally/ethically involved position (in acts of approving/condemning).

intimately connected with their actual experiences in real-life interactions, in which there are always social stakes. And third, the scientist-informant situation itself is not devoid of social stakes. The fact that the researcher is an outsider to the informants, moreover one who investigates, and is interested in how they really think and feel about an issue which is associated with 'proper' behaviour, will contribute to the 'frontstage' character of the situation (Goffman 1959), in which there are definite social gains and losses: in what they say, the informants will be taken to display who they 'really' are. The argumentativity of politeness1 can even be witnessed directly from the results obtained from such situations: all the informants show a clear understanding of 'right' and 'wrong' behaviour, and they always situate themselves, not really surprisingly, on the 'right' side. For example, Blum-Kulka's informants voice:

> [...] recurring complaints concerning the 'impolite' behavior of the Israeli in public places; street behavior is found lacking in restraint (loud voice, bad language) and consideration (not queuing, pushing and shoving), and public service deplorable (phone operators in government offices). (Blum-Kulka 1992:259)

Although these complaints concern "the Israeli" it is clear that the complainers do not consider themselves part of the group of people complained about (otherwise the behaviour complained about would simply be 'expected' and no longer something to complain about). I would argue that this is a general characteristic, not only of metapragmatic politeness1, but of the whole of politeness1, which clearly shows, and derives from, its argumentative character. People never identify with impoliteness, but always see themselves as generally polite.[2] Impoliteness is almost always a property attributed to others. This can also be observed in the famous Discourse Completion Tests (DCT) or role-play situations used in data-gathering throughout the politeness literature. Those procedures boil down to asking informants to give a public display (albeit anonymously in DCTs) of what they consider (or would claim) to be their characteristic behaviour in certain hypothetical situations. Little wonder that everyone always ends up being so remarkably polite to one another.

---

[2] Of course, a speaker can consciously aim for impoliteness in order to achieve some strategic effect. Another exception would be when a speaker acknowledges and positively associates with his or her own 'impoliteness', but as argued earlier in this section, such cases actually involve a definition of 'impoliteness' which is foreign to the speaker.

The argumentativity of politeness1 therefore entails that the common-sense distinction between politeness and impoliteness can never be objective, but is always geared towards some social effect. Blum-Kulka initially indicates an awareness of the phenomenon when she states that informants:

> [...] tend to evoke normative descriptions of the phenomenon and en-gage, to a degree, in positive self-representation (a polite act in its own right) by coming up with what seems to them socially acceptable definitions. (ibid.:257)

However, she eventually fails to incorporate the argumentativity of po-liteness1 into her model, and therefore also into her methodological approach to the data. She fails to take these complaints for what they really are (i.e. 'complaints'), and instead treats them as statements of fact. Since, as we have seen in section 1.1.6, in her model politeness is related to 'cultural scripts', this leads her to conclude that, regarding norms of politeness for interaction in the public sphere in present-day Israeli cul-ture, *"[...] the metapragmatic discourse of informants admits to the lack of cultural scripts in this area"* (ibid.:278). In the light of the foregoing, this is an unwarranted and untenable conclusion. Although exact num-bers are not given, the complaints must be numerous since they lead to a conclusion regarding the whole of 'Israeli present-day culture'. But if they are, then the conclusion becomes paradoxical. Since the complainers are able to identify Others' behaviour in public as 'impolite', they must have some idea of what would constitute polite public behaviour – or they would not be able to make the distinction in the first place. And as politeness is dependent upon cultural scripts, at least the complainers have knowledge of such scripts. So if the complaints are numerous within the corpus, then the conclusion of a *lack* of cultural scripts is unwarranted, and something else must be going on. What that something else is might become clearer when we acknowledge and take into account the argumentativity of po-liteness1, which, as will be argued later on, shows how the complainers are socially positioning themselves *vis-à-vis* the social world.

The examples referred to in this section further illustrate the ontologi-cal difference between politeness1 and politeness2: the child's ToA and the complainers' classificatory acts are part of the practice of everyday social life, and as such always involve social stakes. They are inherently argumentative and can never be socially neutral. Scientific classifications, on the other hand,are part of a completely different world (at least in prin-ciple): the practice of scientific theorizing. Because of this ontological difference, the two should always be carefully distinguished.

'Polite'-ness

Investigations into commonsense conceptions of politeness have shown that in everyday practice the terms 'politeness' and 'impoliteness' are distinct and opposite notions. 'Politeness' always refers to the 'polite' end of the polite–impolite continuum, it never covers impolite forms of behaviour. The latter have their own denominative term: 'impoliteness'. However, again there are two apparent exceptions.

Although in cases where politeness is seen as hypocritical or insincere the term refers to negatively evaluated behaviour, such instances do not really counter the present argument, for there is no doubt about whether the speaker has been 'polite' or 'impolite', only whether or not his or her behaviour was sincere. The question is, 'was the speaker sincerely or insincerely *polite*?' or 'was the speaker *honest* or *only polite*?', not 'was the speaker sincerely or insincerely *impolite*?'. In other words, the speaker's linguistic behaviour is evaluated as 'polite', only there are doubts as to whether this outward appearance matches the speaker's actual intentions or opinions.

A second exception involves cases where (too much) politeness has the effect of being interpreted as impolite, as in Garfinkel's (1972) notorious experiments where he asked his students to behave *"in a circumspect and polite fashion"* (ibid.:9) towards members of their families. As is well known, when the students upheld this behaviour long enough, the family members invariably became angry and generally fumed at the students' behaviour. Among the qualifications flung at them, 'impolite' did figure. But here again, the exception is only apparent, for the politeness the students were asked to display was clearly described: they were told to act as if they were boarders in their own homes, *"[...] to avoid getting personal, to use formal address, to speak only when spoken to."* (ibid.:9). In other words, politeness was equated with formality, behaviour that they would display in other situations, in being polite towards people other than their families. I would argue that only the fact that they behaved as if they were strangers in their own families was interpreted as impoliteness, and whether or not they displayed politeness in their roles of strangers was of little import. The students' aim was to behave as polite strangers, not polite family members. But in spite of their behaviour, they still remained family members, and so their parents and siblings simply observed a family member who treated them as strangers and they evaluated this behaviour as 'impolite' (other adjectives used were 'mean', 'inconsiderate', 'selfish', 'nasty', but never 'polite'). They did not regard the students as 'polite strangers' but rather as 'family members acting as strangers', so their evaluations of impoliteness were not aimed at the politeness of the students' behaviour.

Normativity

Finally, as also noted by Blum-Kulka (1992), politeness1 has a markedly *normative* aspect: it involves social norms. This results directly from the combination of its evaluative nature with the fact that it is oriented towards the 'polite', positive end of the polite–impolite continuum. The normativity of politeness1 is closely connected to its association with 'appropriateness', and its nature and origins become very clear in a historical perspective. Ehlich (1992) argues that politeness involves the evaluation of behaviour against a standard, and shows that in the European late Middle Ages, when an explicit conceptualization of such a standard first emerged, it was related to the sphere of life at the court. Although initially the rules of *courtoisie*/courtesy – as it was called then – were confined to life at court, they later spread throughout other layers of society for which they provided an ideal model on which 'appropriate' behaviour should be modelled. During the following centuries, as social structures changed and the political influence of the court came under siege from the rising urban culture, the concept of *courtoisie* was contested by an emerging notion of *civileté*/civility. The emergence of both concepts, and also the struggle between them, gave rise to an extensive prescriptive literature singing the praises of the respective 'ideal' ways of interacting.

In his overview of politeness research, Fraser groups this popular literature under what he calls the "social norm view" of politeness, the view that:

> [...] assumes that each society has a particular set of social norms consisting of more or less explicit rules that prescribe a certain behavior, a state of affairs, or a way of thinking in a context. (Fraser 1990:220)

This perspective, where politeness is seen as a matter of social norms and which is said to be *"[...] generally embraced by the public within the English-speaking world"* (ibid.:220), is dismissed as unscientific and contrasted to scientific perspectives such as the 'conversational-maxim view' (Lakoff, Leech, Kasher), the 'face-saving view' (Brown & Levinson) and the 'conversational contract view' (Fraser & Nolen). However, contrary to Fraser's claim, the general normative nature of politeness1 is widely accepted in the current literature and, as will be argued below, many theoretical frameworks actually incorporate it in their conception of politeness2 in some way or other – so that Fraser's category of the 'social norm view' will prove to be rather crowded.

Modality and reflexivity

Ehlich (1992) discusses two further basic characteristics of commonsense politeness: modality and reflexivity. The modality of politeness1 refers to the optionality of polite interactional strategies for the actor. The notion of a polite action only makes sense against the background of the possibility of impolite or non-polite action. It is only possible to evaluate an action as 'polite' when that action could have been performed in an alternative way which would have been evaluated as 'impolite'. Therefore, *"[...] non-optional politeness is not possible."* (ibid.:76). This optionality is not an empirical matter, for:

> [...] the actor's choice between alternative actions [...] is established by principle. The alternative actions themselves may be restricted by social conditions, but this does not prevent basic optionality from being a condition of 'polite' activity. (ibid.:77)

However, viewed in this light optionality is not only a characteristic of (im)polite action but rather of action in general: in principle there is always the option of not performing an action at all. As there is always a choice between speaking or not speaking, modality/optionality is a basic notion to be considered by any theory of action. However, although even this basic choice can have evaluative consequences in terms of '(in)appropriateness' or '(im)politeness', because of its general nature modality does not seem to be a characteristic specific to politeness. As for reflexivity, this is already contained in the notions of evaluativity and normativity. Because it involves an evaluative and thus metalinguistic or metapragmatic moment, politeness1 is inherently a reflexive activity, all the more so if the evaluation is based on some behavioural standard or norm.

2.1.2 Politeness2

Since the aim of social science is to capture, understand and explain (aspects of) social reality, it seems self-evident that politeness2 should concern the scientific conceptualization of the social phenomenon of politeness in the form of a theory of politeness1. By means of such a theory we should be able to understand how politeness1 works, what its functionality is, what it 'does' for people and for society in general. As Watts (1991) argues, it involves:

[an] after-the-event assessment of what had occurred. Second order interpretation of this kind engages us in a form of meta-communication in which inferencing processes are at one remove from those that were carried out at the time of the interaction. (ibid.:257)

So although politeness2 should no doubt be *about* politeness1, the concepts developed in a theory of politeness should be able to *explain* the phenomena observed as politeness1. They should provide a view of politeness1 'at one remove', grasping the phenomenon in its totality, revealing its inner workings and its functionality. With this in mind one can derive the minimal characteristics of an adequate politeness2 conceptualization from the characteristics of politeness1.

Since one of the basic characteristics of politeness1 is evaluativity, politeness2 should be able to show the functionality and inner workings of politeness1 *as an evaluative activity*. But in order to be able to do this, it must not itself be evaluative. Evaluation being the object of politeness2, its concepts should at least themselves avoid being evaluative in nature.

This can be illustrated by means of a brief reference to Bourdieu's discussion of ethnic identity:

One can understand the particular form of struggle over classifications that is constituted by the struggle over the definition of 'regional' or 'ethnic' identity only if one transcends the opposition that science, in order to break away from the preconceptions of spontaneous sociology, must first establish between representation and reality, and only if one includes in reality the representation of reality, or, more precisely, the struggle over representations in the sense of mental images, but also of social demonstrations whose aim it is to manipulate mental images (and even in the sense of delegations responsible for organizing the demonstrations that are necessary to modify mental representations). (Bourdieu 1991:221)

Ethnic/regional identity is a concept which classifies human beings into social groups, in a process of classificatory evaluation: it evaluates people against some set of criteria, and classifies them accordingly into this or that group. In this way it superimposes its distinction of ethnic groups on reality. It constitutes a representation of (social) reality which is aimed at a specific social effect: the 'realization' or 'implementation' of the very distinction with which it represents the social world. In other words, the concept is part of the struggle over the representation of reality. Bourdieu warns that in order to properly understand a notion such as ethnic identity, it is crucial that its scientific study should fully acknowledge this aspect. In order to accomplish this the scientist should avoid the trap of making a choice between on the one hand objectivist arbitration, where alternative representations are measured against reality, and on the other hand subjectivist commitment to one or the other representation. Both avenues eventually lead to the objectification of a representation, passing *"[...] from the representation of reality to the reality of the representation."* (Bourdieu 1991:224). Both lead to a view where one representation is claimed to be 'objective', necessarily stigmatizing other representations as erroneous. Both lead to a science which is directly involved in the struggle over reality (by making a choice, by establishing a set of criteria as real), thereby losing its grip on one of the fundamental characteristics of social reality, namely *"[...] the specific logic of the social world, that 'reality' which is the site of a permanent struggle to define reality."* (ibid.:224, original emphasis). In other words, in *getting involved in* the struggle over reality, one loses sight of reality *as* a struggle. In order to avoid this, one should recognize the 'struggle' character of reality by making it the object of research, by including representations, or the struggle over representations, in one's conceptualization of reality. Only by placing itself above the struggle over reality, can science get a grasp on the nature of social reality as a struggle.

This line of reasoning is equally applicable to politeness2 as the scientific conceptualization of politeness1, since the latter also superimposes an evaluative distinction of 'polite behaviour' vs. 'impolite behaviour' on the reality of 'behaviour' *tout court*. So it too involves a representation of reality, and one that is not unequivocal: the same stretch of behaviour is not always unanimously evaluated as polite or impolite. In Ide et al.'s (1992) study of commonsense notions of politeness among Japanese and Americans, the American informants disagree amongst themselves as to the appropriateness of the evaluation 'polite' in the majority of situations examined (10 out of 14), while in 4 out of 14 cases, this disagreement is substantial (in terms of the distribution of informants over the 'yes', 'no', and 'can't say either yes or no' answers). The Japanese informants are even more divided: their judgements are unanimous in only 2 situations, and in 8 cases the disagreement is substantial. In the sense that alternative interpretations coexist, we can say that a struggle over the representation of reality is taking place within politeness1. Therefore, following Bourdieu, an adequate scientific approach should place itself above this struggle, by acknowledging the struggle aspect as one of the basic characteristics of politeness1. It should avoid getting involved in the struggle over representations of reality, and instead incorporate these representations into reality by making the struggle over them the object of research.[3] It should avoid choosing this or that representation either by subjectivist commitment or by objectivist arbitration, since in both cases it would become involved *in* the struggle and inevitably lose sight of reality *as* a struggle.

Since evaluations of politeness are also normative, what has been said about evaluativity is equally applicable to normativity: politeness2, and therefore the concepts in its toolbox, should be non-normative in nature. In this light, Ehlich's argument runs contrary to Bourdieu's recommendations when he states:

> Just as reference to the standard is absolutely necessary for qualifying the individual action as polite, so too is it necessary for *attempting to attribute politeness in cross-group comparisons*. However, whereas in relation to individual actions by individual actors the standard is developed by the group itself and reproduced when politeness is attributed, *the attempt to find a standard beyond those groups* can become caught up all too easily in two different traps: in ethnocentricity or in apparent universality. Both may occur together – and this is more often than not likely to be the case, viz., when an ethnocentric or historically specific standard is raised to the status of a universal. (Ehlich 1992:79, my emphasis)

The danger of the theoretical endeavour losing its way through getting entangled in the struggle over reality instead of acknowledging reality as a struggle is markedly present here. If the aim cross-cultural politeness research sets for itself is (to develop scientific ways or procedures) *"to attribute politeness"*, then it will inevitably need concepts which allow such attributions to be made, i.e. concepts which are evaluative in nature. Evaluation will become not the object, but the instrument of science, which consequently will only be able to present a highly attenuated picture of reality. Likewise, to attempt to *"find a standard beyond [...] groups"* means that the core concepts of the theoretical model will have to be such standards or 'norms', and the theory will inevitably itself become normative as it will claim to present the 'ultimate' or 'scientific' behavioural standard/

---

[3] Of course, this only works up to a point, as the result of such an analysis itself also constitutes a representation of reality (which also becomes a voice in the struggle over reality). But at least it has the advantage of being a representation that takes into account the struggle-character of the reality under investigation, and is thus able to present a richer picture of that reality than an analysis that does not.

norm. In the end we get a scientific theory that is involved in exactly the same activity as the actor it is supposed to study: making normative evaluations. As such it ceases to be 'at one remove' of its object, and the normativity of politeness is so to speak 'taken for granted' instead of questioned; it is 'mimicked' instead of examined; it is instrument instead of object. So what Bourdieu is saying is that one can only grasp the true nature of spontaneous concepts if one acknowledges their argumentative nature, i.e. that they have a social purpose (in the struggle over reality). In order to do this one must include those concepts/representations in reality, in the sense that they are the objects of research, and should not themselves be part of the explanatory apparatus used to grasp that reality.

Finally, since the commonsense notions of politeness and impoliteness are so very closely related that one is labelled by the negative qualification of the other, it seems reasonable that an adequate politeness2 theory should be able to capture both phenomena at the same time. Thus, unlike politeness1, which is restricted to the polite end of the polite–impolite continuum, politeness2 should cover the whole range of the continuum. This becomes possible when politeness2 involves a non-evaluative and non-normative conceptualization, as it is then freed from the positive evaluative connotations of norms and norm-guided behaviour, as well as of the negative evaluation implicit in 'impoliteness'. Concentrating instead on the argumentativity of both notions, studying them as forms or practices of evaluation, the positive–negative distinction between them ceases to exist, allowing both of them to be captured by the same conceptualization.

But the positive–negative distinction is also transcended in a different sense: just as a normative approach to politeness tends to get lost in the struggle over the representation of reality, it also inevitably gets entangled in the positive–negative distinction between politeness and impoliteness (in the sense of the latter being the negative of the former), and is consequently forced to conceptualize impoliteness in a negative manner (as a lack of something), as a sort of negative action. In a non-normative approach however, this is no longer necessary, and both can be considered as 'positive actions'.[4] As we shall see, although many theoretical perspectives argue for just such a broader notion of politeness2, few succeed in

---

[4] The qualifications 'positive' and 'negative', when applied to 'action' are not intended to carry the same meaning as when they are applied to 'evaluation'. Where in the latter case they have the meaning of 'good' and 'bad' respectively, in the former they should be taken to denote actions which 'accomplish something' vs actions which 'fail to accomplish something'. The expressions are

escaping the positive–negative pitfall.

In sum, I have identified three main characteristics of an adequate politeness2 theory, which were derived from the characteristics of politeness1: non-evaluativity, non-normativity, and a broad scope covering the whole of the continuum between polite and impolite.

2.2   The distinction in politeness theory

Let us now turn to the question of how the politeness1–politeness2 distinction can be found in scientific theories of linguistic politeness. Although Watts et al. (1992) maintain that the distinction is simply not made in most cases (except for Watts and Arndt & Janney), a closer look at the implicit claims made by the frameworks reveals that it is always present in the background, albeit sometimes unnoticed, while the overall lack of attention to its consequences implies that it is apparently not regarded as problematic.

2.2.1 Lakoff

Lakoff's framework is a case in point. Although she does not explicitly mention the distinction, on closer inspection we see that it is implicitly present in her conceptualization of politeness. Lakoff's roots in Generative Linguistics – more specifically Generative Semantics – affect her conceptualization in that the rules of politeness she proposes are seen as part of a system of pragmatic rules, which she likens to that of syntactic rules (a "grammar of style" Lakoff 1979). And just as syntactic rules belong to the domain of linguistic theorizing, i.e. are a systematic abstraction from – or abstract systematics of – linguistic data, so politeness rules are primarily seen as a *linguistic tool* to capture the systematics of the process. In Lakoff's own words:

> [...] all we want to do is to understand, say, why word B follows word A in a sentence, why action A generally precedes action B in a non-linguistic transaction. This *understanding* comes in the form of *rule-writing*. (Lakoff 1975:86-87, my emphasis)

So the rules are products of the scientist, part of the scientific way of

---

intended to have the same meaning as, and are used here to stress the relationship with, the positive-negative distinction between politeness and impoliteness, where the latter is the negative of the former as encoded by the prefix 'im-'.

capturing the systematicity of language use; they are not part of the way ordinary people talk about politeness. This uniquely scientific viewpoint is also evidenced in the integration of politeness rules with the Gricean CP and its maxims: rather than capturing ordinary speakers' argumentative evaluations, they are general linguistic principles, involved in the process of how people understand each other.

The scope of Lakoff's concept of politeness is also much broader than ordinary speakers' actual evaluations of (im)politeness, as it includes general notions of situational appropriateness, and is part of a general system of interactional style which classifies people's interactional behaviour according to how they handle interpersonal relationships (Lakoff 1979:62). A similarly broad scope is found in the range of phenomena explained by the politeness rules. To mention only one: the use of technical terms in medical or legal jargon – and of bureaucratese in general – in referring to 'unmentionables' such as sex, elimination or war is adduced as an example of Distance politeness (Lakoff 1973:299; 1990:36). Although Lakoff's claim that technical terms divorce the phenomena referred to from their emotional content seems reasonable enough, it is less evident that the (non-)use of technical jargon would be interpreted as (im)politeness by ordinary speakers. It does not seem to make much sense to claim that a politician's choice of the term 'conflict' instead of 'war' is made out of politeness considerations, or that he or she would be considered 'impolite' were he or she to talk about 'the war' instead.

So Lakoff's notion of politeness derives from the specific viewpoint and goals of scientific investigation – it is specific to the practice of doing science – while it also covers a broader range of phenomena than ordinary speakers' conceptualizations and evaluations of politeness. But there is also a definite connection between her theory and politeness1. Distance politeness is claimed to be *"equivalent to what most people in our society consider 'polite' behavior, since it has been our standard form of politeness for about a millennium, and we are used to it"* (Lakoff 1990:35). In spite of this age-old standard, Camaraderie is said to be rapidly taking over as the preferred form of politeness in 'this [i.e. US] culture' (ibid.:38), although it is not really clear whether those who prefer Camaraderie would spontaneously qualify that style (conventional intimacy, 'mellow', 'laid back', with a lot of 'Y'know's and 'I mean's – ibid.:38-39) as 'polite'. They would probably not qualify Deference as 'polite', however, which is said to be the preferred style of many Asian societies (ibid.:37).

Furthermore, the rules of politeness do seem to capture directly ordinary speakers' politeness1 evaluations, as for example rule 1 ('Don't impose; remain aloof') is associated with social norms for *"proper"* behaviour and *"correct table manners"*, violations of which *"[...] we may describe as 'gross', as 'being familiar', or as 'having no breeding', all somewhat old-fashioned terms, seeming to indicate that this rule of politeness has fallen on evil days here"* (Lakoff 1977:88). The 'politeness' discussed here is no longer about how scientists make sense of linguistic behaviour, but how people evaluate it in everyday interaction. It is an everyday evaluative system located in the heads of ordinary people. Likewise, the claim about rule 1 that *"[...] it is often easier even after long acquaintance to address cleaning women, janitors, and so on by title + last name"* (ibid.:90) implies that this rule is a psychological reality for speakers, making communication 'easier', less awkward. In later work, Lakoff even explicitly claims that *"[...] the rules they [linguists] try to capture are [...] those all fluent speakers of a language use without conscious reflection: rules that are ingrained in the mind, learned effortlessly in infancy"* (Lakoff 1990:24). So the rules which were initially claimed to be an a posteriori (descriptive) derivation by the scientist as a means of *understanding* data, are now – in a gigantic epistemological leap – assumed to reside in the heads of speakers as a priori (predictive) rules involved in *producing* those data.

This duality causes the distinction between politeness1 and politeness2 to become blurred, not only in the sense that the distinction between spontaneous and scientific concepts is not adequately made and maintained, but also in the sense that the scientific concepts designed to capture politeness1 are themselves involved in evaluating behaviour in terms of (im)politeness. In stipulating 'how to be polite', the rules become involved in the very evaluative practices they are supposed to capture and explain.

2.2.2 Brown and Levinson

Like Lakoff, Brown & Levinson do not explicitly make the distinction between politeness1 and politeness2, but again it is present in the background. Their concept of politeness is *"[...] very broadly, and specially defined"* (Brown & Levinson 1987:55), which warns us that it should not be confused with an ordinary or everyday understanding of the concept. What is more, it is not simply about people's judgements of each other's behaviour, it is part of a way of understanding *"[...] the very stuff that social relationships are made of."* (ibid.:55). It is a concept carved out by the linguist, in an attempt to grasp the relationship between language and the social context. Again, the Gricean basis of the theory points in the same direction:

It is a tool for describing, in some much more precise but nevertheless simple way, a phenomenon that has been a persistent interest of anthropologists: the quality of social relationships. And since the tool is here presented with an explanatory account, we hope that its cross-cultural applicability may have more than purely descriptive status. (ibid.:55)

In other words, the concept is a linguistic *tool* for explanation, not a spontaneous concept for evaluation. Moreover, this tool is constructed around the behaviour of a "Model Person", which is not to be confused with a real person, since it is *"constructed"*, a *"cardboard figure"* the analysts *"play around with"* (ibid.:58) in order to derive their hypotheses.

As in Lakoff's case, Brown & Levinson's concept of politeness also has a broader scope than the commonsense notion, as a result of their conceptualization of politeness as FTA redress. On the one hand, this leads to the classification of linguistic acts such as promises, offers, compliments or gossip as politeness strategies. Although the exact relationship between FTA redress and politeness1 is never explicitly discussed, it is doubtful whether a promise, or to preface a request by an offer would ordinarily be evaluated in terms of politeness, or the absence of the preface as impolite. On the other hand, politeness as FTA redress also implies that FTAs without redress would be considered impolite. Since some acts are claimed to be inherently "face-threatening" (ibid.:65), they would also be inherently impolite[5], a notion that does not sit with the observed variability in spontaneous evaluations of politeness (such as in Ide 1992, see above, section 2.1.2). Moreover, inherently face-threatening acts are defined as *"[...] those acts that by their nature run contrary to the face wants of the addressee and/or of the speaker"* (ibid.:65), and the idea of speakers being impolite to themselves does not seem a commonsensically valid notion. Finally, the list of acts threatening the hearer's face contains items such as 'offers', 'promises', 'compliments', 'expressions of admiration' or 'raising dangerously emotional or divisive topics, e.g. politics, race, religion, women's liberation', all of which are highly unlikely to be spontaneously qualified as impolite in everyday situations.

All this indicates that Brown & Levinson do not intend their notion of politeness to cover only politeness1, but aim for something broader and

---

[5] See also Blum-Kulka (1990), who concludes from the high incidence of direct verbal strategies in family discourse that, on the basis of theories such as Brown & Levinson's, this genre would appear to be highly impolite.

more general –Young, for example, interprets their theory as being about *"universal principles of sociability" (Young 1994:18)*. Brown & Levinson themselves also hint at this, for example when discussing negative politeness strategies:

> When we think of politeness in Western cultures, it is negative-politeness behavior that springs to mind. In our culture, negative politeness is the most elaborate and the most conventionalized set of linguistic strategies for FTA redress; it is the stuff that fills the etiquette books. (Brown & Levinson 1987:129-130)

In other words, the commonsense notion of politeness covers only a subset of the phenomena captured by the scientific notion.

However, claims to the contrary can also be found. Although the Model Person starts its life as a hypothetical cardboard figure, not long after its introduction (ibid.:58) it is expanded to encompass *"all competent adult members of a society"* (ibid.:61), where an endnote explains the competence restriction as *"Juvenile, mad, incapacitated persons partially excepted"* (ibid.:285). So the theory is in fact about real human beings, and the Model Person becomes a mini-psychological model of ordinary speakers. Consequently, the whole complex of face-wants, rationality and the notion of politeness as FTA redress is also granted psychological reality, so that ordinary speakers are implicitly assumed to make the same evaluations of speech acts in terms of (im)politeness as the theory does. In other words, Brown & Levinson's politeness notion directly captures ordinary speakers' politeness notions.

This is corroborated by Brown and Levinson's (1987) reassessments of the original (1978) model, based on criticisms by other researchers, where they argue for the validity of their model by referring to empirical analyses in which subjects reproduced the rank order of conventionally indirect speech acts predicted by their theory (Brown & Levinson 1987:17). In fact, such empirically produced rank orders of politeness, as well as ordinary speakers' assessments of (im)politeness in general, have amply been used to investigate the validity of Brown & Levinson's model, e.g. in Ide et al. (1992) ,which can be seen as a substantiation of the critique in Ide (1989), in Blum-Kulka (1987, 1990, 1992), or in Becker et al. (1989). Finally, a link to politeness1 is also provided when Brown & Levinson refer to 'face' as *"[...] the kernel element in folk notions of politeness"* (Brown & Levinson 1987:57) – although this claim is not empirically substantiated in any way.

Although it would appear from the terminology employed – with references to 'folk notions of politeness' while their own concept of politeness is 'specially defined' – that Brown & Levinson are indeed aware of the politeness1–politeness2 distinction, it is never explicitly made, and so it is not consistently carried through in their theorizing either.

2.2.3 Leech

Leech also shows an awareness of the distinction when he qualifies his framework as a *"scientific paradigm"* for which *"[t]here is no clear way of testing the validity"* (Leech 1983:4), and situates it within general pragmatics:

> By this term I mean to distinguish the study of the general conditions of the communicative use of language, and to exclude the more specific 'local' conditions on language use. The latter may be said to belong to a less abstract field of socio-pragmatics, for it is clear that the Cooperative Principle and the Politeness Principle operate variably in different cultures or language communities, in different social situations, among different social classes, etc. One has only to think of the schoolboy taboo against 'telling tales' (*ie* the inopportune telling of the truth!), or the way in which politeness is differently interpreted in (say) Chinese, Indian, or American societies, ... (ibid.:10)

His approach is about the "general" conditions of language use which are opposed to "local" conditions. Since ordinary speakers always and only communicate in local conditions, their concept of politeness, i.e. their local PP will (or at least might) differ from Leech's general PP from which such local conditions are excluded. The 'generality' of Leech's PP should be understood as *"[...] a necessary stage of abstraction between the study of language in total abstraction from situation, and the study of more socially specialized uses of language"* (ibid.:11). The general PP is thus not a derivation from local PPs, it exists *in abstraction from* – regardless of, or disregarding – any local PPs. So at first sight Leech appears to be fully aware of the politeness1– politeness2 distinction in the form of the distinction between local vs. general notions of politeness, in which his own conceptualization is explicitly characterized as residing on the politeness2 side.

On the other hand, his discussion also contains many indications to the contrary, in that the politeness maxims his theory proposes are to be interpreted as residing 'in the heads' of speakers, which implies that the general PP would also be a commonsense concept. For one thing, the PP is defined as a principle of pragmatics, and *"[...] pragmatics is the study of*

*how s communicates with h, it is concerned with what is in s's mind, and
what s assumes to be in h's mind"* (Leech 1980:105). Furthermore, *"[...]
principles introduce communicative values [...] into the study of language"*,
and these values *"[...] are ones we suppose, on empirical grounds, to be
operative in society"* (Leech 1983:9-10). So Leech's theoretical model
does claim to have empirical value (albeit admittedly only 'supposedly'
so) – it is about real people's evaluations based on real social values.
Definite proof that the CP is assumed to be a psychological reality is provided by the many elaborate descriptions of the inferencing processes that
show how the CP and the PP work – as indicated, Leech's PP and Grice's
CP are considered to be epistemologically and ontologically on a par.
These processes are said not to *"[...] happen laboriously and consciously
in the mind of the interpreter"*, but may be to a greater or lesser extent
automatized – the emphasis of the contrast clearly being on 'laboriously'
and 'consciously', not on 'in the mind'.

So, first, the PP is a psychologically real concept which facilitates
communication through enabling people to mean more than they really
say – as will be recalled from section 1.1.3 above, the PP and CP together
enable the communication of indirect meaning. Second, it is also said to
be 'general' in the sense of 'abstracted from any local conditions', indicating that the PP in the heads of ordinary speakers will not necessarily
have the same form as proposed by the theory (recall how in the schoolboy example in the quote at the beginning of this section, local conditions
cause the Gricean maxim of Quality to be reversed). Third, at the same
time, the PP does provide specific stipulations on how to be polite: by
'minimizing the expression of impolite beliefs' and 'maximizing the expression of polite beliefs', where (im)politeness is defined in terms of
(un)favourableness to the hearer. For example, Leech provides the following classification of imperatives (Figure 4) when (un)favourableness
is measured against the cost-benefit scale.

Figure 4. Leech (1983:107) Classification of imperatives

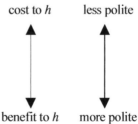

Peel these potatoes
Hand me the newspaper
Sit down
Look at that
Enjoy your holiday
Have another sandwich

cost to *h*   less polite

benefit to *h*   more polite

Leech's theory is thus very specific in predicting not only that these imperatives will be evaluated in terms of (im)politeness, but also which ones will be evaluated as more or less (im)polite.

The question then arises as to how these three aspects are to be reconciled: the PP resides in speakers' heads, although not in any specific speaker's head, but still stipulates a specific definition of (im)politeness and 'how to be polite'. It is exactly here that the theory runs into the intricacies and pitfalls of the politeness1-politeness2 distinction. On the one hand, the nature of the general-local distinction firmly separates theory from practice: real speakers always and only operate in local conditions, while the theory exists in abstraction from such conditions. Although it allows the theory to transcend the empirical variability found in evaluations of politeness, this epistemological choice also causes it not to be about the evaluations of any particular person – it is no longer a theory of real people, but rather of people in general or abstract people. On the other hand, Leech frames his theory as a set of concepts outlining the processes involved in the production of evaluations of politeness – causing it to end up making such evaluations, which clearly is an aspect of the practice of politeness. The final result is an unresolved epistemological duality where the theory claims a politeness2 position while being involved in politeness1 practices.

2.2.4 Ide

Ide is one of the few researchers who has actually carried out experimental research into commonsense notions of politeness (Ide et al. 1992), both as a way of criticizing other approaches as well as laying the foundations of her own theory. Again, this would seem to indicate an (implicit) awareness of the politeness1-politeness2 distinction, but on closer inspection it appears that this awareness remains superficial, as it is not strictly maintained and its consequences are not fully taken into account.

For example, Ide carried out research (reported in Hill et al. 1986) in which utterances were rated by informants not in terms of 'politeness', but on a scale between 'when being most uninhibited' and 'when being most careful', providing a measure of the *"[...] degree of inhibition/ carefulness felt toward a person in a particular situation"* (Hill et al. 1986:352.). The hypothetical addressees of the utterances were further rated on a scale of 'Perceived Distance' – a measure combining perceived addressee status, situation and degree of imposition – which the authors claim is *"[...] useful as a measurable abstract concept for politeness"* while at the same time it *"[...] allows us to establish a common concept of politeness cross-culturally, thus universally"* (ibid.:351-352). So not only are informants not asked for ratings or notions of 'politeness' (the word is never used in the questionnaire – it is even consciously avoided, as explained in a footnote) the investigation does not aim for politeness1 notions either, but rather for something with cross-cultural, universal validity, an abstraction from any local concepts. The fact that the notion of Discernment that is posited on the basis of the examination is part of the researchers' concept of politeness would appear to situate the theory on the politeness2 side of the distinction. However, the experimental results in Ide et al. (1992) were used to establish Discernment as the primary component of the Japanese politeness1 notion – as opposed to the American notion in which Volition is primary, so that the theory's politeness concept is also given politeness1 status.

So overall Ide's position regarding the distinction does not seem to be directly and unequivocally inferable from her own theorizing. However, later in a metascientific state-of-the-art review of politeness research (Ide 1993) she does situate herself explicitly – though not necessarily more clearly – within the distinction. There she argues that early work in politeness research (Lakoff, Leech and Brown & Levinson) was mainly involved in politeness2, whereas her own work aims to rectify this situation by incorporating a concept to account for politeness1: Discernment or *wakimae*. This rather blurs her interpretation of the politeness1–politeness2 distinction. On the one hand she defines politeness1 as *"[...] politeness as an everyday concept, the matter of etiquette and protocol"* while politeness2 is concerned with *"[...] strategies of language use"* thus *"[...] reflecting its focus as a technical term restricted to the academic domain"* (Ide 1993:8). In combination with the (1989) publication, where she argues that Brown & Levinson's and Leech's theories account for the 'Volition' aspect of politeness, and the claim that those theories were involved in politeness2, this results in the overall picture shown in Figure 5.

Figure 5. Ide (1989, 1993) politeness1–politeness2 distinction

politeness1	=	Discernment	=	everyday concept
politeness2	=	Volition	=	academic concept

However, Volition is said to involve *"[...] strategies or maxims which speakers utilize in order to be linguistically polite"* (Ide 1989:350), which would seem to imply that Volition is also part of language users' everyday concepts of politeness – since speakers use it *in order to be polite*. As indicated above, both Volition and Discernment were indeed associated with politeness1 – with the American and Japanese notions respectively.

Moreover, immediately after her definition of the distinction as separating 'everyday concepts' from 'technical terms restricted to the academic
domain', she rephrases it as follows:

> While second-order politeness assumes the speaker's calculation of
> short-term costs and gains, first-order politeness is observed by the
> speaker's calculation of long-term costs and gains. Thus, these two
> types of politeness, which appear diverse in origin and practice, may
> derive from a common cognitive process in the minds of speakers.
> (Ide 1993:8)

Both concepts of politeness are now posited as a psychological reality in
speakers' minds, as strategies resulting from the calculation of costs and
gains, so the distinction between academic and everyday concepts no
longer seems to hold. Instead we are left with a view that separates etiquette or formal politeness, and *"[...] obligatory grammatical usages"*
(ibid.:8) – politeness1 as Discernment – from strategic uses of politeness –
politeness2 as Volition.

In the end, Ide's explicit reference to the politeness1–politeness2 distinction is offset by its equivocal definition, and although by subsuming
both Volition (politeness2) and Discernment (politeness1) her theory appears to place itself above the distinction, this is only seemingly true, since
in order to accomplish this it needs to blur the distinction itself, watering
it down to one between formal and strategic politeness.

2.2.5 Blum-Kulka

Like Ide, Blum-Kulka has also investigated commonsense notions of politeness (Blum-Kulka 1987, 1990, 1992), yet her theoretical model is not
unequivocal as to where exactly her theory is to be situated in relation to
the politeness1–politeness2 distinction. Although her research appears to
be based on empirical findings of commonsense notions of politeness, the
eventual model she arrives at does not fully incorporate many crucial aspects of these findings and contains elements that point to a definition of
politeness that is broader, incorporating behaviour that would not ordinarily be evaluated in terms of politeness. For example, in Blum-Kulka
(1990), she begins with a discussion of ethnographic interviews in which
Israeli families are probed for their notions of politeness, by asking their
opinions about its meaning within family interaction and within Israeli
culture in general. The answers are far from unanimous, in that some informants are reported to see politeness as 'very important' while others

find it 'irrelevant' in the family context. Were the focus of study politeness1, no doubt a major finding would be its variability, which would be incorporated into the theoretical model. However, on the next page, Blum-Kulka states:

> Detailed analysis of the social control acts directed by parents to children in this context has led me to the conclusion that, contrary to the credo of some of our informants, politeness considerations *do* figure strongly in families' ways of speaking. Hence, in essence my argument is that family discourse *is polite*, but it enacts its politeness in culturally and situationally specific ways. (ibid.:261, original emphasis)

In other words, the model runs counter to part of the informants' opinions and, being based on only part of the empirical data, it cannot be a 'theory of politeness1'. This is further confirmed by the phenomena that are classified under the notion of politeness. The conclusion that family discourse is polite is arrived at on the basis of the experimental observation that at dinnertime, Israeli parents use strategies that are classified as 'polite' by the researcher's theoretical model. One such strategy is the use of metapragmatic comments, which are claimed to be:

> [...] one of the ways in which parents socialize children to be polite. They are comments made *to sanction a perceived lack of politeness*, to encourage 'proper' behavior and to prompt the use of politeness formulae. (ibid.:278, my emphasis)

In the pages following this statement, Blum-Kulka defines and categorizes utterances that qualify as metapragmatic comments. One of those categories, labelled 'maxim violation', contains instances of speech in which a mother casts doubt on the truth-value of her child's claim of having seen 'a giant turtle' by saying 'how giant is giant? Did you really see it?', and in which parents try to induce a child to take part in the conversation by saying 'aren't you participating with us today?'. In both cases, it seems questionable whether the parents involved would spontaneously evaluate their children's behaviour as a 'lack of politeness' – or, since in Blum-Kulka's model 'less polite' equals 'more impolite' – as 'impoliteness'.

The same applies to linguistic strategies associated by the model with impoliteness, such as 'aggravation' as it is applied to requests, i.e. the use of linguistic forms that "strengthen" the request, framing it in terms of an "obligation" (Blum-Kulka 1987:139). This leads to claims such as the following:

With mitigated directness representing an independent category, the options parents have in verbalizing their control acts to children vary on an index of politeness as follows:

Impolite. Complete disregard for face-needs is expressed in this context by aggravated-directness. Forms of aggravation include prosody (raised voice) as well as lexical choices:

(10) Father to David (6): Stop it, David, you are making the *most HORRIBLE* noise. (AM)

Said in a raised voice, this direct command is aggravated lexically by the use of the 'expletive' [...] 'horrible'. (Blum-Kulka 1990:271, original emphasis)

Although given the proper situational context (e.g. in the presence of non-family members), it may very well be that the father would consider David's behaviour 'impolite', it seems highly questionable to claim that the father's comment on David's behaviour would be spontaneously evaluated as 'impolite' by either of the participants.

On the other hand, numerous indications can be found to the effect that the notion of politeness proposed by the theory is intended to be a psychological reality for ordinary speakers. For example, empirical investigations in which informants are asked to rate linguistic forms in terms of politeness are adduced in support of the theory (ibid.:270). Also, politeness is defined as something that is *"expressed"* by speakers (ibid.:265, 271), and it is claimed that *"[t]o be polite in speech to children, parents can choose essentially between two modes"* (ibid.:274). In both of these statements, politeness is associated with (ordinary) speakers' intentions. Furthermore, the fourth dimension of politeness – the *"social meanings attached to choices of linguistic encoding in particular situations or speech events"* – is defined as *"the degree to which any linguistic expression is deemed polite by members of a given culture in a specific situation"* (ibid.:275, my emphasis).

The curious mix between politeness1 and politeness2 we have noticed in other perspectives is thus also present in Blum-Kulka's framework and leads to a number of paradoxical claims such as the following:

As a relatively 'young' cultural group, native Israelis seem to be extremely sensitive to the range of social meanings attributable to communicative modes. Such meanings can range from *(possibly*

unnoticeable) social inappropriateness to attributions of strategic or
even manipulative intent. (Blum-Kulka 1992:278, my emphasis)

In light of the fact that Blum-Kulka associates (im)politeness with social
(in)appropriateness, the reference to 'attributions of intent' by 'native Israelis' indicates that Blum-Kulka is talking about politeness1 here.
However, what does the notion of 'unnoticeable inappropriateness' refer
to in that context? Clearly, in a purely politeness1 frame of reference,
'inappropriateness' is the result of an evaluation made by (one of) the
participants. If inappropriateness goes unnoticed by both participants in
an interaction, then there is simply no inappropriateness present: a linguistic choice that is not evaluated as inappropriate by the interactants is
not inappropriate. The only way a statement such as the above ceases to
be nonsensical is when it is interpreted in a politeness2 frame of reference. Inappropriateness that goes unnoticed by the participants, but is
nevertheless claimed to be there, can only result from interpretation by
the researcher's theoretical framework, not that of the participants. But in
that case, the concept of politeness we are talking about is no longer that
of the interactants, but a purely theoretical and academic one.

2.2.6 Gu

Gu's approach is analogous to Ide's in that it is built on a culture-specific
notion of politeness: the Chinese concept of *limao* is adduced to argue
that existing universalist theories are either inadequate (Brown & Levinson)
or should at least be amended (Leech) if they are to account for Chinese
data. Gu's intention is to *"[...] describe politeness phenomena in Modern
Chinese"* (Gu 1990:237), the officially standardized variant of Chinese
that is taught at schools and universities and used in the media, and so
*"[...] the politeness phenomena [Gu's theory] captures can be said to be
generally prevailing among the (fairly) educated."* (ibid.:256). In providing a description of "generally prevailing" politeness notions, Gu clearly
aims for politeness1, for politeness as it manifests itself in ordinary speakers' minds. This is further confirmed by the examples from natural data
that are brought in to support the theory's claims.

As with the other frameworks, however, no matter how natural the
data may be, there are also indications that the stipulations of the theory
are not as ordinary or commonsensical as they purport to be. Gu's notion
of politeness is based on Leech's, in that it consists of a number of maxims, with the addition of an explicitly moral component: the maxims are
moralized, socially sanctionable norms. Behaviour that follows the maxims is interpreted in terms of politeness, while not abiding by them results

in impoliteness. This view leads to a number of intuitively awkward claims. For example, Gu incorporates the choice between performing or not performing an action into the system of politeness under the header of 'content-regulating maximization (minimization)', which refers to the actual cost/benefit involved in an action.[6] Since making an offer or invitation is always more costly to Self and more beneficial to Other than not doing so, offers and invitations are always (and necessarily) interpreted in terms of politeness – they are intrinsically polite acts, which is explicated at length by means of an example where someone offers another person a lift (ibid.:244-245). However, since politeness is a matter of moral, sanctionable norms, this entails that (1) offers and invitations are always made out of politeness considerations, (2) they will always be interpreted as such, (3) not offering/inviting will be interpreted as impoliteness and (4) not offering/inviting is socially sanctionable. This paints rather a surreal, counter-intuitive picture of social reality, and is contradicted by another example in which Gu discusses a Chinese invitation/acceptance interaction sequence. Such an interaction typically consists of three exchanges: a first one where A invites and B declines, a second one where A repeats the invitation and B declines again, and a final one where A insists and B accepts. Gu states:

> Note that we are considering only those cases in which A sincerely invites B, and B wants to accept the invitation. Since B desires it, why does B not accept it immediately instead of going through this lengthy procedure?
> [...]
> Although issuing an invitation places the inviter's face (positive face according to Brown and Levinson) at risk, it is intrinsically polite, since it manifests the inviter's observance of the Generosity maxim, i.e. maximizing benefit to other (at the motivational level). (ibid.:253-254)

---

[6] For example, the actual value of a gift, or the actual effort a host makes to prepare a delicious and copious meal for a guest. This principle contrasts with 'speech-regulating maximization (minimization)', which refers to how the effort is treated in language – the guest emphasizing the deliciousness of the meal regardless of its actual taste, or the happiness and gratitude expressed by the receiver of a gift regardless of its actual value – and 'manner-regulating maximization (minimization)', which refers to, for example, the degree of urgency with which one makes a request – 'Will you do X for me now?' vs 'When you have time, could you perhaps do X for me?'.

So, contrary to what the theory would predict, it is possible for a Chinese speaker to 'sincerely' invite someone, as opposed to doing this *"out of sheer consideration of formality"* (ibid.:254). In fact, the lengthiness of the procedure is said to allow the invitee to discover whether the invitation was sincere or not, whether it was made out of a sense of moral or social obligation rather than sincere liking. In light of Gu's definition of politeness as a set of moral rules and obligations, the declinations thus serve the purpose of finding out whether the inviter was 'being sincere' or 'being polite' in issuing the invitation. This directly contradicts the notion that invitations are intrinsically polite, and the latter can only be maintained if the evaluation of politeness does not emanate from the interactants themselves, but from the theory. As a consequence, because this evaluation of politeness contradicts that of ordinary speakers, it can only be a purely academic notion, i.e. politeness2. The same conclusion must be drawn from the claim that *"[…] it is possible in Chinese to criticize someone (i.e. being impolite in content) in a polite way (i.e. using indirect speech acts, hedges, politeness markers, etc...)"* (ibid.:240), as it is unlikely that ordinary speakers would reproduce the evaluation of the criticism as being *both* polite and impolite.

Although these few examples already illustrate the same unquestioned mix of politeness1 and politeness2 characteristics found in the other frameworks, one final aspect specific to Gu's theory deserves more detailed attention, as it touches upon general epistemological issues for the study of politeness. The meaning of the term *limao* with its four basic constituents of respectfulness, modesty, attitudinal warmth and refinement is historically traced back to the writings of philosophers such as Confucius (± 500 BC) and Dai Sheng (West Han Dynasty) and is characterized by Gu as follows:

> Some Chinese cultural anthropologists [...] observe that western philosophers tend to pursue knowledge for the sake of it, whereas Chinese philosophers' (especially ancient ones) pursuit of knowledge is often motivated by moral or/and political goals. The Chinese conception of politeness is a good example. Dai's *Li Ji* mentioned above is a treatise on politeness and rituals written for the purpose of attaining political goals. As a result, it is by no means descriptive (in the sense usually employed in linguistics); it is prescriptive: it aims to lay down rules of conduct. The four essential elements of politeness are basically derived from this book, and handed down from one generation to another through formal or informal pedagogical channels. In the last ten years or so, the so-called 'beautification of speech' campaign has tried to revive the four elements as cultural heritage and explicitly appealed

> to the nation to abide by them [...]. At least in the Chinese context rules for politeness are moral maxims, the breach of which will incur social sanctions. (ibid.:239-240)

The argument for the moral nature of politeness refers to normative philosophical literature concerned with rules of proper conduct. At least as far as subject and intention is concerned, this genre is comparable to the European tradition of socially prescriptive literature as described by Burke (1993:chapter 4). Although Burke's analysis of publications on good behaviour, good manners, civility, courtesy and politeness mainly focuses on sixteenth-century Italy, seventeenth-century France and eighteenth-century Britain, the tradition can be traced back to the Ancient Greeks and Romans and extends into our present time with examples such as Glass (1991) or Vanderbilt & Baldridge (1978). Whatever the specific background of their writers (philosophers, politicians, literary writers, etc.), all of these books have the same political goal of telling their readers how to speak or how to behave properly. All of them are prescriptive in providing their readers with norms or guidelines for polite conversation.

However, before treating such literature as a representation of 'common sense' or of 'cultural' ways of speaking, as is done by both Burke (1993) and Gu (1990), one needs to consider carefully the relationship between such etiquette manuals and the actual everyday practice of the members of the culture or society from which the literature stems. This relationship is a far from obvious one, although the number of agreements between different authors (even across time) do make it tempting to think of the precepts as a common stock of cultural norms.

Of course, the authors will have based their recommendations on observed behaviour: a book of precepts that bear no relation to actual practice would have little chance of getting published, and would certainly not be as well received as some of those publications were. And no doubt they will have had at least some influence on at least some of their readership, just in the same way (as Burke (1993:120) adduces) that the dialogues presented on television nowadays can be expected to affect everyday speech habits to a certain extent. But a number of caveats do stand in the way of too close an equation between the precepts and any practice so widespread as to deserve the qualification 'common' or 'cultural'.

As Burke remarks, it is highly implausible that everyone followed the precepts at the time of publication, since in that case there would have been no need for the manuals in the first place – who would be interested in reading a book on, say, *"L'art de plaire dans la conversation"* (The art of pleasing in conversation – Ortigue 1688), if everybody has already mastered that art? But neither can the manuals be expected to articulate a social – let alone a cultural – consensus. Not only may different social groups within one society follow different rules of communication, the manuals in question also have rather a limited scope and audience. Obviously, their audience is confined to literate people, but the manuals also seem to be addressed to specific social groups – the socio-economically better-off – and they pertain to a very specific type of interactional situation only. This situation usually involves a semi-public setting (such as the *salon* in seventeenth-century France or the coffee-house and club in eighteenth-century Britain) where a mixed and partly non-intimate company gather for the purpose of free and equal discussion, leisurely enjoyment or mere sociability. And even within this socially restricted target group, a social consensus about the norms of conversation can hardly be assumed to have existed, as contemporary writers each have their own hints, principles or *règles*; 'language' and 'conversation' were among the favourite topics of discussion during such encounters, especially in the French *salons*. Burke further recounts the poignant fact that Molière – whose plays were certainly as popular as most of the etiquette books – makes fun of people who follow the etiquette precepts of two of his contemporaries, Bouhours and Vaugelas (Burke 1993:104). Some writers of etiquette manuals rejected the propriety of certain speech acts on the basis of their association *"with the common people or at best with the bourgeoisie"*, and advised their readers *"to take care what they said in order to distinguish themselves from their social inferiors"* (ibid.:107).

Of course, the arguments adduced here all pertain to the European cultural framework, and it is far from obvious that they can be transposed to the Chinese social context without modification. But they do provide a few insights into the general relationship between morally prescriptive literature and everyday commonsense values and practices. And that is precisely what both traditions have in common: they are both broadly political in that they attempt to achieve some social goal; both aim to produce a certain social effect.[7] Gu explicitly mentions this in respect to Confucius' writings. Confucius lived at a time when social chaos reigned, and he aimed to restore the social order and stability of the Zhou Dynasty (dating back to 1100 BC), which he regarded as an ideal social model. The behavioural precepts he formulated were intended to restore this social order and stability. In other words, the precepts referred to an ideal

---

[7] For an interesting and in-depth discussion of the politics of linguistic prescriptive practices, see Cameron 1995.

social model that no longer existed, rather than to any common or cultural practice of the time. Thus the very fact that they were political already denies the common nature of those prescriptive norms. And, as appears from the above quote, this still holds for the present situation in China, where for the past few decades the 'beautification of speech' campaign *"has tried to revive the four elements as cultural heritage and explicitly appealed to the nation to abide by them" (Gu 1990:240)*. Clearly, social norms that need to be 'revived' by 'appeals' to abide by them are not established cultural practice.

2.2.7 Fraser & Nolen

From the epistemological foundations of Fraser & Nolen's approach, one could conclude that they aim for a politeness2 approach. In Fraser & Nolen (1981) the authors examine the notion of 'deference', and although deference and politeness are not to be equated, they are very closely related through the notion of a Conversational Contract (CC). Fraser & Nolen define politeness as 'staying within the then-current terms of the CC', where 'the expected amount of deference' is one of those contractual terms. So the CC determines the proper amount of deference to be paid, while the actual amount of deference paid determines whether a speaker is 'polite' or 'impolite'. In their analysis, Fraser & Nolen attempt to set up empirically a rank order of linguistic structures on a high–low deference scale. An empirical investigation would normally point to a politeness1 approach, but in the introduction to this study, Fraser & Nolen specify that:

> [...] it is very clear that one cannot follow the linguistic tradition and appeal directly to the intuitions of the native speaker to sort out the degree of deference associated with particular expressions. (ibid.:93)

Although native speakers can be expected to agree on big differences in the amount of deference conveyed by different linguistic structures, *"[...] the use of such intuitions quickly breaks down on the more subtle cases, and judges are inconsistent"* (ibid.:93), so ordinary speakers' intuitive notions of deference cannot be trusted.

Fraser & Nolen's solution to this problem is the usual sociolinguistic one: large amounts of such intuitions are collected and statistically analysed into some 'mean' measure. But reliance on any such mean measure also implies reliance on a hypothetical mean speaker. Although the notion of deference arrived at in this manner will no doubt approximate to that of at least some part of the group of real speakers/informants, others may have widely differing notions, and the resulting rank order of linguistic structures may well not be held by any of the informants at all.

This becomes clear when we take a closer look at the specific method-ology employed in the experiment. It considers 25 different linguistic forms of a general request asking the hearer to 'do that': 'Can you do that?', 'Could you do that?', 'Would you do that?', 'I must ask you to do that' and so on. Informants are not asked to produce the rank order as a whole, but instead are presented with only two sentences at a time. For each pair of sentences they are asked to indicate which of the two they consider to be the more deferential one – with deference defined as 're-spect for the hearer' (ibid.:100). With 25 different structures, there are 300 possible combinations, but each of the 40 respondents is presented with only 45 to 50 pairs, meaning that no single respondent gets to com-pare all the sentences. Instead, for each pair, the number of respondents that choose one or the other of the sentences is taken as a measure of the relative distance between the sentences in the subsequent rank order. The more unanimous the vote, the greater the assumed distance between any two structures. This eventually leads to the construction of a rank order that includes all the sentences.

However, this resulting rank order is not an average of the rank orders produced by each respondent, since no respondent actually constructs a complete rank order. Furthermore, as each respondent is presented with 50 pairs, he or she judges only $1/6^{th}$ of the total of 300 possible pairs – assuming that all pairs are equally represented in the sample. So at least 6 respondents are involved in the construction of one 'complete' hypotheti-cal rank order. With 40 respondents x 50 pairs per respondent, the resulting 2000 pairs involved in the experiment comprise only 6 such hypothetical complete rank orders. Thus each pair figures 6 to 7 times in the whole sample and is judged by only 6 to 7 people out of the group of 40 – assum-ing that no respondent gets the same pair more than once.

This method introduces a considerable margin of error into the experi-ment. Suppose that 30 out of 40 respondents (i.e. 75%) would judge sentence X to be more deferential than sentence Y, while the remaining 10 respondents would make the opposite judgement. Since only 6 people get to judge each pair, they could theoretically all belong to the latter category, producing a 100% vote of Y over X instead of the 75% vote of X over Y, a serious distortion of the average opinion of the whole popula-tion. In the end, the empirical nature of the analysis, which would indicate a concern with what goes on in speakers' heads, is strongly qualified by the fact that the methodology employed leads to a result which does not necessarily match that of any ordinary speaker.[8]

Of course the experiment was concerned with deference, not politeness. And since judgements of (im)politeness depend on whether or not the hearer perceives the speaker to have used the appropriate amount of deference, they are completely independent of any ranking of linguistic structures on a deference scale. Indeed, Fraser & Nolen themselves claim that *"no sentence is inherently polite or impolite"* (ibid.:96). However, the discussion of the methodology behind the experiment does contain indications of how Fraser & Nolen see the relationship between commonsense judgements and their scientific analysis, that is between commonsense notions and their scientific counterparts. Their method of analysis brings into practice their conviction that ordinary speakers' judgements cannot be trusted, and need to be somehow 'corrected' by scientific analysis.

Another indication that the scientific notion of politeness cannot be equated with ordinary speakers' notions can be found in the claim that:

> Politeness is a state that one expects to exist in every conversation; participants note not that someone is being polite [...]. Being polite [...] simply involves getting on with the task at hand in light of the terms and conditions of the CC. The intention to be polite is not signaled [...] (Fraser 1990:233)

This statement indicates that the theory's judgements of politeness do not depend on ordinary speakers' judgements, as behaviour can very well be theoretically polite without being evaluated as such – without being 'noticed' – by the interactants. Examples provided by Fraser & Nolen testify to the way in which the equation between the normal course of events – abidance by the CC – and politeness leads to a dissociation between the theoretical notion of politeness and the commonsense notion. Terms of the CC relating to social structure, such as the rule that *"[a] child [...] does not ordinarily authorize a parent to do something; [...] and an atheist does not excommunicate a wayward parishoner"* (Fraser & Nolen 1981:94), which involve social power differences and the rights and duties connected to socio-structural positions, are most eloquent in

---

[8] Note that I abstract here other problematic aspects of the experiment, such as the decontextualized form of the phrases, which in actual practice would occur within a specific context. Different informants may presuppose different contexts when producing the rankings.

this respect. It is hard to fathom how an atheist's not excommunicating someone would ordinarily be interpreted in terms of politeness. And if a child authorizes his or her parents to do something – which, in view of the social power relations between them, the child simply cannot do success-fully – it would take pretty stuffy parents to interpret this authorization as impolite (and would probably cause them to rather miss the point of their child's behaviour).

The incorporation of such socio-structural terms into the CC and the consequent dissociation between scientific and commonsense notions of politeness strongly contradict Fraser & Nolen's explicit claim that *"whether or not an utterance is heard as being polite is totally in the hands (or ears) of the hearer"* (ibid.:96). By itself, this claim would indicate that the notion of politeness talked about is the commonsense one that operates in the minds of ordinary speakers: politeness1. The rest of their framework, however, contains many clues to the contrary.

Fraser & Nolen's ambiguous epistemological relationship with ordi-nary speakers identified at the start of this section – they are the object of analysis, but their intuitions cannot be trusted to be accurate – is reflected in the general layout of their framework. While the power over politeness is explicitly laid in the hands of ordinary speakers, the very structure of the scientific concept intended to capture that notion takes it away again.

2.2.8 Arndt & Janney

Arndt & Janney make a strong case for a politeness1 approach, in that they reject existing theoretical frameworks on the basis of their plac-ing politeness outside actual speakers and hearers, locating it in abstract notions of 'language', 'society', or 'situation' (Arndt & Janney 1985a: 285). They argue for *"[...] a shift from a logical approach to a socio-psychological approach."* (Janney & Arndt 1992:22) in which people are the locus of language and politeness (Arndt & Janney 1985a:285). This emphasis not only affects their conceptualization of politeness, but is part of their general approach to language and linguistics. This can be seen from their argument for a "non-autonomous linguistics" in which the em-phasis is on speakers' "intuitive knowledge" (Arndt & Janney 1981a), and from their rejection of *"excessive abstraction of language away from speech"* on the grounds that *"[...] if linguistic theories are to avoid being merely intellectual games they ought to be about what human beings do."* (Arndt & Janney 1983:367). As an example, the methodology of their experiment (Arndt & Janney 1981a), in which intuitive evaluations of utterances are used to examine the notion of 'group role identity' is based on the idea that:

> Observation is important in the formulation of linguistic theory inso-
> far as it enables the linguist to determine which theoretical concepts
> are intersubjectively valid and which require more thought. (ibid.:108)

In other words, concepts only have scientific value if they are also meaningful to non-linguists.

This explicit focus on intuitive concepts is balanced by claims that
imply the opposite point of view, such as their rejection of folk notions
that equate politeness with style, a legacy of the nineteenth century
which – erratically – is *"[...] still broadly accepted among nonlinguists"*
(Arndt & Janney 1985a:283). In their view there is no such thing as a
'polite style' at all, for *"[h]ow a given style is interpreted depends on the
momentary expectations of the interpreter, not on the style itself"*
(ibid.:283). Note the ambiguity in rejecting the 'broadly accepted' notion
that a style can be interpreted as polite, while simultaneously claiming
that the evaluation of style depends on the interpreter. To complicate matters even further, the claim that:

> [...] every normal speaker knows there are virtually any number of
> ways of being polite or impolite, or combinations of these, in a given
> situation, and that many of these have nothing whatever to do with
> language styles or social conventions (ibid.:285)

directly contradicts the idea that the politeness-as-style notion would be
'broadly accepted'.

Besides these general theoretical arguments, the examples adduced by
Arndt & Janney also contain indications of a dissociation between the
scientific and commonsense notions of politeness, as the structure of their
concept often leads to counterintuitive (im)politeness evaluations. Recall
that Arndt & Janney focus on 'interpersonal politeness', which refers to
the interactional practice of being 'supportive'. Supportiveness is not a
function of *what* you say, but of *how* you say it, and is conveyed through
'cross-modal emotive cues': verbal, vocal and kinesic characteristics of
the message/utterance signalling emotional support. Emotive behaviour
is an important part of Arndt & Janney's effort to define an 'interactional
grammar' of spoken (English) language, in which verbal, prosodic and
kinesic aspects of speech are integrated (Arndt & Janney 1983, 1987). In
their discussion of such a grammar, they claim that in order to capture the
interpretation of emotive cues, it is necessary to postulate a 'sincerity condition' and assume that speakers are not intentionally misleading hearers
by issuing false signals (Arndt & Janney 1983:373). In other words, in

interpreting specific emotive cues as 'supportive', the assumption is that the speaker is being 'sincerely supportive'. Since supportiveness and politeness are interchangeable in their framework (Arndt & Janney 1985a:282, 295), politeness also becomes a matter of sincerity.

Apart from the fact that Blum-Kulka's (1992:257) investigations reveal that commonsense notions of politeness are associated with hypocritical, insincere behaviour, contradicting Arndt & Janney's sincerity condition, the equation of politeness with supportiveness also leads to the theoretical interpretation of any instance of supportiveness as politeness. This can all too easily create a discontinuity between the theory's and ordinary speakers' evaluations, as was already demonstrated for Fraser & Nolen's equation of politeness with 'abiding by the terms of the CC'. That the danger is real appears from the following example of a supportive message:

(1)   Supportive positive message:
        'Jane, I agree with you completely'
        (smiling, full gaze, emphasis on 'Jane' and 'completely',
        both with falling intonation) (Arndt & Janney 1985a:294)

for which an interpretation as 'polite' seems counter-intuitive, especially in light of the sincerity condition.

Besides sincerity and supportiveness, politeness in Arndt & Janney's theory is also a matter of conforming to expectations:

> Whether a particular utterance is more or less 'polite' than another in a given situation is thus largely a question of the stylistic group role expectations of the hearer at the moment the speaker makes his utterance. 'I beg your pardon?', for instance [...] is no more inherently polite than 'Huh?', 'What?', 'What's that?' and so on. That is, 'I beg your pardon?' is more polite than the other utterances only in those situations where the hearer expects an extremely distant, nonintimate group role relationship [...] to the speaker, i.e., where he expects a detached, impersonal speaking style. [...] the imputed politeness or impoliteness is not the result of utterance style *per se*, but rather of the speaker's perceived willingness or unwillingness to coordinate his stylistic choices with his hearer's stylistic expectations. (Arndt & Janney 1981b:445)

Elsewhere, hearer expectations are further related to situational norms in that *"[...] previous choices provide the norms against which subsequent choices are measured" (Arndt & Janney 1980:44)*. These 'previous choices' may refer to a habitual speaking style previously established be-

tween two specific interactants, but also to the immediately previous utterance, as when one interactant suddenly deviates from the previously
established norm. In the latter case, the speaker's deviation from the norm
signals interpersonal meaning, while the deviant utterance at the same
time sets a new norm. Now, consider Arndt & Janney's example about the
negotiation of interpersonal distance (they themselves do not explicitly
relate this example to politeness, but it obviously can be related to it since
it involves stylistic negotiation):

(2)   A: Hold on Lady, Jack wants to talk.
        B: I beg your pardon, young man?
        A: Uh, excuse me, would you mind letting my friend talk
        for a minute Ma'am? (Arndt & Janney 1981b:438)

Since the authors do not specify the interactional context of this interchange, I will assume that there is none, that is, that A and B did not talk
to each other before. A opens the interaction in a more or less informal
style, so one can assume that this matches his expectations. At the same
time, his initial utterance sets the situational norm to informality. B immediately deviates from this norm, and resets it to a formal style, to which A
then conforms. B apparently expects a formal style, indictating that A's
initial turn can retrospectively be seen as a deviation from B's stylistic
expectations regarding the interchange. Since impoliteness is defined in
terms of deviation from expectations, A and B would evaluate each other's utterances as impolite. Intuitively it makes perfect sense to say that B
interprets A's initial utterance in terms of '(im)politeness'. In fact, her
own utterance is a way of making this clear to A, who apparently gets the
message and changes his style accordingly. But the line of reasoning does
not seem to hold the other way around. It somehow does not make sense
to claim that A interprets B's utterance as 'impolite'. Even if A were to
insist on the norm of informality he set for the interaction and retort to B's
utterance with 'I said: hold on Lady, Jack wants to talk', B might well be
shocked ('Oh!') and either walk away or continue the rest of the interaction
in her formal style, despite A's insistence on informality. But then it still
would seem unlikely that A would find B's formal behaviour 'impolite' –
although he might find her 'stuffy' of course. It remains perfectly sensible, however, to say that B would find A's insistence on informality highly
'impolite', to show a 'lack of manners', etc. So again Arndt & Janney's
concept of politeness does not seem to square with intuitive, commonsense notions.

    In sum, Arndt & Janney seem to want it both ways. They want their concept of politeness to be a scientific representation of what goes on inside speakers' heads, but when their conceptual line of reasoning is continued far enough, and put to the practical test of exemplification, it leads to evaluative results which are commonsensically highly questionable.

2.2.9 Watts

Like Fraser & Nolen, Watts is quite clear as to the ontological status he claims for his concept of politeness. His general epistemological and methodological approach to research indicates a concern for understanding and capturing ordinary speakers' assessments of the interactional process. For instance, in an analysis of status in conversation (Watts 1992b), Watts validates his conceptualization through several references to the subjective assessments of observers of the videotapes on which the analysis is based (ibid.:475, 476, 502). Although they are not the actual participants in the interaction, they are ordinary speakers, and their observations are drawn into the analysis as a touchstone for the scientist's notion of status. So ultimately, it is ordinary speakers' notions that the scientist is after.[9] Analogously, Watts' approach to politeness is claimed to be one *"[...] in which forms of behavior conventionally termed 'polite' in a 'Volition culture' are seen to be marked forms of elaborated speech codes in open groups"* (ibid.:134). Because such marked forms are exactly what his theoretical framework defines as politeness (see above, section 1.1.9), the claim that they are conventionally interpretable as polite suggests that this interpretation is not restricted to the community of scientists, but widespread among ordinary speakers.

The theoretical aim thus seems to be politeness1, which is further confirmed by the relationship between the polite–politic and the politeness1–politeness2 distinctions, where the mere choice of terms suggests a parallelism. Whereas 'polite' is a commonsense term (it can be used in experiments without startling informants), 'politic' is not, at least not with the meaning it receives in Watts' theory – 'behaviour directed towards the goal of establishing and/or maintaining in a state of equilibrium the personal relationships between the individuals of a social group' (see above, section 1.1.9). In order to use that notion successfully in an experiment,

---

[9] Of course, there is still a difference between an observer and an actual participant in the interaction, but the observers' non-scientist status together with the qualification of their observations as subjective judgements – contrasting with the scientist's 'objective' method of counting certain topic-related conversational moves – indicates a belief that those ordinary speakers' observations would also be made by the participants themselves.

informants would have to be briefed on its exact meaning and interpretation.

On another occasion, Watts (1992a:43) criticizes other frameworks for presenting definitions of politeness which do not correspond with native English speakers' perceptions of the notion. The latter are said to often involve negative attitudes, which are lost in modern theoretical accounts. This negative side of politeness is traced back to eighteenth-century British English society, where politeness was also a mark of social status, regulating membership of the societal elite. Thus the adoption of a 'polite style' was also a means of access to that elite. In this light, polite behaviour was often seen as 'selfishness in a veil of considerateness', the proverbial velvet glove hiding an iron fist. Watts' notion of politeness is presented as an attempt to remedy the inability of other frameworks to capture this 'negative side', in that it regards politeness as essentially egocentric behaviour, geared to enhance the speaker's social status in the eyes of the hearer (ibid.:57). In this way, Watts' notion actually attempts to bring the theoretical concept back in line with the commonsense concept.

But there are also indications that point away from an identification of Watts' concept of politeness with commonsense notions. One of these indications lies in its definition as 'marked behaviour'. Recall that politic behaviour is intended to cover socio-culturally appropriate behaviour, geared towards the maintenance of the interpersonal equilibrium, while polite behaviour is seen as 'more-than-merely-appropriate' behaviour (ibid.:50-51). Thus, whereas politic behaviour is unmarked socially appropriate behaviour, politeness is 'marked' in that it does more social interactional work than mere politic behaviour. Indeed, politeness is essentially egocentric, in that it represents the attempt by Ego to enhance his or her social standing in the eyes of Alter. Ego wants to stand out from the grey mass of people, wants to be noticed by Alter and therefore 'goes the extra mile' so that Alter will have a better-than-average impression of him or her. In this light, honorifics, or ToAs (terms of address) in general, are primarily politic and only interpretable as 'polite' *"[...] if they go beyond their normal usage as socio-culturally constrained forms of politic behavior"* (ibid.:52). Indeed, ToAs such as those exemplified by the pronominal choice between T/V variants in many languages,[10] can be seen as

---

[10] See Brown & Gilman (1960). 'T/V' refers to the second person pronouns *tu* (singular) and *vous* (plural) in French. Both can be used singularly, i.e. to address a single person. The distinction is usually thought of as representing 'informal' or 'intimate' (T) versus 'formal' or 'non-intimate' (V) ways of addressing someone. It is found in many languages besides French, including German *Du/Sie*, Spanish *tú/usted* or Russian *ty/vy*. The distinction can take on a somewhat different form

socio-culturally determined in that the appropriateness of their choice is often more a matter of social contextual factors than the speakers' free will. In general, French 'vous' (V-variant) will be more appropriate (and more heard) on formal occasions or with strangers than 'tu' (T-variant), while 'tu' will more often be heard among peers; likewise, in Dutch the V-variant ('u') will be used by the employees of banks, shops, etc. to clients, at least where interactants are not familiar with each other. This may be qualified as the normal usage, in that under those circumstances, the speaker will not be seen as making any special effort towards the hearer. In Watts' framework, it thus fully qualifies as politic but not as polite behaviour. This position, however, can arguably deviate from commonsense notions of politeness in at least two ways.

Firstly, contrary to Watts' theoretical classification, appropriate or adequate use of ToAs does appear to be commonsensically associated with polite behaviour by informants, and this for both the T-variant as well as the V-variant, for example, the V-variant used to superiors and the T-variant used to family members are both qualified as 'polite' (Braun & Schubert 1988:49). Analogously, although it is part of normal appropriate interactional practice in languages such as English or Dutch to express one's gratitude upon being given a present, or to greet one another upon meeting, it does not seem implausible that a parent might admonish his or her

---

in different languages. For example, whereas French has only one plural form (*vous*), so that in the plural the distinction is not made, in Dutch a speaker has the choice between plural *jullie* (T) and *u* (V). The Dutch singular T/V distinction comprises the forms *jij* (T) and *u* (V). Note that the V-variant is the same in both the plural and the singular. Unlike French, however, where the singular V-variant consists of the plural pronoun (the verb is also pluralized: *Vous pouvez entrer* - You$_{(sing; V)}$ may$_{(plur)}$ come in), in Dutch the singular form is primary. The plural V-variant consists of the singular V-pronoun: when the plural V-variant is used, the verb is singularized (*U mag binnenkomen* - You$_{(plural; V)}$ may$_{(sing)}$ come in). In Portuguese the distinction is even more complex, in that the singular offers three possibilities: apart from the pronominal forms *tu/você*, the impersonal (nominal) form *o senhor - a senhora* (Mr/Mrs or Sir/Madam) can also be used. The plural takes only the forms *vocês* and *os senhores/as senhoras*. Note that the singular V-variants do not consist of plural pronouns, but of third person pronouns/nouns. The third person is also used in Polish for the V-variant *pan - pani* (Sir - Madam) versus *ty* (thou) for the T-variant (Wierzbicka 1985). In other languages the T/V distinction is also applicable to third person referential pronominal usage (i.e. for people who are not present in the interaction), such as in Yoruba (Ajiboye 1992). In line with, for example Braun (1988), I use a broad definition of the term 'ToA' which includes forms such as personal pronouns and Japanese honorifics.

child for failing to express gratitude by saying "Be polite: say 'Thank you'!". Thanking and greeting are often cited by children as tokens of politeness (Blum-Kulka 1992:260), which implies that these practices are taught as elementary forms of politeness rather than as 'more than adequate' forms, used to show 'extra interactional effort'.

Secondly, classifying 'normal' address behaviour as politic means that according to Watts the phenomenon of Discernment in Japanese – identified by Ide (see above, section 1.1.5) – is part of politic but not polite behaviour, because it involves socio-culturally determined grammatical choices – in Ide's words, it is "automatic" socially appropriate behaviour. Volition on the other hand involves the speaker's free choice of verbal strategies, and therefore Watts holds the position that *"[...] wherever volition supersedes discernment in the choice of specific linguistic forms such as honorifics, terms of address, ritualised expressions, etc., we are dealing with politeness phenomena."* (Watts 1992a:52). Thus, Discernment constitutes politic behaviour, while Volition strategies are polite behaviour. Furthermore, politeness being 'more-than-merely-appropriate' can be paraphrased in Watts' framework as 'being extra-friendly' or 'particularly considerate' towards the hearer, and always involves putting in a more than casual effort. However, as appears from the ordinary speakers' ratings in Ide et al. (1992), the Japanese commonsense notion of politeness is more closely associated with appropriateness and casualness than with considerateness or friendliness. What is more, friendliness is even negatively correlated with politeness. Since Ide et al. (ibid.) associate friendliness with Volition, it would appear that for Japanese ordinary speakers, Volition is less closely associated with politeness than Discernment, i.e. exactly the opposite of Watts' theoretical classification.

So when we take a closer look at the kinds of behaviour that would be classified as 'polite' on the basis of Watts' conceptual definition, it appears from intuition as well as from other investigators' empirical research that ordinary speakers would often not agree. In spite of theoretical claims to the contrary, Watts' concept of politeness seems to have more of a politeness2 than a politeness1 character.

2.3 Discussion

A number of general observations can be derived from the discussion of each of the theories' specific orientation towards the politeness1–politeness2 distinction. Although only very few theories make explicit statements about their orientation towards the distinction, it was nevertheless seen to be implicitly present in each account. Some frameworks claim a politeness2 viewpoint (e.g. Leech's 'abstract', 'general', 'non-local' principles) but in the actual course of their analysis end up making claims and statements about what goes on in speakers' heads. Other frameworks claim the opposite: their intention is to represent 'local' or commonsense notions of politeness (e.g. Fraser & Nolen, Watts), but they end up with systems or models that lead to counterintuitive results or theoretically contradictory statements when consistently applied to actual cases, or confronted with ordinary speakers' definitions and evaluations. So the theoretical accounts invariably occupy an ambiguous position in relation to the distinction.

The fact that the politeness1–politeness2 distinction is always present in the background indicates that it is a highly salient aspect of scientific theorizing. The presence of both sides of the distinction in each and every account further suggests that both are intrinsic and thus inevitable aspects of scientific accounts. They are inseparably interconnected, so that any theory necessarily incorporates aspects of both, and an unequivocally one-sided position is in practice impossible. The ambiguous position of the theories can be explained by a general lack of awareness of the importance and influence of the distinction. Exactly because the distinction is inherent to scientific theorizing, a thorough awareness of its presence, form, and influence is necessary in order to avoid becoming entangled in its intricacies. At each point in the analysis one must remain thoroughly aware of the position of one's concepts in relation to the distinction, and the possible conclusions or next steps this position warrants. If this is not properly done, one runs the risk of arbitrarily jumping from one side to the other without taking the necessary precautions, which ultimately results in confusion regarding the status of the concepts. In practice, such an awareness thus takes on the form of making explicit what in most current approaches is left implicit.

Emic vs etic
In order to explain the inevitability of the politeness1–politeness2 distinction, it is illuminating to trace its relation to another distinction: that between 'emic' and 'etic'. This distinction originated in anthropological linguistics, and was coined by Kenneth Pike (1967[1954]) as a derivation from the terms 'phonemic' and 'phonetic'. Although it is highly controversial, in that over the years the terms 'emic' and 'etic' have been interpreted in many different ways by different researchers (for an overview, see Headland 1990), it can nonetheless be helpful for the present discussion. Pike defines an emic unit as *"[...] a physical or mental item or system treated by insiders as relevant to their system of behavior and as the same emic*

unit in spite of etic variability" (Pike 1990:28). The key point here is that emic units are relevant to insiders. As the distinction originated in anthropology, the term 'insider' is to be taken to mean 'cultural insider', i.e. the members of the culture under investigation, the 'natives'. Emic knowledge or the emic viewpoint are thus sometimes also called 'native knowledge' or the 'native viewpoint'. Despite what other observations or measurements (by the anthropologist, of course) may reveal in terms of differences, if two behavioural or mental units are perceived or treated as one and the same by insiders, then both can be said to belong to the same emic unit. 'Emically' there is no difference between them. The most obvious example of the distinction can of course be found in the domain from which the terms were derived:

> Kenneth Pike formed the words 'etic' and 'emic' from the suffixes of the words phon*etic* and phon*emic*. Phonetic accounts of the sounds of a language are based upon a taxonomy of the body parts active in the production of speech utterances and their characteristic environmental effects in the form of acoustic waves. Linguists discriminate etically between voiced and unvoiced sounds, depending on the activity of the vocal cords; between aspirated and nonaspirated sounds, depending on the activity of the glottis; between labials and dentals, depending on the activity of the tongue and teeth. The native speaker does not make these discriminations. On the other hand, emic accounts of the sounds of a language are based on the implicit or unconscious system of sound contrasts that native speakers have inside their heads and that they employ to identify meaningful utterances in their language. (Harris 1979:34, original emphasis)

Note that there is a slight nuance in the meaning of emic in Harris' account as opposed to Pike's. The emicness of a unit is not necessarily a function of conscious evaluation by the insider, but can also refer to *unconscious* distinctive practices. 'Emic' can thus refer both to how a native informant conceptualizes his or own behaviour, as well as to what actually goes on in the native informant's head while performing the behaviour in question. In terms of politeness, this difference refers to, on the one hand, the informants' conscious statements about his or her notion of politeness (as elicited, for example, in Blum-Kulka's 1992 investigation), and on the other to his or her spontaneous evaluations of (im)politeness (of his or her own or someone else's behaviour), made in the course of actual interaction. In section 2.1.1, I labelled the former 'metapragmatic politeness1', while the latter covers both 'expressive' and 'classificatory' politeness1. In this sense, 'emic' and 'politeness1' appear to be closely related, although different aspects can certainly be distinguished, which are lost if they are all subsumed under 'emic'. Etic accounts refer to outsiders' accounts of insiders' behaviour, involving distinctions not relevant to those insiders. In this sense it is identical to the way in which I used the notion of politeness2 in section 2.1.1 above: if theoretical evaluations did not match those of the participants, a politeness2 framework was said to predominate.

If we accept Harris' definition of emics as including participants' unconscious distinctive practices, then it is clear that any research effort necessarily has an emic dimension: the object of investigation is always human behaviour. On the other hand, science also attempts to understand or explain human behaviour, and this usually involves etic categorizations, since scientific accounts always intend to have some kind of surplus value over lay accounts. At the very least, a description of human behaviour involves making explicit the actor's unconscious distinctive practices, which in itself already entails a description in analytical as opposed to folk categories. But scientific descriptions mostly aim to achieve more than this: they aim, for example, to integrate the description in a cross-cultural comparison, or to trace the relationship of behaviour to psychological or sociological insights and so on. In all of these cases, the description will necessarily be etic.

Consequently, both aspects can also be seen to be present in the politeness theories under investigation. The emic side of research is present in both the search for (conscious) commonsense concepts of politeness, as well as in the study of actors' (unconscious) distinctive social interactional practices. Although only very few theories investigate the former, all of them study the latter – after all, what sociolinguistic theory would claim *not* to study human behaviour? But they also involve etic concepts and categorizations, be it Distance, Deference and Camaraderie (Lakoff), FTAs (Brown & Levinson), the PP (Leech, Gu), the CC (Fraser & Nolen), Volition vs. Discernment (Ide), cultural scripts (Blum-Kulka), emotive (Arndt & Janney) or politic (Watts) behaviour. In each of these cases, the scientific description or understanding involves concepts and categorizations that are not folk notions.

Ambiguity in politeness theories

But if both aspects are necessarily part of politeness research, then where is the confusion? Why did I label the presence of both aspects as 'ambiguity'? The answer lies in how the frameworks handle the presence of both aspects, in how the two aspects are related to each other within the

theories. Since there is hardly any explicit awareness (or at least treatment) of the importance of the two aspects, this relationship is established
implicitly, in the practice of theorizing, in the way in which concepts are
derived, handled and applied. Two approaches can be observed, depending on the presence or absence of research into conscious commonsense
concepts of politeness.

Theories that involve such research, notably those of Blum-Kulka and
Ide, take observed regularities in empirical data of informants' conscious
discussions of politeness, or their evaluations of utterances in terms of
politeness – i.e. emic conceptualizations and distinctive practices – and
interpret these using etic notions: cultural scripts (Blum-Kulka) and the
Volition-Discernment distinction (Ide). Note the transition from emics
('spontaneous' conceptualizations and distinctive practices) to etics (de-
scription/interpretation in analytical terms). The bulk of scientific work
then goes into the elaboration of the etic conceptualization, through extensive discussion of the notion, tracing its relation to other scientific
concepts and theories and so on. Afterwards, these etic notions are transferred back into speakers' minds, in that they are claimed to be
representations of what politeness is in everyday practice, showing how it
works, the mechanisms by which and because of which speakers produce
polite utterances. In other words, etics become emics again. For example,
Blum-Kulka's cultural scripts are claimed to be involved in determining
*"[...] the degree to which any linguistic expression is deemed polite by
members of a given culture in a specific situation"* (Blum-Kulka 1992:275).
They represent the *"usually tacit"* *"cultural expectations for what constitutes appropriate social behavior"* (ibid.:276) that determine evaluations
of verbal behaviour as '(im)polite'. And when such scripts are lacking, as
Blum-Kulka claims to be the case for Israeli public behaviour (see above,
section 2.1.1), *"Israelis alternatively rely either on the ethos of solidarity
or on individuated scripts true to personality"* (ibid.:269). In other words,
the cultural scripts are no longer the scientist's interpretive tool to understand human communication but rather become the speaker's own tool,
by means of which he or she arrives at appropriate behaviour. The etic
notions are, so to speak, implemented back into speakers' minds; they
become part of the way speakers arrive at their everyday distinctive practices regarding politeness; they are notions the speakers rely on in making
distinctive evaluations.

In Ide's framework, the transition from etics back to emics follows a
slightly different path, which involves the automaticity and obligatoriness
of Discernment choices and the identification of Discernment with specific linguistic units such as honorifics. At first, Volition and Discernment

are deployed as (etic) scientific notions to capture individual vs social aspects of social interaction. These notions are then claimed to be the basic constituents of politeness. Subsequently, the association of Volition and Discernment with 'free' (conscious) vs 'automatic' (unconscious) behavioural choices roots them firmly back in the speaker's mind. Where at first they represented the way in which the scientist interprets regularities in speakers' behaviour, they now become mechanisms inside those speakers' minds. Indeed, the scientist's definition of politeness is presented as the 'Japanese' concept. Moreover, Discernment is connected with specific linguistic units (honorifics), so the etic concept of politeness also includes these linguistic forms. However, when Discernment becomes a psychological reality of the speaker, the use of honorifics also becomes a matter of politeness for this speaker. When using honorifics, the speaker is doing this 'in order to be polite'.

On the other hand, theories that do not incorporate empirical examinations of commonsense notions of politeness simply skip the first step from emics to etics. They start off by immediately positing certain notions on the basis of which they develop a concept of politeness. As these notions are basically etic, the derived concept of politeness is also etic. For example, in Brown & Levinson's framework, politeness consists of specific ways of handling FTAs in specific social contexts. Obviously FTAs are not commonsense notions, but scientific constructions. Therefore the notion of politeness as FTA-related is also clearly an etic notion. However, since science is supposed to be about reality, about real human behaviour, the scientific notions are necessarily (and mostly unquestioningly) converted into emic ones. The same is true for the Model Person, who is first framed in the scientist's etic world, and then converted into 'every competent member of a culture'.

In this conversion process, the relationship between etics and emics is assumed to be a one-to-one relationship. In fact, since the etic/emic distinction is not explicitly discussed by the frameworks, there is no such thing as a conversion *process*. The conversion is immediate and direct: etics and emics are simply treated as one and the same. FTAs become psychological realities, the basis of speakers' distinctive practices. By extension, the notion of politeness as FTA-related is also given emic status. The latter becomes evident in the discussion of specific examples, where linguistic strategies that fall within the etic definition of politeness are attributed to speakers' (emic) intent to be polite. The same argument can be made about the other theories, but as this was done sufficiently in the detailed discussion above of each framework, it will not be repeated here. The important thing to note is that in each case politeness is defined on the basis of etic concepts. It is defined by the scientist as behaviour related in a specific way to those concepts. Consequently, each instance of behaviour that falls within that category – i.e. that can be interpreted as being related to those concepts in that specific way – is treated as an instance of politeness. When concrete examples are discussed, this notion of politeness is simply transferred to the speaker, as the utterance is said to result from 'politeness considerations'. As etics and emics are never discussed, the relationship between the scientist's and the ordinary speaker's concepts of politeness can be direct, immediate, straightforward, one-to-one. Only when the distinction is made explicit does the need arise to actually think about or conceptualize it in more depth. By making explicit the distinction between etic and emic aspects of research, the two are effectively separated and their relationship problematized. A line is drawn between them which can no longer be crossed unquestioningly.

The fact that this is not done in current theorizing leads to the ambiguous status of the theoretical concepts it proposes. Although they are basically etic in origin, they are claimed to be emic. The ambiguity is thus ontological (regarding the status of the concepts) as well as epistemological (regarding legitimate practices of scientific theorizing). The resulting confusion is nicely illustrated by the following research question formulated by Snow et al.:

> The question arises how children acquire this complex system. The problem can be conceptualized in a way similar to that in which linguists have presented the problem of language acquisition; the child receives data about use, yet the competent adult has achieved an understanding of a set of rules. How does the input, which is limited in amount and does not come equipped with information about the dimensions of interest, get elaborated into a systematic theory which is both abstract and more complex than the input data ever fully reveals?
> [...]
> Must children derive the theory which governs the use of these forms for themselves, or does parental teaching ever make explicit the rule system as well as the output of that rule system?
> [...]
> How do children come to understand the operation of the dimensions of social distance and power under these circumstances? (Snow et al. 1990:290)

Although the question is asked here in reference to Brown & Levinson's theory, it is clear that it could equally apply to any of the other frameworks, since they all involve complex systems of some sort. For example, in Fraser & Nolen's perspective, the speaker must need to be aware not only of the existence of a Conversational Contract and the fact that politeness consists of 'abiding by its stipulations', but also of the specifics of those stipulations, which involve situational, societal, etc. variables or dimensions – akin to the 'power' and 'social distance' dimensions mentioned by Snow et al. Similarly, in Watts' framework, the speaker must be aware of what the 'interpersonal equilibrium' consists of, of how it can be maintained and how this can be done in marked vs unmarked ways. The latter in particular requires knowledge about cultural or societal rules of politic behaviour, and of ways of deviating from these in order to establish polite behaviour.

The question then arises of how children ever manage to learn these complex systems. Because the etic concepts have been transformed into emic ones, they are assumed to be required in order for speakers to be able to produce polite behaviour. People need (the scientist's) theory in order to be able to be polite. Applied to the process of socialization, this means that children are in fact thought of as 'little scientists': just like their grown-up colleagues, they construct theories of politeness on the basis of observed behaviour, which they can then rely on in producing their own behaviour. They come to be aware of people's face-needs, of levels of imposition associated with specific speech acts and their face-threatening aspect (which also implies knowledge of power and social distance relationships), as well as of indirectness and other means of redressing such face-threats. In short, they gradually come to have Brown & Levinson's formula – as well as the rest of their theory – inside their heads. Note that not only children, but adults too are portrayed as scientists – in fact, the more they reproduce the scientist's evaluations, the more competent they are deemed to be. The transfer from etics to emics implies that ordinary speakers not only share the scientist's notion of politeness, but also his or her epistemological perspective, even up to the point where they are assumed to construct a theory of social interaction, on the basis of which they subsequently act.

Thus, where at first the theories were a posteriori derivations of observed behaviour (means of etically interpreting behaviour), they have now become a priori factors of production of that behaviour (means of emically producing behaviour). No need to stress the fact that, although the theories seem to take this step for granted – or at least do not make much ado about it – it actually involves a giant epistemological leap. Only by making explicit and thereby problematizing the etic/emic distinction does this feature of current scientific theorizing in the field of politeness become apparent.

However, as with the theories on which their research is based, Snow et al. also take the legitimacy of the transformation of etic into emic concepts for granted, and even attempt to substantiate it through empirical research on parent–child interaction. It is therefore instructive to take a more in depth look at their explanation of how children acquire the politeness system. Not surprisingly, the parents in the empirical study are found to rarely or never actually discuss the nature of the rules or the system directly:

> Explicit discussion of the abstract principles themselves rarely took place in the conversations we analyzed. The following example could be considered a lesson about the need for mitigation when imposing anything on others. In this example a white middle class mother was teaching her son that using the word 'please' helps mitigate the burden imposed on others by asking even a small favor of them.

> Mother: Well maybe if he'd asked please, could I have one, Morton would have given him a cookie, but the phony said I want one, he demanded it, and when you demand things what happens?
> Child:　He won't give it to him.
> Mother: Yeah, that's right. You know, when people are polite and they ask certain things, in nice ways, they get it. Right?
> Child:　Right.
> Mother: Well...
> (Snow et al. 1990:302)

The mother equates 'polite' with 'asking certain things in nice ways', exemplified by 'please, could I have one', and qualified as a way to 'get things you want'. She does not explicitly say anything about the fact that asking for a cookie constitutes an imposition, let alone about the smallness of the imposition (in fact, it would seem that cookies can be pretty important to children – at least they're higher on their list of wants than, say, a million dollars). If anything, the only lesson the child could learn from this interaction is that if you want something, it is safest to ask nicely (which equals politely), otherwise you may not get it. Of 'face', 'imposition', 'weightiness', 'power' or 'distance' there is absolutely no overt trace. So it would seem that what is presented as an example of a parent directly discussing the nature of the rules can only validly be interpreted as such by someone who *already knows* these rules and the system behind them.

Direct discussion is not the only kind of evidence presented. Other kinds that are more 'plentiful' in the data consist of parents' *"[...] manipulation of the dimensions in such a way that the child can observe*

their correlation to language form; [and] direct teaching of the child
about what forms to use in various situations" (ibid.:303). The latter can
be argued to belong to the same category as the direct discussion example
above. It is exemplified by a father refusing to hand his child the ketchup until the child is willing to say 'please may I have some ketchup'
(ibid.:295) – which is actually a practical version of the above theoretical
lesson to 'ask nicely or you will not get what you want' – and by a mother
forbidding her child to say 'shit' and 'puck you' [*sic*] because *"it's not*
nice" (ibid.:300). In each of these cases, the child is simply taught to (not)
say something, with the statement that it is '(not) nice' as the only overt
explanatory note.

The other kind of evidence, where parents are said to manipulate the
dimensions so the child can observe their correlation to language forms,
consists of instances of parental behaviour that can be interpreted along
the lines of Brown & Levinson's model. Two forms of such evidence are
presented. On the one hand there are cases such as that in which a mother
attempts to get her child to stop singing by saying *"Okay, that's excellent,*
thank you. Now let's put away those..." (ibid.:295) which is claimed to be
an instance of the parent addressing the child's positive face; or on in
which a father's request *"Martin, can daddy have some of your milk for*
his coffee? 'kay'?" (ibid.:296) is claimed to instantiate attendance to the
child's negative face-needs. On the other hand, parents were also observed
to issue unmitigated requests to their children, which are explained as
being cases where the children were not *"conforming to basic norms of*
civilized behavior" (ibid.:303). This practice is claimed to teach the child
the difference between imposing and non-imposing requests (asking for a
favour versus asking for normal civilized behaviour, i.e. what is expected
of anyone) while at the same time being a reflection of the parent–child
power relationship – presumably teaching the child about the influence of
the power variable in Brown & Levinson's model.

So on the one hand there are cases where parents attend to children's
face-needs, and on the other cases where parents display power-related
behaviour. Both are said to provide the child with background information about the system of politeness, because they exemplify the rules of
Brown & Levinson's model. But the line of reasoning employed in arguing this claim is circular. The parents' attendance to children's face-needs
can only be interpreted as such (i.e. as face-attendance) by the latter if
they *already have* face-needs, if they already think or function in terms of
such face-needs. For example, the father's request for milk does not in
and of itself teach his son that requests for favours constitute impositions,
are therefore face-threatening, and must thus be redressed. The child can

only interpret the request as face-threatening if he already thinks in terms of face-needs, i.e. if face-needs *already are* an emic reality. Claiming that the child interprets the request as face-threatening boils down to saying that, as a result of the request, his face *is actually* threatened (and the child realizes this), which in turn implies the emic reality of face-threats. Likewise, in order for the mother's qualification of her daughter's singing as 'excellent' to be able to provide the child with information about the system of politeness, the child needs to *recognize* it as an instance of that system. But in order to be able to do so, the child needs to know that (1) her mother wants her to stop singing, (2) the compliment is not genuine but strategic, (3) the compliment is used in order to get her to stop singing. If moreover she is able to associate it with the system of politeness, she needs to already have a notion of politeness which includes strategic compliments as politeness strategies. In short, since the mother's behaviour does not contain any overt references to 'face' or 'politeness', it can only be interpreted as an instance of Brown & Levinson's system of politeness if one already knows this system.

The crucial missing link in all of these examples is an account of *exactly how* the child gets from the overt behaviour to the underlying notions of 'imposition', 'face', 'face-threat', 'face-redress', 'weightiness', etc. How does the child derive the mere existence or salience of these notions from the behaviour displayed by his or her parents? Since there is no explicit mention of these concepts, this is only possible if they are already present in the child's mind. In other words, the child can only learn from such behaviour if he or she already knows how to interpret it. Consequently, the examples can only be said to constitute evidence for the emic validity of Brown & Levinson's model *if one first assumes* the emic validity of the model. They only exemplify the model for interpreters who already know its rules. They presuppose rather than evidence the emic saliency of the theoretical model. This is most strikingly demonstrated in the conclusion, where Snow et al. maintain that:

> [C]learly children do learn about the dimensions of power, social distance, and degree of imposition; by the time they are adolescents these dimensions govern their public interactions just as they do adults'. (Snow et al. 1990.:304)

The fact that children gradually come to display behaviour that can be interpreted using Brown & Levinson's model is taken as evidence for the fact that they actually learn about and learn how to employ this model. But by the same line of reasoning, the fact that adults' behaviour can be described using the model would be equally valid evidence for the claim that they actually use it. In the end, this amounts to the claim that because behaviour can be described using certain concepts, these concepts must necessarily be emic.

Just as in the theoretical models themselves, the transition from etic to emic here is immediate, direct and presupposed. The failure to recognize that this step actually involves bridging an epistemological divide results in what I have termed the 'confusion' or 'ambiguity' between etic and emic concepts, between politeness1 and politeness2.

Also note that the equation of etic and emic conceptualizations leads to a behavioural model where theory precedes behaviour, where thinking precedes acting. People act on the basis of a conceptual system: they think first, then act. Action is rational, based on (albeit unconscious) conceptual reasoning. This is most clearly and explicitly so in Brown & Levinson's model, where speakers are claimed to actually have a formula in their heads with which to calculate the weightiness of an act before being able to produce it. But it is also the case in other theories, where the formula takes the form of a 'cultural script', 'Conversational Contract', etc.

Finally it should be pointed out that the preceding discussion used the notions of politeness1 and politeness2 in rather a crude sense, with politeness1 denoting the commonsense concept of politeness and politeness2 referring to the concept as it figures in scientific theories. That this does not do justice to the more detailed explication of both notions at the start of this chapter is owing to the fact that the theoretical frameworks simply do not make the distinction, and thus cannot be expected to engage in a detailed discussion of evaluativity, normativity, variability and argumentativity. Just like the distinction itself, these notions are in some way or other taken for granted or treated implicitly in the practice of theorizing. Likewise, the present discussion has only focused on the output stage of the theoretical process, where the move is from politeness2 to politeness1 (see above, section 2.1), while the input stage of theorizing, where the move is from commonsense to scientific notions, has been left undiscussed. Nevertheless, it was claimed to be equally dangerous, in that insufficient awareness of its presence and importance could equally engender epistemological confusion between the ordinary speaker's and the scientist's positions. That this danger is all too real and is ignored by all of the theories will be argued in the next two chapters.

Chapter 3: Conceptual bias

In this chapter, another distinction enters the picture: that between politeness and impoliteness. Although the politeness-impoliteness distinction is explicitly discussed by most theories, it is as a rule not thoroughly analyzed, meaning that many aspects of its nature are taken for granted or left implicit. Just as with the politeness1-politeness2 distinction, this situation creates a number of problems. A more in-depth examination of its nature and treatment will also lead to the discussion of a few other conceptual issues, such as the theoretical roles allocated to speaker and hearer, and the associated conceptual importance of language production vs language reception. For each of these distinctions, a definite conceptual bias towards one side can be identified, which causes the other side to effectively disappear from the theoretical picture. This bias results from the unquestioning retention of certain aspects of politeness1 notions in the construction of politeness2 theoretical frameworks. The present chapter provides an analysis of how the theories handle the emic-etic distinction at the input stage of the analytical process, where the move is from politeness1 to politeness2.

3.1 The focus on 'polite'

As already argued in the discussion of politeness1, in practice emic politeness always refers to polite and never to impolite behaviour. This is not only exemplified by dictionaries, where politeness is usually defined as 'the quality of being polite', but also by the plain fact that impolite behaviour is covered by a separate noun: impoliteness. Furthermore, when informants are asked to provide definitions or descriptions of politeness, they invariably come up with definitions of polite behaviour, or descriptions of what 'to be polite' consists of (Blum-Kulka 1992). When impolite behaviour is mentioned, it is invariably associated with a lack of politeness, implying that impoliteness does not qualify as an instance of politeness, but rather as its absence. As their morphology testifies, the two terms are thus not only distinct, but also opposites.

This emic bias towards the polite side of the polite-impolite distinction is retained in scientific conceptualizations. Blum-Kulka's framework is a case in point: although her theoretical notion of politeness intends to cover the whole spectrum from "extensively polite" over "polite" to "impolite" (Blum-Kulka 1992:276), the latter is notably absent from the discussion. Not that impoliteness is not discussed at all, but it does receive strikingly less attention than polite behaviour. While the introduction explains that *"student interviews elicited definitions and descriptions of polite and impolite speech and behaviour"* (ibid.:256), the subsequent text only explicates definitions of polite behaviour. And the Hebrew terms proposed as equivalents to politeness (*nimus*, referring to formal etiquette, and *adivut*, which is associated with *"tolerance, restraint, good manners, showing deference and being nice to people"* ibid.:257) do not seem to cover impoliteness either. Furthermore, when behavioural indicators (the 'how') of politeness are discussed, all of the attention is focused on ways of being polite; the social motivations (the 'why') behind politeness are investigated through the question *"Why be linguistically polite?"* (ibid.:270); the social meanings of politeness (the 'what for') are paraphrased as *"the degree to which any linguistic expression is deemed polite by members of a given culture in a specific situation"* (ibid.:275); and the social differentials (the 'when') of politeness treats the social contexts that affect the appropriateness of behaviour – appropriateness being associated with the centre ('polite') part of the continuum only. So polite behaviour occupies centre stage, while impolite behaviour only has a walk-on part. Of course it is not totally absent. Just as the extensively polite end of the continuum is said to result from excessive use of polite strategies, the impolite end is conceived as resulting from diminished use of such strategies (ibid.:276); and the reasons why a speech act can be considered impolite are also discussed – because it defies culturally interpreted face concerns, or because it deviates from culturally conventionalized expressions. Even so, the *focus* of the whole framework is entirely on polite behaviour. The theoretical conceptualization starts and ends at the polite side of the polite–impolite distinction, and the concept itself is completely centred on the definition of polite behaviour.

The same can be said of Ide's framework, where the notion also covers the whole continuum between 'polite', 'nonpolite' and 'impolite' (Ide 1989:225; 1992:281). Again however, this position is not fully maintained in the practice of theorizing. Her empirical investigation into the Japanese concept of politeness (Ide 1992) is entirely focused on a comparison of the (American) English term 'polite' and its Japanese equivalent *teineina*, while the title presents it as a study of 'the concept of politeness'. Although the terms 'rude' and its Japanese equivalent *bureina* are also present, they only figure as part of a list of associated adjectives used to compare 'polite' with *teineina*. The latter are at the centre of the study, and thus of the whole ensuing concept of politeness. This is confirmed by Ide's definition of linguistic politeness as:

> [...] the language usage associated with *smooth communication,* re-
> alized 1) through the speaker's use of intentional strategies to allow
> his or her message *to be received favorably by* the addressee, and 2)
> through the speaker's choice of *expressions to conform to the expected
> and/or prescribed norms of speech* appropriate to the contextual situ-
> ation in individual speech communities. (Ide 1989:225, my emphasis)

1) and 2) refer to Volition and Discernment respectively. The latter comprises obligatory or automatic choices of *appropriate* honorific forms,
and the former strategic intentional choices for *making the hearer feel
good*; these two conceptual foundations of Ide's theoretical approach do
not really appear to be successful descriptors of impolite behaviour.

So although both theories explicitly claim a neutral conceptualization of politeness which is intended to cover polite as well as impolite
behaviour, in practice their theorizing starts at, and throughout remains
completely centred on, the polite side of the distinction. This conceptual
bias can equally be found in the other theoretical frameworks. It must be
added, however, that most of them do not claim such a neutral politeness concept at all, and are thus more 'openly' biased towards the polite
side of the distinction. In Lakoff's theory, the second 'rule of pragmatic
competence' – intended to complement the Gricean CP – reads *"Be Polite!"* (Lakoff 1977:86), while the three rules of politeness (Don't impose;
Give H options; make H feel good) are all stipulations leading to polite
rather than impolite behaviour. In later work Lakoff defines politeness as
*"a system of interpersonal relations designed to facilitate interaction by
minimizing the potential for conflict and confrontation inherent in all human interchange"* (Lakoff 1990:34). Again, this definition displays the
positive thrust of polite behaviour, rather than the negative one associated with impolite behaviour. The same can be said of Brown & Levinson's
definition in terms of face-redress, where politeness strategies avoid threatening the hearer's face by removing any such threat inherent in speech
acts. They see politeness as a means of interactional conflict-avoidance,
based on the avoidance of imposition (off-record politeness) or the display of solidarity (positive politeness) and restraint (negative politeness).
Again the focus is entirely on being polite. To wit, in explaining the connection of their model with the Gricean framework, they claim to be
concerned with the explanation of 'polite ways of talking' as deviations
from the Gricean maxims (Brown & Levinson 1987:4). Positive politeness strategies are paraphrased as ways of being "positively polite"
(ibid.:104), while negative politeness is qualified as "the stuff that fills the

etiquette books" (ibid.:130) – both strategies that stipulate how to be polite rather than impolite.

In Watts' and Arndt & Janney's frameworks a similar conceptual bias
can be found. Arndt & Janney think of politeness as consisting of social
conventions for achieving smooth interaction ('social politeness'), as well
as interpersonally supportive emotive behaviour or 'interpersonal politeness', 'tact', that is, *"knowing how to express positive and negative feelings
without threatening one's partner emotionally"* (Arndt & Janney 1985a:
292). Both these notions only explicate polite behaviour, impoliteness is
never even explicitly discussed. A similar bias is observed in Watts'
theory, where politeness is defined as a marked form of normal politic
behaviour. In his own words, politic behaviour *"includes as a subset polite verbal behavior"* (Watts 1989a:136-137), so again politeness equals
polite behaviour. Impoliteness never really enters the picture, although
we are given an implicit hint that it may have something to do with
non-politic behaviour. Gu's statement that his framework is about *"the
essential elements of politeness, or what counts as polite behavior"* (Gu
1990:239) speaks for itself. Not only are the 'essential elements' all 'positive' (respectfulness, modesty, attitudinal warmth and refinement),
politeness is also a matter of moral maxims, of socially prescriptive rules
that define "appropriate" ways of interacting (ibid.:240).

Although Leech's PP resembles Lakoff's second rule of pragmatic
competence in urging people to 'Be Polite', his framework seems to be
more accommodating to impoliteness, in that 'being polite' is defined as
'minimizing the expression of impolite beliefs'. So impoliteness is no
longer out of the picture, or even relegated to peripheral status, but is
rather right at the heart of the definition of politeness. Unfortunately its
role is limited to that of a mere possibility, as a possible course of action
that should in practice be avoided, since the PP only explains the why and
how of polite behaviour. Impoliteness is also explicitly present in Fraser
& Nolen's theory, as the terms of the CC delineate which behaviours will
be interpreted as polite and which as impolite. Because the CC determines impolite as well as polite behaviour, with no apparent conceptual
preference for either, Fraser & Nolen's framework is by far the most neutral in terms of the politeness-impoliteness distinction. However, this is
only true for the *definition* of (im)politeness. As we will see later on, when
it comes to explaining how politeness and impoliteness work, the CC ceases
to be all that neutral.

So, only four out of nine theories explicitly incorporate impoliteness
(Blum-Kulka, Ide, Leech and Fraser & Nolen), and of those four only the

last provides a definition that is not conceptually biased towards the polite end of the distinction. In all the other theories politeness equals 'polite'. A further clarification is in order, however, for this does not mean that in conceptually biased frameworks the term 'politeness' always refers to 'polite behaviour' exclusively. Nor is it true that in a non-conceptually biased theory such as Fraser & Nolen's, 'politeness' refers to both polite and impolite behaviour. All in all, three different cases can be distinguished.

First, in Ide's and Blum-Kulka's frameworks, politeness is explicitly claimed to comprise the whole continuum between impolite and polite (or "extensively polite" in Blum-Kulka's case), so the field of study is delineated as incorporating polite as well as impolite behaviour. In practice, however, the definition of politeness is completely focused on the polite side of the continuum: the interactional phenomenon identified by the notion comprises polite behaviour only. So the delineation of the field does not match the conceptual definition. The use of the term 'politeness' thus becomes ambiguous: from the perspective of the field of study, it should refer to both polite and impolite behaviour. But as a result of the definition, in reference to actual phenomena it covers polite behaviour only, while impolite behaviour is referred to as 'impoliteness'.

Second, other theories also incorporate impolite behaviour but do not claim to use the term 'politeness' neutrally. Both Leech and Fraser & Nolen use it to refer to polite behaviour only, while 'impoliteness' is used to refer to impolite behaviour. Neither of them explicitly claims that politeness should cover both. However, their conceptual definition does accommodate both. In a sense this is the reverse situation of Ide and Blum-Kulka above: they do not claim a neutral concept, but in practice their conceptual definition does cover both phenomena. Owing to the fact that they are united by a common definition, the field of study of politeness is factually delineated as including both. Leech does not go as far in this as Fraser & Nolen, since his core concept – the PP – still accounts for polite behaviour only.

Lastly, for a third group of theories, 'politeness' and 'polite' are really synonyms. This group comprises Lakoff, Brown & Levinson, Gu, Arndt & Janney and Watts. The thrust of their research efforts is entirely and solely aimed at accounting for polite behaviour. Their models allocate virtually no space to impolite behaviour, nor do they make any explicit claims that they intend to do so. Both the field of study of politeness as well as the conceptual definition of the phenomenon refer to polite behaviour only.

3.2   Conceptualizing the distinction

It could be argued that since the theories in the third group do not aim for a neutral concept of politeness, their exclusive focus on polite behaviour would not seem to be problematic. Rather, it merely fits the commonsense use of the term: since polite behaviour is nominalized into 'politeness', while impolite behaviour is referred to as 'impoliteness', it only seems natural that a theory of politeness should focus on polite behaviour. It is not of course my intention to criticize theories for not doing something they do not claim nor intend to do in the first place. Nevertheless, I believe there are certain advantages to a conceptual approach that simultaneously captures politeness and impoliteness. For one thing, commonsensically the two phenomena are closely related. This can be seen not only from the terms' lexical relationship, but also from their dictionary definitions, where impoliteness is usually defined as the inverse or negative of politeness (impolite = not polite). The phenomena are merely two sides of the same coin, and therefore any theory that pretends to say something valuable about one side, automatically needs to deal with the other side as well. All the more so for a theory that proposes a model that purports to explain or account for one side entirely: surely it must take into account the whole coin. And sure enough, as we have already seen, most theories do include some reference to impoliteness.

From this perspective, it may be illuminating to examine just how impoliteness and its relationship to politeness are conceptualized by theories that take them into account, and how they could or would be integrated into frameworks that do not explicitly cover them. Let me start by repeating that commonsensically speaking politeness and impoliteness are each other's opposites, with politeness as the 'positive' and impoliteness as the 'negative' term. This positive–negative relationship not only holds for the kind of evaluation they involve (polite behaviour being positively evaluated, impolite behaviour negatively evaluated), but also for their lexical meaning, as inscribed in their morphological structure (impoliteness being the negative derivation – through the prefix 'im' – of politeness). The reverse relation does not hold directly, only by implication: politeness is not defined as 'not impolite'. The unmarked term thus seems to be 'politeness'.

When we compare this with theoretical conceptualizations of impoliteness, a striking resemblance emerges. For Fraser & Nolen impoliteness results from *not* abiding by the terms of the CC. For Leech impoliteness consists of *not* abiding by the PP, while impolite beliefs are beliefs that

are *un*favourable to the hearer. Gu seems largely to uphold Leech's definition: in one of the few remarks on impoliteness, 'to criticize someone' is
equated with *"being impolite in content"* (Gu 1990:240), which agrees
with Leech's definition in terms of unfavourableness to the hearer. Moreover, analogous to Leech's approach, speech acts are ranked along a
continuum from 'beneficial to the hearer' to 'costly to the hearer', which
is said to correspond to degrees of politeness – from 'more polite' to 'less
polite' (Gu 1990:243; Leech 1983:107), where 'less polite' equals 'more
impolite'.

For Blum-Kulka impoliteness is associated with a *lack* of cultural
scripts, with defying culturally interpreted face concerns and deviating
from culturally conventionalized ways of expression. Ide's conceptualization involves a continuum between 'polite' and 'impolite', where
'polite' is defined in terms of conforming to prescribed norms (Discernment) and making the hearer feel good (Volition). Since the polite end of
the continuum is associated with positive scores on these points, presumably impoliteness consists of not conforming to norms and not making the
hearer feel good. Lakoff claims that not following the politeness rules
may be interpreted as being impolite (Lakoff 1977:88) or 'rude', 'having
no breeding' etc. In later work, 'rude' is opposed to 'polite' and characterized as *"behavior that does not utilize politeness strategies where they
would be expected, in such a way that the utterance can only or most
plausibly be interpreted as intentionally and negatively confrontational."*
(Lakoff 1989a:103).

The status of impoliteness in Brown & Levinson's framework is less
clear, as it is hardly ever explicitly mentioned. In their discussion of indirect speech acts, for example, they state that *"[s]o far, beyond the
categorization 'polite/impolite' we have not properly investigated what
makes some conventionally indirect expressions slightly more or less polite than others"* (Brown & Levinson 1987:142). From the juxtaposition
of the polite-impolite categorization with the qualifications of 'more or
less polite', it can be surmised that 'impolite' equals 'less polite'. Also, in
light of the conceptual bias towards polite behaviour, the claim that their
model categorizes expressions in terms of polite-impolite, seems to indicate that impoliteness results from the non-application of their politeness
strategies: not redressing an FTA when the calculation of its Weightiness
(W_x) stipulates doing so. But there seems to be more to Brown & Levinson's
conceptualization of impoliteness. In a discussion of possible flaws of,
and necessary amendments to, their original model on the occasion of
its second edition (Brown & Levinson 1987), the problem of over-
generation of strategies is mentioned: some strategies lead to unrealistic

predictions about what would qualify as polite utterances. For example, the strategy 'be pessimistic about the success of the FTA' would lead one to expect that 'You don't want to pass the salt' constitutes a polite way of requesting for the salt. *"That it is not, of course, is due to the fact that it attributes impolite desires to the addressee"* (ibid.:11). It is not very clear how the notion of 'impolite desires' could fit in with their definition of politeness in terms of the *performance* of speech acts. A possible solution could be to argue that such unwillingness to cooperate with a request would threaten the requester's positive face, although in that case it is still not clear how a mere *desire* could constitute a face-threatening *act*. Apart from this lack of clarity, however, the interpretation would fit the image of impoliteness as the blunt performance of an FTA, without any redress, i.e. as the negative of politeness.

There are two points at which Arndt & Janney mention impoliteness. They claim that whereas politeness consists in conforming to situational or hearer-expectations, impoliteness is associated with deviations from them. Impoliteness is thus a matter of *not* doing that which is expected. Impoliteness is also mentioned in the statement that *"[...] almost any normal adult can be polite in impolite ways, or be impolite in polite ways"* (Arndt & Janney 1992:22). This statement is intended to illustrate the difference between the notions of social and interpersonal politeness, with the first part being an instance of social politeness, while the latter is politeness from an interpersonal point of view. If we incorporate this distinction into their statement, it reads 'it is possible to be socially polite in interpersonally impolite ways, or to be socially impolite in interpersonally polite ways'. In the light of Arndt & Janney's metaphorical characterization of social politeness as a system of social traffic rules and interpersonal politeness as an interpersonally supportive driving style, it would seem that social impoliteness results from not abiding by the social traffic rules, while interpersonal impoliteness consists of not maintaining an interpersonally supportive driving style. In both cases, impoliteness equals *not* being polite.

As an aside, it can be remarked that Arndt & Janney's statement is not as clear as it seems. For they maintain that its reverse is not possible – a logically necessary condition if the statement is intended to illustrate a difference between the two kinds of politeness. However, intuitively it does seem possible to be interpersonally impolite in socially polite ways, or to be interpersonally polite in socially impolite ways. For example, in the situational context of a lecture, the former would be the case if a member of the audience were to shatter the speaker's arguments while respecting all the rules of social etiquette. On the other hand, a member of the audience complimenting the speaker about his or her 'most interesting, fascinating presentation', sending highly supportive emotive cues (big smile, direct gaze, confident intonation), but doing so during the lecture, without invitation, by blatantly interrupting the speaker, would qualify as a case of the latter. So in the end the remark about impoliteness seems to be more confusing than enlightening.

Finally, in Watts' framework impoliteness is not given much attention either. It shows up only once, in a remark on deviations from politic behaviour, where Watts claims that *"those points at which the verbal interaction is perceived not to be functioning as it should are potentially open to interpretation as revealing non-politic, possibly also explicitly impolite, behavior"* (Watts 1989a:136). Recall that politic behaviour is unmarked behaviour, geared towards maintaining the interpersonal equilibrium, of which polite behaviour is a marked subset, while non-politic behaviour consists in deviating from politic behaviour. Both polite and non-politic behaviour are marked forms. Politeness can be seen as exemplifying "extra care" for the interpersonal relationship, since it does more than mere politic behaviour (Watts 1992a:51). In being explicit about its aims for maintaining the interpersonal equilibrium, it foregrounds that equilibrium, and the speaker's positive intentions are made the focus of the interaction. The reverse can be said to be true about non-politic behaviour: it is a marked form which threatens or reassesses the equilibrium: it is geared towards (temporarily) destabilizing the interpersonal relationship. Since it appears from the quote that impolite behaviour is some kind of explicit form of non-politic behaviour, politeness and impoliteness can again be seen as each other's opposites. Whereas politeness is explicitly involved in maintaining the equilibrium – i.e. positive towards the interpersonal relationship – impoliteness is explicitly involved in reassessing, or threatening the equilibrium, i.e. negative towards the interpersonal relationship – in Watts' own words, non-politic behaviour "disturbs" the relationship (Watts 1989a:137), and those points at which it occurs are open to interpretation as "attempts to disrupt the fabric of the interpersonal relationship" (ibid.:136).

In sum, the commonsense relationship between polite(ness) and impolite(ness) – inverse and opposite – is mirrored by the scientific conceptualizations. (Im)politeness is associated with, or represented as (in)appropriateness, (un)favourableness, (un)supportiveness, (non)-abidance by the CC, the PP or other soci(et)al rules, (non)-politicness, (lack of) cultural scripts or (lack of) FTA-redress.

3.3   The focus on production

Another factor that needs to be considered for a proper understanding of how the theories conceptualize the polite–impolite distinction, is their treatment of the speaker–hearer interactional dyad. For there are two sides to (im)politeness: the production of behaviour by a speaker and the evaluation of that behaviour by a hearer. Both are essential and indispensable elements of any notion of (im)politeness, as they constitute the two sides of the communicative process. At first sight, most theories seem to recognize this duality, as their conceptualizations reserve a place for the speaker (the production side of politeness) as well as the hearer (the evaluative side of politeness). Although it would be hard to imagine a theory that does not incorporate the evaluative (the 'hearer') side of politeness, in many cases the central concepts or the models that are developed are primarily those of production. In some cases these concepts or models can also be applied to reception, and provide an explanation for how and why behaviour is evaluated as (im)polite, but even then their primary mode of existence still seems to be as productive concepts. In other words, politeness is primarily conceptualized as a form of speaker behaviour rather than hearer evaluation.

This speaker behaviour bias is clearest in Brown & Levinson's theory, where one of the main prerequisites for politeness (and thus one of the main assumptions of the framework) is that the speaker is endowed with rationality, a specific kind of means-ends reasoning based on the hierarchical ordering of different politeness strategies. Politeness is thus an aspect of speech act production, where the speaker anticipates the hearer's reactions and formulates his or her utterances in such a way that any threat to the hearer's face is either removed or redressed. This anticipatory process even takes an objective form in the formula with which the speaker is said to calculate the Weightiness (W_x) of the speech acts. So politeness is all about making appropriate linguistic choices in the performance of speech acts, and Brown & Levinson's framework provides a model for how that decision-making process develops. Of course, for these choices or strategies to be effective, the hearer is still required to interpret them properly, but exactly how this happens is never addressed by Brown & Levinson. From the fact that politeness strategies actually 'work', it can be derived that they assume the hearer applies the same concepts as the speaker.[1] The

---

[1] In the 1987 reissue of their original publication, Brown & Levinson do point

hearer's interpretative processes are simply taken for granted, and remain absent on the theoretical conceptual level.

The association of politeness with speech production is also found in other frameworks. For example, it finds expression in the specific formulations of rules, maxims, principles, etc. Lakoff's rules ('Remain Aloof!', 'Give Options', etc.); Leech's PP ('Minimize the expression of impolite beliefs'); Gu's Self-Denigration maxim ('Denigrate Self and elevate other') all stipulate strategies the speaker should follow in order to be polite. And as argued in the previous section, most theories attempt to explain or model polite behaviour – this time our attention goes not so much to the term 'polite' but rather to 'behaviour'. Even in Fraser & Nolen's relatively neutral framework, (im)politeness results from the *speaker's* staying within or deviating from the terms of the CC, although they do mention that no matter how much the speaker aims for polite behaviour, the hearer can always interpret it as impolite (Fraser & Nolen 1981:96). In Arndt & Janney's framework, politeness is a matter of *conveying* messages in a supportive way, so again politeness resides with the speaker, as it does in Watts' theory where politeness is an explicit ('marked') way of the speaker's maintaining the interpersonal equilibrium. Although Blum-Kulka's cultural scripts can arguably be conceived as playing a role in politeness perception as well, their primary function lies in regulating the production of behaviour. This can clearly be seen from the fact that Israeli informants' perceptions of widespread impoliteness in the public sphere (Blum-Kulka 1992:259) are explained through a lack of cultural scripts. Had cultural scripts been intended to account for the perception of politeness, surely complaints of impoliteness would imply not the lack, but rather the clear presence of such scripts. In fact, if scripts were perceptual notions, their absence would lead to the perception of neither politeness nor impoliteness – to the 'undefinedness' of the behaviour in question in terms of (im)politeness. Finally, the speaker-bias in Ide's framework can be read directly from her definition of politeness (Ide 1989:225, see above, section 3.1), which explicitly refers to the speaker's strategic (Volition) or automatic (Discernment) choice of linguistic expressions.

---

out their awareness of the problem that the hearer's understanding of the speaker's intentions must involve running their means-ends reasoning 'backwards' so to speak (Brown & Levinson 1987:8). They do not offer any solution, however, but merely admit that the hearer's understanding of politeness would constitute a 'conceptual mystery' to their framework.

So the theoretical models all describe what speakers have to do in order to be polite. In general, this can also be seen from the fact that politeness is often defined as a means to 'avoid conflict' or 'achieve smooth communication' (Arndt & Janney 1985a:282; 1992:22-23, 34ff; Brown & Levinson 1987:1; Ide 1989:225, 230; Leech 1983:17, 82; Lakoff 1990:34; Gu 1990:239) and arguably also Blum-Kulka and Watts). This definition establishes politeness as a tool with which speakers achieve certain communicative or interpersonal goals. True, the attainment of these goals still depends on the evaluative or interpretative practice of the hearer, but these interpretations are anticipated by the speaker. So the hearer's interpretative activity is only present as part of the speaker's productive activity, insofar as it plays a role in influencing the speaker's construction of utterances. Politeness is primarily conceptualized as a productive activity – an aspect of speech production – instead of an evaluative activity – an aspect of speech reception. It needs to be stressed once more that in each of these cases the hearer is of course not completely absent. The frameworks do recognize the fact that communication is a two-sided process. The present point of interest is not that the hearer would be totally absent from the picture, but rather that he or she is only present by implication. Moreover, the hearer's presence seems to be rather a passive one: in all frameworks, except Fraser & Nolen's, the hearer's role is restricted to that of a mere 'recognizer' of speaker behavioural choices.

3.4   Theoretical implications

So far this chapter has argued three points in relation to the frameworks: (1) that they involve a conceptual bias towards the polite end of the polite-impolite distinction; (2) that they conceptualize politeness and impoliteness as each other's opposites; and (3) that their conceptualizations of politeness are biased towards the production of behaviour, or towards the speaker in the interactional dyad. In combination, these three characteristics have a number of theoretical consequences.

3.4.1 The mystery of impoliteness
The combination of the speaker behaviour bias and the conceptualization of impoliteness as the opposite and negative of politeness, results in the implicit definition of impoliteness as the non-performance of an act, as the lack or absence of something. Impoliteness results from not redressing FTAs, not applying politeness rules, not abiding by the PP or the CC, etc. As a lack or absence, impoliteness becomes a 'non-act'. It consists in

'not doing something' or failing to display a specific kind of behaviour. This basically creates two possibilities for the status of impoliteness: either 'not being polite' is considered an act in its own right, or it is not. The question here concerns intentionality. If politeness is something the speaker consciously *does*, and impoliteness consists of 'not behaving politely', the question arises whether this behaviour is also consciously performed by the speaker or not. If not, the positive-negative conceptualization of the polite-impolite distinction is pursued to its extreme and impoliteness becomes pure absence. It then consists in the absence of both politeness and intentionality. This seems to be the case in a few frameworks where the specific conceptualization of polite behaviour makes the occurrence of impoliteness hard to imagine.

Ide's Discernment consists of "obligatory" or "automatic" linguistic choices (Hill et al. 1986:348) which form a system of sociopragmatic concordance (Ide 1989:227) that functions like a grammar. But as they are part of the constituent factors of speaking a language, syntactic and grammatical concordance are not really a matter of speaker choice. Although it may be intelligible, a statement such as:

(3)   Yesterday me sleep late

does not constitute grammatical English and, except in cases of known syntactic incompetence, will be taken as an attempt at saying:

(4)   Yesterday I slept late

rather than as a strategy of speaking in its own right. Syntactic concordance is what makes a sentence an instance of 'English'. In defining Discernment as a form of 'sociopragmatic concordance' and likening it to syntactic concordance, the same line of reasoning is applied to politeness. The 'obligatoriness' and 'automaticity' of Discernment are of the same nature as those of syntactic concordance: the rules of Discernment are an integral part of speaking Japanese, they are part of the structure of the Japanese language. Just as a fluent speaker of English would say (4) rather than (3), so a fluent speaker of Japanese would follow the rules of Discernment rather than not. Impoliteness as the absence of Discernment would therefore not be regarded (by the theory, and presumably also by the hearer) as an 'act' of the speaker, but rather as an indication of incompetence. Apart from the stumbling of the non-fluent, impoliteness has no real place in Japanese: 'proper' or 'real' Japanese is always 'polite'. Note how this contrasts strongly with Ide's explicit claim of politeness being a neutral term designating the whole continuum between polite and impolite. The association of politeness with cultural scripts and of impoliteness with a lack of such scripts in Blum-Kulka's framework has the same implication. Impoliteness is not the result of the speaker's intentional strategic choice, but rather of some kind of cultural deficiency. By default people are polite, provided they have scripts that tell them how. In this case, impoliteness is doubly negatively defined: as the absence of politeness which results from the absence of cultural scripts.

The second possibility involves the conceptualization of impoliteness as a conscious act in its own right. In this frame of thinking, impoliteness is still the opposite of politeness, but the two are ontologically on a par. They are equal but opposite strategies open to any speaker at any time. This seems to be the case in Leech's framework, where the possibility of impoliteness is manifest in the fact that the PP tells people to avoid it as much as possible. Likewise, Brown & Levinson's framework does not exclude the wilful 'bald on-record' performance of an FTA where its Weightiness would advise the application of face-redress. In the remaining frameworks, impoliteness can equally be conceived of as an act in its own right, whether it involves *"intentionally and negatively confrontational"* behaviour (Lakoff 1989a:103) where the actor does not follow the politeness rules, the intention to 'disrupt' the interpersonal equilibrium (Watts), defiance of socially prescriptive norms (Gu) or hearer expectations (Arndt & Janney), or non-abidance by the terms of the CC (Fraser & Nolen).

So the theories can conceptually accommodate impoliteness with varying degrees of ease. In spite of explicit claims to the contrary, for some it would in practice be quite difficult to fully integrate impoliteness, while for others it is a behavioural choice on a par with polite behaviour. But regardless of how well they can accommodate the occurrence of impoliteness, none of the theories is really able to adequately *explain* it, because the bias towards polite behaviour results in concepts geared to explain polite behaviour only. This is most clear in Blum-Kulka's account, where the notion of cultural scripts can only be used to explain why people display polite behaviour. There are no scripts for impoliteness, that is, scripts that people use as a guide to achieve impoliteness. On the contrary, impoliteness is explained by the absence of such scripts. So although the scripts-concept does not as such render impoliteness unimaginable, it cannot itself *explain* its occurrence in the same way as it does for politeness. Politeness is there *because of* cultural scripts, but the same is not true of impoliteness. Likewise, Leech's PP, Lakoff's rules, Gu's social norms, Arndt & Janney's social politeness rules or Ide's Volition and Discern-

ment cannot offer a real explanation for the occurrence or even the existence of impolite behaviour in the same way as they do for polite behaviour.
If these concepts were developed to explain impoliteness, one would have
to posit an Impoliteness Principle, or a system of Rules of Impoliteness,
and so on. Since they are all based on some kind of 'norms' – as I shall
collectively call norms, rules, maxims, principles, scripts, etc. – and norms
qua norms can never explain their own breaching, none of these theories
is able to explain impoliteness adequately. The best they can do is capture
it as the 'lack', 'absence', or 'violation' of norms. So even when politeness and impoliteness are both seen as instances of behaviour, their
occurrence still cannot be explained uniformly by the central theoretical
concepts. This is illustrated by Arndt & Janney's metaphor of traffic rules:
although traffic rules can certainly explain why people at a crossroads
give right of way to traffic coming from the right, they cannot explain
why so many other people do not.

Four frameworks seem to escape this dilemma: Arndt & Janney (at
least partly), Brown & Levinson, Fraser & Nolen and Watts. As they are
not based on maxims, scripts, rules or principles, they seem to be more
open to the incorporation of impoliteness. However, closer examination
reveals that this openness to impoliteness is largely superficial, as each of
them contains elements that hamper its full integration into the explanatory framework.

Brown & Levinson's notion of rationality as a means-ends reasoning
does not exclude the pursuit of conflictive goals. As it moreover not only
conceptualizes face-redress, but also face-threats, it seems all the more
capable of theoretically accommodating impoliteness. If a speaker aims
for conflict, he or she should avoid face-redress, and instead aim for as
blunt a face-threat as possible. So the conflictive concept of FTA enables
a non-negative conceptualization of impoliteness, with Weightiness even
becoming a direct measure of impoliteness: the higher its value, the more
redressive action would be required for the act to be polite, so the more
impolite its unmitigated performance would be.

However appealing this view may be, there is one major stumbling
block to the full incorporation of impoliteness: the centrality of the notions of face and face-wants. The basic explanatory factor for the existence
and occurrence of politeness lies in the fact that people have face-wants.
People want their wants to be satisfied (otherwise they would not be wants),
and you can only get others to satisfy your wants if you in turn satisfy
theirs – by means of politeness. Not satisfying people's face-wants is self-
destructive and almost unnatural behaviour, as it will lead to those others

not satisfying your wants, not complying with your requests, etc. If face-wants were to account for impoliteness in the same way as politeness, they would need to include the want not to satisfy one's own face-wants, which is a contradiction in terms. As such, impoliteness cannot be a consequence of face-wants. Although Brown & Levinson do acknowledge that face-wants can be ignored, *"[...] not just in cases of social break-down (affrontery) but also in cases of urgent cooperation, or in the interests of efficiency"* (Brown & Levinson 1987:62), this does not dispel with the fact that wants *qua wants* can never explain their own non-fulfilment. In this sense the notion of face-wants has the same effect – and can thus be subsumed under – the general notion of 'norms'.

Fraser & Nolen go even further than Brown & Levinson in the incorporation of impoliteness, in that they explicitly define it as the violation of the terms of the CC (Fraser & Nolen 1981:96). However, what was said about face-wants can equally be applied to the notion of a Conversational Contract. Not only is the CC focused exclusively on polite behaviour in that its terms outline what is expected and thus polite, the notion of a contract itself can only explain why both parties would abide by its terms, not why they would violate them. In the economic sphere, if a sales contract stipulates that the buyer of some goods is not to use those goods for commercial purposes, one can very well say that party X does not use the goods in question for commercial purposes 'because he or she is under contract not to do so'. To say that party X *does* use the goods for commercial purposes 'because he or she is under contract not to do so' would be contradictory.[2] Analogously, the concept of a Conversational Contract can *qua contract* not explain its own violation, and thus it can equally be subsumed under the general category of 'norms'.

In Arndt & Janney's approach, the 'traffic rules' of social politeness exhibit all the characteristics of norms discussed above, so only interpersonal politeness (or tact) seems a viable candidate for explaining impoliteness. However, tact is claimed to be connected to face concerns, and to result from the universal (pan-cultural) human desire to avoid conflicts and maintain and protect each other's face. Consequently, what has been said about Brown & Levinson's approach also applies here. Moreover, the principles and techniques of interpersonal politeness are said to

---

[2] Of course, conditions can be envisaged under which this statement would be acceptable, for example, when the actor is known to consistently and deliberately violate any contract he or she signs. However, the argument here is that the point of a contract is to ensure its abidance, not its violation.

be learned through socialization and stored in the mind as cultural assumptions about normal communication. Their influence on communication is "almost automatic", so that deviations from 'normal' practice are interpreted by others not as merely 'different' but rather as incorrect, incomprehensible or abnormal (Janney & Arndt 1992:23-32). And when impoliteness is seen in terms of deviation from situational or hearer-expectations (as is maintained in Arndt & Janney 1979:31; 1980:42), we are again faced with the problem that expectations as such can directly account for politeness only. So because the inner workings of tact are highly similar to concepts found in other frameworks, with expectations (cf. Fraser & Nolen), automatic (cf. Ide) cultural assumptions (cf. Blum-Kulka) and universal face-related desires (cf. Brown & Levinson), the notion of 'tact' can equally be categorized as a variant of the norms-related approach.

Watts' framework also contains elements that warrant its classification with the norm-based approaches. Recall that polite behaviour is seen as a marked, conventionalized form of politic behaviour, while impoliteness is associated with non-politic behaviour. Politic behaviour is unmarked (goes largely unnoticed by the participants), and is geared towards establishing or maintaining 'interpersonal equilibrium'. It is explained through the claim that it answers a "fundamental need" to uphold the fabric of interpersonal relationships (Watts 1989a:133), and as such it is a universal phenomenon that permeates all verbal interaction. It is what gives verbal interaction its cohesion and continuity (ibid.:135-136). On the other hand, *"[…] those points at which behavior is perceived by the co-interactants to be nonpolitic are open to interpretation as attempts to disrupt a. the verbal interaction itself; b. the smooth functioning of the social event and c. the fabric of interpersonal relationships"* (ibid.:136). So whereas politic behaviour is productive, non-politic behaviour is destructive. It cannot be associated with any 'fundamental need' lest it be a pathological, destructive one. Impoliteness disrupts the continuity and cohesion of verbal interaction (whatever this may mean), and even goes against the grain of society and social being as such. Where politic behaviour is the product of *"[...] a process of socialization from a biological into a cultural being"* (ibid.:135), surely non-politic behaviour must constitute the failure of that process, or at least is not included in the characteristics of a cultural being. Again, politic behaviour and thus politeness ultimately result from a fundamental and universal cultural need, a notion which cannot explain the existence of impoliteness.

Summarizing, I have argued that the polite bias influences the structure of the conceptual scheme to such an extent that its concepts are primarily geared towards accounting for politeness, which causes the theories to lose their theoretical grip on impoliteness. Even in theories which explicitly claim to cover impolite behaviour as well, the bias towards polite behaviour still either makes the incorporation of impoliteness in practice impossible, or at least results in a conceptualization that is not on a par with that granted to polite behaviour. The concepts involved can never explain impoliteness in the same way or to the same extent as they explain politeness. So the polite bias is not just a matter of differential attention, it goes far deeper than that: it is a conceptual, theoretical-structural matter. It is not so much a quantitative, but rather a qualitative problem.

3.4.2 The elusive hearer

Just as the focus on polite behaviour causes impoliteness to disappear from theoretical view, so the focus on the speaker's behaviour causes the hearer's behaviour to disappear. The hearer is absent from the theoretical models in the sense that politeness is always seen as a *behavioural practice with which the speaker tries to achieve something*, rather than as *a behavioural practice with which the hearer tries to achieve something*. This is even the case in Fraser & Nolen's theory, in which the hearer is given a comparatively more active role than in the other frameworks. Although Fraser & Nolen maintain that the ultimate power over (im)-politeness lies with the hearer, their framework is still entirely devoted to describing (im)politeness in terms of *behavioural* constraints – the terms of the CC. The focus is thus always on the activities of the speaker rather than those of the hearer.

By conceptualizing politeness in terms of speaker behaviour, the theoretical viewpoint comes to closely resemble that of the 'ordinary hearer', since the latter's evaluations are also focused entirely on the speaker.[3] Commonsensically speaking, politeness is always a matter of what 'other people' do: it is their behaviour that is (im)polite, it is their behaviour that triggers our evaluations. So by describing the kinds of speaker behaviour that are evaluated as (im)polite, the models actually (aim to) provide an outline of hearers' evaluations, and as such the viewpoints of the theory

---

[3] In his or her evaluations of the speaker the hearer may of course consider aspects pertaining to him- or herself, such as his or her own status. In this sense these hearer characteristics also determine 'politeness'. But the important point for the present argument is that for the hearer, evaluations of (im)politeness are triggered by the speaker's behaviour, so that for the hearer, politeness is a characteristic of speaker-behaviour.

and the hearer are conflated. The theories effectively take the place of the hearer, they try to be the hearer, in that their theoretical models are designed to replicate the hearer's judgements. This is particularly manifest in some of the theories' methodological practices, more specifically in the way they use empirical data for theory-building. In both Blum-Kulka's and Ide's investigations, the informants' judgements are used as direct input for the theoretical notion, so their models are built on information from the hearer's point of view. In Ide's empirical study (Ide et al. 1992), informants are provided with descriptions of interactional situations which they are asked to judge in terms of a number of adjectives including 'polite', 'friendly', 'appropriate', etc. In each of these situations, they are asked to rate behaviour that some hypothetical other directs at them. In other words, they are asked to produce judgements from the interactional position of the hearer, at moments when they are hearers in the interactional dyad. A few examples from the English version of the questionnaire will illustrate this:

> You and your close friend planned to go to see a movie one evening.
> That morning, your friend called you and postponed the date because...
> (A)   he/she was asked out for dinner by his or her boyfriend/girl friend.
> (B)   something urgent had turned up.

> Suppose you were an assistant professor. You gave a student a C on a term paper. The student came to you and...
> (A)   asked the reason why the paper was a C.
> (B)   said to you, 'What's wrong with this term paper? You only gave it a C. I worked hard and it should get at least a B.'
> (C)   said to you, 'I'd like to ask you about my term paper. The C was a little disappointing after all the care I gave it. I wonder if you could show me where I went wrong.' (ibid.:295)

In each of these cases, the informant is approached by a speaker whose performance he or she is asked to judge. In the accompanying instructions, informants are told to *"[...] circle the appropriate answer for each of the adjectives based on **how you might interpret the described behavior had it been directed to you**"* (ibid.:294, original emphasis). So the information provided by the informants, and thus the input for the theoretical model of polite speaker behaviour derives from the hearer's interactional point of view.

But since the models in practice take the hearer's interactional position, one could argue that the hearer can hardly be claimed to be absent from the theories. On the contrary, because of their crucial role as information providers, hearers seem to occupy a central position in the models. This would be a highly unwarranted conclusion, however, because by looking at the world from the hearer's position, the theories focus entirely on the speaker. By looking 'through the hearer's eyes', so to speak, they effectively *look through* the hearer and consequently fail to see him or her. All attention falls on the speaker, while the hearer's act of judgement disappears from view. As a result the theories cease to be neutral to the interaction: they do not stand outside speaker and hearer, looking at both of them from a distance, but rather become involved. They choose sides by joining one of the interactional parties and looking at the interaction through that interactant's eyes.

Consequently, in practice the distinction between the ordinary hearer and the theorist is to some extent blurred. While the theories take the interactional position of the hearer, the hearer (as represented by the theories) in turn takes on some characteristics of the theorist. Whereas the strategic nature of the speaker's behaviour is readily recognized and minutely scrutinized – this makes up the gist of the frameworks – the hearer's evaluations are assumed to be (and are conceptualized as) non-strategic. They do not depend on the hearer's strategic aims, but are disinterested and objective. In a sense, the conflation of the positions of the theory and the hearer causes the hearer's evaluations to become like scientific observations. Although the speaker is fully acknowledged to have a stake in the situation, as he or she twists and turns in his or her formulations so as to please or at least not offend the hearer, that hearer seems to have no such stakes in performing his or her evaluation. Of course, the hearer does have a stake in the situation in the sense that he or she is definitely interested in whether or not the speaker is being (im)polite to him or her (the hearer can be offended, pleased, have face-needs, etc.), but the *act of evaluation itself* is not a function of the hearer's argumentative-strategic aims. It is a function of the speaker's behaviour only: it directly and linearly depends on, for example, the indirectness of the speaker's formulation, on the use of formal forms, or in general on whether or not the speaker's formulation is in accordance with whatever the model stipulates to be (im)polite. Hearers are assumed not to vary their judgements according to their own strategic aims, they merely recognize the speaker's strategies and produce the associated evaluation. Their interpretations are only informed by the factual reality of the speaker's behaviour, as if they were involved in a scientific investigation, aiming at a scientific description of the speaker's behaviour. So the focus on speaker production causes not only the hearer to disappear from view, but also the hearer's evaluative practice, which is turned into scientific observation. As such, the evaluative moment of politeness is completely lost in the theoretical conceptualization.

But if the hearer becomes part-scientist, the scientist also becomes part-hearer, and adopting the hearer's interactional position also means taking the hearer's argumentative position. By attempting to theoretically capture the hearer's evaluations, these evaluations become the very basis on which the theoretical model is built. As concepts intended to reproduce the hearer's evaluations, norms, scripts, rules and other 'norm'-like constructions become the theoretical counterparts of those evaluations, and thus not only the *results* of those evaluations are brought into the theory – the '(im)polite behaviours' – but also the *practice* of evaluating itself. The hearer's evaluations effectively become part of the analytical process, and the resulting model is therefore also the result of such evaluations. As such, (im)politeness in its ultimate theoretical form *already incorporates* the evaluative moment, and therefore that moment is lost as an *object* of analysis. Consequently, the theoretical models themselves are basically evaluative in nature: because they aim to model the hearer's evaluative decisions, to mimic them through some abstract theoretical model, they themselves become engaged in the evaluation of speakers' behaviour. In short, they are no longer at one remove. To quote Bourdieu once again (see above, section 2.1.2), in their conceptualization of reality the theories take the hearer's representation of reality as a model of reality. And as the hearer's representation of reality thus effectively becomes 'reality',[4] they lose sight of that representation *as a representation*.

3.4.3 Predictiveness

By taking the interactional position of the evaluating hearer and conceptualizing (im)politeness in terms of speaker behaviour, the theories also become basically predictive. Although their models are primarily intended to explain politeness through revealing its underlying linguistic, social or psychological principles (norms, scripts, the PP, etc.), their primary focus on describing what kinds of behaviour are (im)polite causes

---

[4] Bearing in mind that for the most part the theories do not work with actual conversational data, but with elicited judgements in non-natural settings, it could be argued that in practice the theories do not really take the actual conversational viewpoint of the hearer – his or her representation of conversational reality. But this represents a further critique that does not as such touch on the point to be made here.

them to implicitly claim to be able to predict the hearer's evaluations. Claiming that 'behaviour X is (im)polite' boils down to claiming that any (competent) hearer will evaluate X accordingly. This is obvious for frameworks that explicitly mention specific polite linguistic choices (such as Brown & Levinson's 'indirectness' or Ide's use of honorifics) and that are therefore openly predictive, but it equally applies to those that do not. Fraser & Nolen maintain that there are no inherently (im)polite linguistic choices, because what will be evaluated as (im)polite depends on the specific terms of the CC between any speaker and hearer at any specific time in the interaction. But even in their framework the hearer is predicted to evaluate a speaker's behaviour as impolite *whenever that speaker violates the then-current terms of the CC*, whatever the specific form or content of those terms. So in that sense, even their theory is predictive. Analogously, and regardless of how (im)politeness is conceptualized, whenever a speaker displays behaviour that conforms to the definition of (im)politeness, any hearer is always assumed, and thus predicted, to evaluate that behaviour accordingly.

As a corollary, the theories can be examined in terms of the commonsense plausibility of the evaluative judgements they engender and/or predict, as was often done above in the investigation of their positions *vis-à-vis* the politeness1-politeness2 distinction. This is also mirrored by the fact that theories are often criticized or defended on the basis of empirical investigations involving informants' politeness ratings of specific utterances (for numerous such criticisms of Brown & Levinson's theory, see their introduction to the 1987 reissue of their original 1978 thesis – Brown & Levinson 1987:1-50), or on the basis of the researcher's intuitive judgements (as in Wierzbicka 1985). Ide uses this technique to argue that Brown & Levinson's framework needs to be expanded in order to capture the Japanese notion of politeness, but it is equally abundant in other studies that examine politeness in specific cultural contexts.

But the frameworks are also predictive in a more fundamental sense. For speaker behaviour and hearer evaluation stand in a temporally sequential relationship, with hearer evaluation occurring after speaker behaviour. So because behaviour is sequentially situated *before* the (hearer's) evaluative act, any theory that defines (im)politeness as a characteristic of speaker behaviour almost naturally becomes predictive. Since the post-behavioural evaluation in terms of (im)politeness is directly and functionally linked to the pre-evaluative behaviour, the link between the two (a time vector from the latter to the former) is necessarily predictive. Again, the notion that 'X is (im)polite' already subsumes the (subsequent) evaluation of X as (im)polite.

This notion of predictiveness is not the same as the one sketched earlier, although the two are intimately related. The first form of predictiveness involves the link between (abstract) theory and (practical) reality: the abstract theoretical model predicts the evaluations of any real hearer. The predictive link in that case runs from theory to practice, from theoretical concept to empirical datum. This outward or extra-theoretical predictiveness is now matched by an intra-theoretical one, situated within the theoretical conceptualization itself. This conceptualization is temporally oriented or 'vectored' from act to evaluation, and thus from present (the behaviour under scrutiny) to future (the evaluation of that behaviour). This kind of predictiveness is an entirely theoretical matter, rather than a posited relationship between theory and reality. But the two are intimately related, in that internally predictive theories are almost naturally also externally predictive. For the concept of politeness as a characteristic of behaviour implies a world where behaviour determines its own evaluation, so hearers are automatically assumed to all make the same evaluations. Both forms of predictiveness thus result from the theories' interactionally 'involved' position. Taking the place of the hearer not only implies a view of reality from a particular interactional role/position (that of 'hearer'), which causes the models to become extra-theoretically predictive, but this interactional position also involves a view from a particular temporal position, and as this position is situated after the definitional centre of their notions of politeness (speaker behaviour), the models also become intra-theoretically predictive.

3.4.4 Enter evaluation

In section 2.1.1, evaluativity was argued to be an important characteristic of politeness1. In everyday practice (im)politeness occurs not so much when the speaker produces behaviour but rather when the hearer evaluates that behaviour. I will go even further and claim that the very essence of (im)politeness lies in this evaluative moment. Whether it involves hearers evaluating speakers, speakers evaluating themselves, or informants evaluating hypothetical speakers or utterances, the evaluative moment is always present. Indeed, in practice it proves to be the only way in which (im)politeness can be studied. Evaluation is thus the basic, primordial mode of being of (im)politeness.

Since the traditional theories lose track of the evaluative moment by defining (im)politeness in terms of speaker behaviour, which itself results from their involved position in the interactional dyad, an obvious way of acknowledging or reintroducing the evaluative nature of (im)politeness is to follow Bourdieu's advice and 'take a step back' from the interactional dyad. By assuming a heuristic position outside the interactional dyad, the whole dyad becomes the focus of attention rather than one side only. As both interactional parties are considered in the theoretical model, (im)politeness becomes not only a matter of speakers producing behaviour, but also of hearers evaluating that behaviour. So by bringing the hearer back into view, a position 'at one remove' also exposes the importance of the evaluative moment.

Besides constituting a more comfortable heuristic position by avoiding interactional involvement, such a view also provides a more complete picture of the interactional dyad in the sense that speakers and hearers are now ontologically on a par. The hearer is not only brought back into view, he or she can also be approached from the same angle as the speaker, examined by the same concepts and assigned the same psychological characteristics. After all, in reality the interactional roles of speaker and hearer constantly change hands, with the same persons alternating between both positions, so obviously both should have similar characteristics. By conceptualizing one position as 'strategic' and the other as 'powerless', the traditional theories implicitly create a view of interactional reality where the same individual can instantly change from a cunning (even deceptive) manipulator to an innocent and powerless observer and back again, which is not a very realistic picture.

But when speaker and hearer are psychologically on a par, their interactional practices must also be interpreted using the same criteria. So if the speaker's behaviour can be strategically informed, so can the hearer's evaluations. An evaluation-centred approach thus fully recognizes the hearer's argumentative position and no longer relegates him or her to the role of a passive recognizer of behaviour. His or her evaluation is no longer automatic, objective and disinterested, a direct and linear function of the speaker's behaviour, but rather subjective and interested, an active judgement of that behaviour. As the hearer becomes master of his or her evaluations, he or she is empowered, in the sense that the speaker's (im)politeness becomes relative to his or her judgements instead of those judgements being relative to the speaker's behaviour. So Fraser & Nolen's view, in which (im)politeness is entirely in the hands (ears) of the hearer, can now be fully realized.

Of course, because the focus is not shifted from the speaker to the hearer but rather to a position outside the interactional dyad, in a view that includes both speaker and hearer, the question of what the speaker does is still valid. It would be unwise not to acknowledge the fact that a speaker can aim for politeness and structure his or her behaviour accordingly. An evaluation-centred approach does not remove the speaker's behaviour from the picture (which would merely lead to an opposite and equally deficient conceptual bias), but fully acknowledges the possibility of reflexive situations in which the speaker plans his or her behaviour to be (im)polite. In such cases, the hearer and speaker would coincide, as the evaluative act is carried out by the speaker him- or herself, as a 'hearer' of his or her own planned speech. Note that in such a view, the speaker's evaluation of his or her own contribution and the hearer's evaluation of it become separate instances of politeness, which can and even must be examined separately. However, the fact that a speaker aims at politeness is ultimately still a function of the hearer's evaluation. The speaker attempts to steer the hearer's evaluation in a certain direction, but whether or not he or she succeeds ultimately depends on the hearer. So the hearer's evaluation remains the at heart of the matter, both in determining the eventual outcome and in engendering the speaker's behaviour.

And through this focus on the hearer in its definition of politeness, an evaluation-centred model also becomes non-predictive. As politeness is relative to the hearer's evaluative judgement, the model no longer situates it prior to the evaluation, but at the evaluative moment itself, so that speaker behaviour can only be (im)polite in retrospect, from the post-behavioural position of the hearer's evaluative practice. But although non-predictive in the intra-theoretical sense, it is not necessarily also outwardly non-predictive. As it no longer assumes that a specific behaviour will automatically trigger a specific hearer evaluation, it has to wait for a hearer evaluation to occur in reality before it can examine its link with the preceding speaker behaviour. Although in the end this can still lead to predictions in terms of the relationship between specific behaviours and specific evaluations, these predictions would be arrived at a posteriori; they would not result from a priori theoretical assumptions. As such they would also require explanation.

Finally, note also that a non-predictive evaluation-centred perspective permits the researcher to actually *question* the link between behaviour and evaluation, something which is not possible in an intra-theoretically predictive account, where the association is a priori fixed by the conceptual makeup. Because the notion of polite behaviour already carries within it the evaluation of that behaviour as 'polite', the evaluative act is actually performed by the theory (as an a priori assumption) and therefore remains unquestioned and even unquestionable without also questioning the conceptual makeup of the theory. In an evaluation-centred approach on the other hand, the starting point is the evaluative act, so polite behaviour becomes relative to such a 'known-to-have-occurred' evaluative act.

3.4.5 The mystery solved

Through bringing the hearer and the evaluative moment into view, a heuristic position 'at one remove' from the interactional dyad not only resolves the conceptual bias towards speaker behaviour, but can do the same for the conceptual bias towards polite behaviour. Analogous to its effect on the interactional dyad, such a perspective avoids becoming involved in the polite–impolite distinction by bringing both sides into view and elevating them to equal ontological status. The acknowledgement of the importance of the evaluative moment leads to a view where politeness and impoliteness both result from the hearer's evaluative act. Since they both reside in the hearer's evaluative judgement rather than in the speaker's behaviour, they can both be captured by the same conceptual tools.

An evaluation-centred approach also does away with the negative definition of impoliteness prevalent in current theorizing. Regardless of whether the evaluation is one of 'politeness' or of 'impoliteness', it is always the result of a positive act of the hearer – in the sense of 'doing' as opposed to the negative 'not doing'. Note that this does not exclude the commonsense definition of impolite as 'not polite', since the hearer's evaluation of 'impoliteness' can still be based on the speaker 'not being polite' in a situation where politeness is expected. And through the recognition of the hearer's interactional-argumentative position, politeness and impoliteness can both serve argumentative goals, they can both be used to achieve something – for example, some social-interactional effect. Whereas in a speaker-behaviour conceptually biased model impoliteness can only have negative, (self-)destructive argumentative goals and effects (because it involves a negative evaluation of the speaker, and it is the speaker who causes impoliteness to happen), an evaluation-centred model also allows impoliteness to serve positive, constructive goals. Although the evaluation of a speaker as 'impolite' is still negative for that speaker, it can be used to create a positive image for the hearer. When Blum-Kulka's (1992) informants complain about widespread impoliteness in Israeli public contexts, they implicitly claim higher moral standards and practices for themselves. More generally, (im)politeness rules and evaluations can be used as tools of social distinction (see, e.g. Burke 1993).

But what about the relationship between the speaker's behaviour and impoliteness? First of all, an evaluation-centred approach does not exclude the occurrence of impoliteness owing to misunderstanding. It is true that the speaker can aim for politeness but miss because the hearer has a different understanding of politeness. This is a direct and logical consequence of the fact that such a situation actually involves two separate instances of (im)politeness. But impoliteness is no longer confined to such cases of genuine misunderstanding, as the hearer's evaluation can also be argumentatively inspired. Because the hearer's evaluation is functionally disconnected from the speaker's behaviour, no matter how much the speaker aims at politeness, nothing can keep the hearer from evaluating it as impolite should his or her argumentative goals dictate it. Secondly, an evaluation-centred approach does not exclude the possibility of the speaker aiming for impoliteness. Since the conceptual toolbox no longer caters exclusively for the goals of polite behaviour, but is broadened to include argumentative goals in general, the study of the interactional effects and argumentative goals of the speaker's aim for impoliteness is made possible.

3.5 Origins of the conceptual bias

The conceptual bias towards speaker behaviour and towards the polite side of the polite-impolite distinction is not restricted to the theories discussed here, but is a characteristic of the field of politeness research in general. It can be found in the overwhelming majority of publications that carry the term 'politeness' in their titles, regardless of whether research is explicitly based on one or other of the theoretical perspectives presently under investigation.[5] Given its extensive penetration, it may be interesting to look for possible causes of this phenomenon. It seems that at least two contributory factors can be identified. The first is a feature of sociolinguistic scientific thinking in general, while the second is specific to commonsense thinking about politeness.

3.5.1 Sociolinguistics
The contribution of (socio)linguistic scientific thinking to the conceptual bias is epistemological as well as methodological in nature. A first

---

[5] As witnessed by state-of-the-art publications such as Held (1992) or Kasper (1990). Even frameworks that differ substantially from the core theories, such as those discussed in section 1.3, fail to escape the conceptual bias. It also underlies investigations of politeness in a variety of cultures (Adegbija 1989; Ajiboye 1992; Braun 1988; Chen 1991, 1993; El-Sayed 1989; Garcia 1993; Krummer 1992; Mao 1994; Matsumoto 1988, 1989; Nwoye 1989; Rhodes 1989; Sifianou 1992a, 1992b, 1993; Smith-Hefner 1988; Srivastava & Pandit 1988) or in various specific social or interactional contexts (Aronsson & Sätterlund-Larsson 1987; Berk-Seligson 1988; Chilton 1990; Coupland et al. 1988; Knapp-Potthoff 1992; Stalpers 1992), in studies investigating developmental aspects of politeness (Ervin-Tripp et al. 1990; Kwarciak 1993; Snow et al. 1990), or in studies that focus on purely theoretical matters (Held 1989).

element has to do with the commonsense, observable, even trivial – and therefore also immensely influential – fact that language only exists when someone speaks or writes – only the product of language (text, discourse, speech) can be observed. Throughout the history of linguistics the focus has thus largely (necessarily) been on this product, whether it is regarded in isolation from its social context of production, as in the tradition of autonomous (formalist) linguistics, or whether it is seen as intimately re-lated to that context, as in the majority of sociolinguistic (functionalist) theorizing. Not surprisingly then, when politeness is taken up as an object of study in linguistics, it is also studied in connection with that product, it is conceived as an aspect or characteristic of text/discourse/speech. So even if evaluations of (im)politeness are studied, it is only natural that the focus would also be on 'that-which-is-evaluated' (the language product) rather than on the act of evaluation.

However, as Figeroa (1994) shows, sociolinguistics (and the function-alist paradigm in general), distinguishes itself from formalist linguistic thinking in that it focuses not on the isolated, abstract product, but rather on the product as intimately interconnected with its social context of production – the broader process of 'communication' (Hymes 1974:4). The object of study is no longer Saussurian langue, but rather parole. This distinction also finds expression in the basic unit of analysis, which in sociolinguistic theorizing is the (contextualized) 'utterance', as opposed to the centrality of the abstract 'sentence' in the formalist paradigm. In Figeroa's own words, *"sociolinguistics is the study of utterance (**spoken, written, signaled**). An utterance is language **performed** in a particular context"* (Figeroa 1992:26, my emphasis). So the contextualizing of the sentence (resulting in the utterance) within the functionalist paradigm finds expression mainly in the fact that the utterance is now seen as 'the product of a speaker-in-context', as 'performance', but still not as the product of a hearer.

True, it is readily acknowledged that the form of the utterance will be tailored to its intended hearer, but the meaning of any utterance ultimately lies with the speaker, it resides in what the speaker signals. This is the case in spite of the fact that, in focusing on communication rather than language, the hearer is to a certain extent brought into the picture. Hymes' 'ethnography of speaking/communication', for example, in concentrating on the societal organization or patterning of communication, is concerned simultaneously with speakers' behaviour and hearers' interpretation pro-cesses. However, the main focus is still *"the act of speech"* (Hymes 1974:90), *"including writing, song and speech-derived whistling, drum-ming, horn calling, and the like"* (Hymes 1972:53), seen as *"means, resources, which different groups and individuals make different use of"* (Hymes 1986:51). Meaning is taken to reside in the socioculturally framed contextualized performance of speech, and although both speaker and hearer are endowed with a socioculturally defined "communicative competence" (Figeroa 1994:51-56), the hearer's role is limited to appropriately inferring the speaker's intended meaning.

Although in the Hymesian tradition this is only true to a certain extent, since Hymes' focus on 'text' and his notion of 'performance' are substantially broader than 'speaker-production' alone, in many other linguistic research traditions the speaker-centeredness remains much more central. This is especially true for Searlean Speech Act Theory (e.g. Searle 1969) with its basic claim – deriving from Austin (1962) – that *"[...] to speak is not only to **say** something but also to **do** something"* (Taylor & Cameron 1987:44, original emphasis). Illocutionary acts – utterances invested with some kind of communicative force (such as 'requests', 'promises', 'warnings', etc.) – are acts of and by the speaker, their force being determined by the speaker's intentions and their success depending on certain 'felicity conditions' – the conditions under which the hearer will interpret the speech act for what it is. *"Searle assumes that to communicate successfully, speakers must get each other to 'recognize what we are trying to do', that is to say, what illocutionary act is being performed/what illocutionary force some utterance possesses"* (ibid.:47), so the hearer is relegated to the status of a rather passive recognizer of the speaker's intentions. This basic speaker-centredness is retained in (speech-act based) research focusing on the analysis of conversation as well as in large areas of pragmatics, where it is most notably found in the Gricean tradition, which informs much of current politeness theory.

The view whereby meaning is created by the speaker's act, while the hearer never seems to be doing much apart from obediently and innocently deriving the utterance's socioculturally appropriate communicative meaning results in an image of what I would call the 'innocent' or 'powerless' hearer: while the speaker creates meaning, the hearer is assumed to sit back and receive. Although interpretation is admittedly seen as something the hearer needs to *do* – and in this sense the hearer is surely active – his or her creative freedom is severely restricted or even numbed. To elaborate on a famous phrase: in the study of 'how to do things with words', it is always the speaker that does the doing; the hearer never seems to be doing anything much with the speaker's words.

As a corollary, a second 'scientific' factor that lies at the basis of the conceptual bias is methodological in nature. Because speech/writing is the only 'visible' form of language, it naturally becomes the main source of information for theories of language, which consequently run a high risk of becoming in essence theories of (the processes of) speech/writing. For politeness, such data come in different forms. One can ask informants about politeness in interviews, either in free (e.g. Blum-Kulka 1992) or restricted (e.g. Sifianou 1992a) formats. One can also present informants with utterances and ask them to rate these as polite/not polite (e.g. Ide et al. 1992) or more/less polite (as in Fraser & Nolen's 1981 examination of 'deference' – see above, section 2.2.7). Or one can use techniques such as the Discourse Completion Test (DCT) and the role-play, which for all practical purposes can be regarded as a spoken or 'enacted' DCT[6] (e.g. Sifianou 1992a; or the Cross Cultural Speech Act Realization Project: Blum-Kulka et al. 1989 and especially Blum-Kulka & House 1989a). Although DCTs are never used to examine politeness directly, in that informants are never asked to produce a 'polite' turn, but rather to 'fill in what you would say' often with a specification to the effect that *"[...] what is important is to be natural, where possible using responses you have employed in relevant, real-life situations"* (Sifianou 1992a:227), their results are often drawn upon to formulate conclusions about politeness (as in Sifianou 1992a), or politeness theories are called upon to explain and interpret the results (as in many studies in Blum-Kulka et al. 1989 and Kasper & Blum-Kulka 1993). In any case, the data resulting from these empirical methods are always linguistic behaviour (utterances) that are evaluated as '(im)polite' by the informants: in interviews the informants provide examples, in rating experiments they evaluate given utterances, and in DCTs they produce utterances. As these utterances are then used as input for theorizing about politeness, politeness becomes conceptually associated with speaker behaviour rather than with hearer evaluations.

Note that strictly speaking, the outcome of the experimental methods is not so much speaker behaviour, but rather informant evaluation, as the (im)politeness of the utterances crucially depends on the informants' evaluation. Nevertheless, it is always the evaluated behaviour that is used for theorizing. This implies that in practice the informants' evaluations are not questioned, but taken as statements of fact. Their evaluations are treated

---

[6] Of course there are marked differences between the two that will undoubtedly influence the nature or status of the data that are obtained. For example, role-playing situations are enacted in 'real time', whereas in DCTs informants have more time to think about their answers. Role-plays also involve real conversational partners whereas DCTs do not, and so on. However, for the present argument, such differences are of no consequence.

as objective statements, in the sense that they are taken to provide information about the character of their object (the utterances). In a sense then,
just as sociolinguistic theorizing assumes an 'innocent hearer' (and arguably also as a result of this), the employed empirical methodology assumes
an 'innocent informant'. In making their evaluations, informants are not
taken to be doing anything other than recognizing the characteristics of
the utterances and conveying these to the analyst. In this way, informants
(and hearers in general) are again assumed not to be *doing* anything.

3.5.2 Common sense

The second explanatory factor for the conceptual bias is related to
commonsense thinking about politeness. Apart from the rather scarce
empirical scientific studies (and of course our own intuitions), the major
source of information on commonsense notions of politeness consists of
popular publications on the subject. Although these etiquette manuals are
not always specifically or solely about politeness (and certainly not about
concepts of politeness), they are relevant in that they are about appropriate ways of speaking/behaving. They have not only been published
widely and sold successfully throughout European history (Burke 1993;
Elias 1978) into our present times, but can also be found in other cultures.
For example, Gu (1990) describes Chinese prescriptive literature from
the time of Confucius to the present, while Japan also has a rich tradition
on the subject (Coulmas 1992). The genre is also very much alive in various newspaper and magazine columns (the famous Miss Manners'
column), as well as on the Internet.[7] Politeness as it relates to etiquette
manuals can even be argued to extend to broad social phenomena such as
the currently ubiquitous practices of and debates over so-called politically
correct language use (Cameron 1995). The question of whether or not all

---

[7] From a quick search on the Net it would seem that politeness manifests itself
there in at least four forms. First there are theoretical discussions of the concept
from a linguistic-theoretical angle. These usually emanate from university cam-
pus sites and take the form of explications of existing linguistic theories on the
subject. Second, politeness surfaces in an (inter)cultural context, in advice on
how to interact with members of foreign cultures and as part of general descriptions of those cultures. A third form closely resembles etiquette manuals, and
consists of practical advice on how to behave in various situations (weddings
seem to be very popular) or towards different persons (from the proper term of
address for a retired army colonel to guidelines for interacting with disabled people). Finally, a rich literature can be found on how to behave on the Internet, for
example in composing electronic mail messages – the emerging discipline of
'netiquette'.

of these phenomena can legitimately be conflated into 'commonsense politeness' is not of much consequence for the present argument, for they all provide a firm commonsense basis for the different forms of conceptual bias that were identified in current scientific theorizing on the subject.

As for the 'polite' conceptual bias, the emphasis in such popular publications is always on normative guidelines on 'how to be polite' rather than 'how to be impolite'. Of course impoliteness also surfaces occasionally, but when it does, it takes a purely negative form, as a discussion of behaviour that is 'not done'. Such publications also all implicitly define politeness in terms of speaker behaviour. At best, the evaluations of the hearer are taken for granted, but in most cases the hearer simply does not enter the picture at all. The hearer's absence is due to the specific nature of etiquette literature as a genre that does not pretend to study, model or otherwise *conceptualize* the phenomenon of politeness, but instead *prescribes* how people should behave. It is not and does not in any way claim to be at one remove from the social phenomenon of politeness, but on the contrary is completely and thoroughly involved *in* that social phenomenon: its aim is overtly political. This was already the case in the time of Confucius (see above, section 2.2.6), it was the case for seventeenth-century French treatises (which were often intended to be of educational value, for example, for schoolboys; see Burke 1993:103), and it is no different for the high-tech phenomenon of Internet-etiquette or 'netiquette', which basically consists of people telling other people how to behave when interacting on the Net. As a political enterprise trying to influence its readers' interactive behaviour, etiquette literature is therefore naturally focused on speaker behaviour. It does not reserve a space for the hearer-evaluator, because *it is itself* that hearer-evaluator. When such literature is then used as a basis for a conceptualization of politeness (as in Gu's case), it is all the more understandable that this results in a speaker behaviour biased conceptualization of the phenomenon.

But etiquette literature can of course be expected to have the same effect on the commonsense politeness conceptualizations of its readers. In this it merely complements and reinforces what they were already taught in childhood socialization. As Snow et al. (1990) indicate, one of the main sources of information about politeness for children lies in their parents telling them what (not) to do 'because it is (im)polite'. So the link between politeness and behaviour is forged from early on in childhood, as attested by Blum-Kulka's (1992) empirical investigation in which the younger informants invariably responded to the question of what politeness is with an enumeration of specific types of behaviours (see above, section 2.1.1). But also in later life, when we ourselves produce evaluations of others' behaviour, this link remains intact, for as far as we are concerned it is those others and their behaviour that trigger our evaluations: it is they who are (im)polite. We do not usually look at our own evaluations in a reflexive way but tend to take them for granted.

Although I have argued above that a more adequate scientific conception of the phenomenon would have to see both the behavioural and the evaluative side of politeness, this does not mean that the behavioural bias of commonsense conceptualizations would be 'wrong'. Rather it tells us something important about the very nature of commonsense politeness. When as in Blum-Kulka (1992) informants state that in Israeli public contexts impoliteness (impolite *behaviour*) abounds, they are not so much conceptualizing politeness (in terms of behaviour), but rather taking an argumentative social and moral stance in relation to impolite people and Israeli social life. In that they are acting *as* evaluators, they effectively *are* the hearer-evaluator at that particular time, and so necessarily look at politeness through the hearer's eyes. Indeed, 'taking a moral stance' means taking an argumentative position *vis-à-vis* someone else, and the very act of taking such a position precludes a contemplation of that position 'at one remove'. One *is* the hearer, and thus one cannot be a third party looking on from a position 'at one remove', as scientists usually are. In this way the behavioural conceptual bias is natural to commonsense politeness: it is a direct consequence of its fundamentally evaluative and argumentative nature.

3.6 Summary

Current theories of politeness manifest a triple conceptual bias: towards the polite side of the polite-impolite distinction, towards the speaker in the interactional dyad and towards the production of behaviour rather than its evaluation. This triple bias was shown to have a number of theoretical consequences.

Most readily visible is the fact that the explanatory power of the approaches cannot readily be stretched to provide a satisfactory account of impoliteness, at least not without encountering serious theoretical problems. The fragility and limitations of such a one-sided approach are also manifest in the conceptual bias towards speaker behaviour and the consequent neglect of the interactional role of the hearer, and thus of the evaluative moment. By assuming the hearer's interactional position in their descriptions of the world, the theories focus entirely on the speaker, and fail to see the hearer's evaluative act, which is treated as self-evident and unquestioningly incorporated in the conceptual makeup of the theoretical model. By subsuming the hearer's evaluative act in their definitions of (im)politeness, the theories become predictive, not only in the sense of outward empirical predictiveness, but also of internal conceptual predictiveness. As politeness is conceptualized in terms of speaker behaviour, the act of evaluation becomes a direct function of the evaluated behaviour, and the whole approach becomes temporally vectored from present (behaviour) to future (evaluation).

The triple conceptual bias and its associated problems can be resolved by an approach that acknowledges the crucial evaluative moment of politeness. Such an approach can be attained by assuming a heuristic position at one remove from the interactional dyad and the polite-impolite distinction. By not taking sides in the interactional dyad, the theoretical approach avoids argumentative involvement, so that evaluativity and argumentativity become objects of analysis rather than fundamental characteristics of its conceptual tools. Such a view also puts politeness and impoliteness on a par, as they become manifestations of essentially the same (evaluative) behaviour. An evaluation-centred model thus constitutes a view where communication is seen as a bi-directional and interactional process in which both speaker and hearer have an active part which deserves full attention. It does not reduce politeness to either of those interactional positions, but examines it as a truly social interactional phenomenon located in both positions and in neither of them at the same time – as a matter of 'speaker-action', of 'hearer-action', as well as of 'inter-action'.

Chapter 4: Normativity

Besides evaluativity and argumentativity, normativity was claimed to be a third fundamental aspect of politeness1 (section 2.1.1). Blum-Kulka's (1992) informants tended to answer questions about politeness with normative statements, Ehlich (1992) argues that throughout history politeness has always involved some standard against which behaviour is evaluated, and Fraser's (1990) category of the 'social-norm view' of politeness covers notions held by the 'general public in the English speaking world'. Furthermore, etiquette manuals, as well as parents' directives to their children, are obviously normative.

In the previous chapter the prescriptive nature of politeness1 was causally related to its speaker behaviour biased view of politeness, which in turn was posited as a possible factor underlying the conceptual bias of current scientific theories. In this light the obvious next question concerns the relationship between scientific concepts of politeness and the normativity of commonsense politeness. How do the theories handle the normativity of commonsense politeness? For if the behavioural conceptual bias of commonsense politeness is unquestioningly retained in scientific conceptualizations, the same might very well be expected for normativity. In order to examine this, it is first necessary to present an outline of exactly how normativity figures in scientific theories.

4.1 Norms in politeness theory

The most clear-cut case of normativity is Gu's theory, where politeness is explicitly conceptualized as a system of moral norms emanating from society:

> [...] in interaction, politeness is not just instrumental. It is also normative. [...] it would be a serious oversight not to see the normative aspect of politeness. [...] Politeness is a phenomenon belonging to the level of society, which endorses its normative constraints on each individual. (Gu 1990:242)

This normative aspect of politeness is conceptually translated as a set of (moral) maxims, subsumed under one 'Politeness Principle' or PP, which itself is defined as *"[...] a sanctioned belief that an individual's social behaviour ought to live up to the expectations of respectfulness, modesty, attitudinal warmth and refinement"* (ibid.:245). The PP and its maxims thus describe the norms used by Chinese speakers in assessing their own and others' behaviour. The relationship between ordinary speakers' norms and theoretical concepts is one-to-one: theoretical concepts are moulded so as to directly capture the behavioural norms operative in society.

But norms also figure in other theories. As outlined in section 3.4.1, all the frameworks contain elements that can be captured under a broad and general notion of norms – including scripts, rules, principles, etc. But most are not as openly accommodating as Gu to the normative aspect of politeness. Gu's approach is inspired by Leech's, and Leech's conceptualization of politeness as maxims can be easily reinterpreted in moral terms. Leech himself, however, opposes such an interpretation. Just like Grice's CP, Leech's PP is claimed to be a "principle of language use" (Leech 1983:4), or a "conversational principle" (ibid.:7). It is part of the linguistic system, in that it is involved in enabling understanding by regulating the relationship between the semantic meaning of an utterance (for example, a question about someone's ability to pass the salt) and its pragmatic sense (a request to be handed the salt by that person). It is a purely technical principle:

> One element, although it is part of the everyday interpretation of the terms 'principle' and 'maxim', has been carefully omitted from the above definition. This is the implication that such constraints are of a moral or ethical nature. The requirement to tell the truth might, indeed, be regarded as a moral imperative; but the reason for including it in a scientific account of language is descriptive rather than prescriptive. The maxims form a necessary part of the description of linguistic meaning in that they explain how it is that speakers often 'mean more than they say', [...]
> In saying that people normally follow the CP, then, one is by no means taking a moral stance. But one thing that cannot be denied is that principles introduce communicative values, such as truthfulness, into the study of language. Traditionally, linguists have avoided referring to such values, feeling that they undermine one's claim for objectivity. But so long as the values we consider are ones we suppose, on empirical grounds, to be operative in society, rather than ones we impose on society, then there is no reason to exclude them from our inquiry. (ibid.:9-10)

Analogous to Gu's theory, the CP (and by extension also the PP) thus represents values taken to be operative in society. But although these values and the maxims that express them receive a moral interpretation in everyday life, this ethical aspect is carefully omitted from their scientific formulation. Whereas in everyday life a maxim such as 'minimize the expression of impolite beliefs' would constitute a normative, prescriptive rule, its scientific counterpart is claimed not be prescriptive. Although the two look exactly alike, they are not identical twins. Two strategies are employed to establish this.

In the first it is argued that the scientific maxims merely *describe* values operative in society, and a description of a prescription is not itself a prescription. So the PP and its maxims, although descriptive of ethical values, are not themselves ethical values. The second strategy is built on the explanatory character of such a scientific description. The CP, the PP and their associated maxims are endowed with linguistic-technical functionality: they enable understanding and communication. They are principles that allow people to 'mean more than they say' and to be understood as such. Without them, people would not be able to go beyond the semantic meaning of utterances. Everyday moral/ethical values becoming technical conversational principles in scientific theory is of course a restatement of Leech's general-local distinction which, applied to politeness, becomes the difference between absolute and relative politeness. In everyday life, people *"[...] typically use 'polite' in a relative sense: that is, relative to some norm of behaviour which, for a particular setting, they regard as typical. The norm may be that of a particular culture or language community[...]"* (ibid.:84). Science, however, is concerned with absolute politeness: the 'inherent', linguistic-technical (im)politeness of illocutions.

What is true for Leech also counts for other theories based on Grice's CP: they too need to develop a strategy for handling the values which the CP introduces. Lakoff's 'rules' closely resemble Leech's maxims: compare rule1/distance politeness ('Don't impose, remain aloof') with Leech's Tact maxim ('Minimize cost to other'); rule2/deference politeness ('Allow the addressee his options') with Leech's Generosity maxim ('Minimize benefit to self') and Agreement maxim ('Minimize disagreement between self and other'); rule3/camaraderie politeness ('Act as though you and addressee were equal/make him feel good') with Leech's Agreement, Approbation ('Minimize dispraise of other') and Sympathy ('Minimize antipathy between self and other') maxims (Lakoff 1977:88; Leech 1983:132). Aware of their probable interpretation as prescriptive statements in everyday life, Lakoff feels the need to explicitly deny any prescriptive intent for her scientific approach, again through the argument that her theory is descriptive rather than prescriptive:

> We're not, as everyone should know by now, setting up prescriptive
> rules for the way people are supposed to behave, any more than the
> rules in Chomsky's *Syntactic Structures* told people how to form nice
> sentences. We are describing what we see...(Lakoff 1977:86)

She further attempts to avoid a moralist stance by acknowledging that the
rules are not general but that *"[...] different ones are applicable in different real-world situations"* (ibid.:86). This situational variance is then
combined with an intercultural one through the position that each of the
three rules constitutes a basic strategy of politeness, and that each culture
adopts one of these three as its dominant strategy:

> While distance politeness has been characteristic of the middle and
> upper classes in most of Europe for a very long time, deference has
> been typical in many Asian societies. But it is also the preferred mode
> of interaction for women in the majority of societies, either always or
> only when talking to men. (Lakoff 1990:37)

But as with Leech and Gu, the theoretical concepts (rules) capturing politeness are still a direct reflection of norms operative in society.

Ide's account also readily acknowledges the normative aspect of politeness, as Discernment reflects social conventions that capture *"[...] the
speaker's choice of expressions to conform to the expected and/or prescribed norms of speech appropriate to the contextual situation in
individual speech communities."* (Ide 1989:225). So when Ide explicates those rules for Japanese society as 'Be polite to a person of a higher
social position'; 'Be polite to a person with power'; 'Be polite to an older
person'; 'Be polite in a formal setting determined by the factors of participants, occasions, or topics' (Ide 1989:225; 1982:366ff), she is describing
the conventional norms operative in Japanese society. Again, the theory
itself is not prescriptive, for the rules of Discernment reflect 'the *speaker's choice* of expressions *to conform* to the prescribed norms'. The norms
are out there, in society, and the speaker conforms to them (prescription).
Ide's role is merely to document the speaker's choices (description).

In Blum-Kulka's framework normativity is handled by the notion of
'cultural script', which is intended as the linguistic counterpart of societally
operative norms of behaviour. In fact, the terms 'norm' and 'script' are
used interchangeably:

> The central zone is that of 'polite' behaviour; included in this zone is
> the range of *cultural expectations* for what constitutes appropriate

social behavior relative to changing social situations. Since such expectations are usually tacit, polite behavior is largely taken for granted,
at most noticeable as showing an actor's 'tactfulness'. It is deviations
from the *cultural norms* which will arouse attention; thus non-
fulfillment of a given *politeness rule*, [...]
It is in *norms of politeness* for behaviour in the public arena that Israeli present-day culture seems less consolidated; the metapragmatic
discourse of informants admits to the lack of *cultural scripts* in this
area [...] (Ide 1992:276, 278, my emphasis)

Politeness is subject to cultural expectations arising from cultural norms,
and cultural scripts provide speakers with the means to meet these expectations. The scripts thus become the operational (linguistic-technical)
counterparts of the norms: they represent the way norms manifest themselves in actual behaviour.

Norms are relevant to Arndt & Janney's theory in at least four ways.
Not only are they the essence of social politeness, which is associated
with *"socially appropriate communicative forms, norms, routines, rituals, etc."* (Arndt & Janney 1992:24), norms are also important for
interpersonal politeness – tact. On the one hand tact relies on cultural
assumptions concerning the interpretation and evaluation of communicative behaviour. And such cultural assumptions are normative ways of
interpreting behaviour which establish a common base of "communicative knowledge", which in turn allows speakers to "foresee" the impact of
their communicative techniques and thus allows them to apply "tact"
(ibid.:30-31). On the other hand this conceptualization of tact in terms of
cultural assumptions also allows the precise description of tactful techniques within specific cultures, as is done in Arndt & Janney (1985b) for
American English and Anglo-American culture. Finally, norms are also
relevant to tact in that tact *is* the norm: *"[i]n normal intracultural conversation people more or less automatically edit their verbal and nonverbal
output so as to project a certain definition of the situation for the partner's benefit"* (Arndt & Janney 1992:35). Tact is a basic means of
conflict-avoidance (ibid.:23), and as people strive to avoid conflict, they
tend to be tactful.

In the latter sense, norms are also present in Brown & Levinson's account where:

[...] normally everyone's face depends on everyone else's being maintained, and since people can be expected to defend their faces if
threatened, and in defending their own to threaten others' faces, it is

> in general in every participant's best interest to maintain each others'
> [...] face [...] (Brown & Levinson 1987:61)

Nevertheless, Brown & Levinson explicitly deny any normative dimension for their framework. Although they acknowledge that norms may be the prevalent commonsense explanation for politeness (ibid.:59), they reject a value-based interpretation in favour of a goal-oriented (means-ends) model – with conflict-avoidance as the goal and strategic face-attendance as the means to reach it (ibid.:62, 85-87). A model where politeness is not an absolute value can better accommodate the fact that politeness can be omitted from verbal interaction, not only in cases of plain affrontery but also for the sake of urgency or efficiency. In this sense, Brown & Levinson's approach resembles that of Leech, as a phenomenon that is commonsensically interpreted in terms of social norms receives a scientific conceptualization in terms of a (social-) technical principle.

On the other hand, the validity of face and rationality is based on the claim that they are *"[...] assumptions that all interacting humans know that they will be expected to orient to"* (ibid.:58). Face and rationality are standards people are expected to live up to – in simple terms, social norms. In this light the Model Person becomes a normative being, an 'ideal' interactant to which every real interactant is expected to orient. And as the Model Person is generally polite (albeit for strategic reasons), this leads back to the initial observation of polite behaviour as the interactional norm. The Model Person thus takes on more or less the same ontological function as 'cultural assumptions' in Arndt & Janney's theory. Both represent normative social expectations which enable speakers to calculate the effect their own contributions will have on others.

Fraser (1990) distances Fraser & Nolen's 'conversational-contract view' from the 'social-norm view' on politeness, which is said to be the prevalent commonsense interpretation of politeness. So again the commonsense normativity of politeness is paired to an explicitly non-normative scientific approach. However, their theoretical model is not free of normative aspects either. For one thing, it accepts the Gricean Cooperative Principle (Fraser 1990:232), and as we have seen, the CP introduces values into the theoretical conceptualization. And as argued in section 3.4.1, the notion of a Conversational Contract itself has a normative dimension, in that it stipulates behaviour that is *expected* of interactants. Whether the terms of the CC derive from social conventions, from institutional constraints, or are specific to particular interactants, they all outline *"[...] what types of speech acts can be seen as appropriate"* (Fraser & Nolen 1981:94), i.e. they stipulate the norms of behaviour the interactants are expected to uphold. Moreover, because people normally abide by the terms of the CC, politeness itself becomes the norm:

> Politeness, on this view, is not a sometime thing. Rational partici-
> pants are aware that they are to act within the negotiated constraints
> and generally do so. […] Politeness is a state that one expects to exist
> in every conversation; participants note not that someone is being
> polite – this is the norm – but rather that the speaker is violating the
> CC. (Fraser 1990:233)

So in dealing with the normative aspect of commonsense politeness, Fraser & Nolen construct concepts that do not explicitly refer to norms but that, on closer inspection, do take on the same role. Just as in Gu's theory, the terms of the CC – especially conventional and institutional terms – are direct representations of social communicative norms.

Although Watts never explicitly mentions social norms as relevant to politeness, norms do have a place in his theory. Politeness is a form of politic behaviour, and the latter is behaviour *"[…] deemed to be socially and culturally appropriate in any given social activity"* (Watts 1992a:48), a definition which allows Watts to classify Ide's Discernment as politic behaviour (ibid.:52). As argued above, Discernment is closely related to social norms because it stipulates the rules for socially appropriate com-municative behaviour, so analogously, politic behaviour can be said to capture or represent such norms of behaviour. Furthermore, although Watts never goes into great detail about how politic behaviour is operationalized in actual interaction – how people know what is politic and what is not – the notion involves "cultural assumptions" (ibid.:137) and "cultural expectations" (ibid.:51) for appropriate behaviour, notions which were already linked to normativity in the discussion of other frame-works. As politeness is defined relative to politic behaviour, it too becomes connected with those norms of behaviour. Being 'more than merely poli-tic', it even crucially relies on them to achieve its effect, as an act can only be interpreted as 'polite' in the light of the social norms for the activity in which the act occurs.

4.2 Theoretical norms

So the normativity of commonsense politeness is reflected in the scien-tific theories in the sense that norms in some form or other always find their way into the various conceptualizations of politeness. However, what I have up to now conveniently designated by the unique term 'norms' appears to cover different kinds of phenomena. Let us therefore take a closer look at the different notions through which normativity is captured by the theories, and see what norms are actually made of.

4.2.1 Appropriateness

A term one encounters throughout the entire field of research is 'appropriateness': to be polite is always 'to act appropriately'. Even in an individualistic model such as Brown & Levinson's, where speakers are only polite in order to realize their personal goals, communicative success depends on the right amount and kind of politeness applied at the right time to the right speech act, as determined by social norms that stipulate what is appropriate for a specific interactional situation.

And because a polite communicative act is always aimed at some addressee on which it intends to have some effect, the hearer's expectations about politeness need to be met in order to be successful. Social appropriateness is thus closely related to hearer expectations. In fact, in the literature the term 'expectations' is encountered almost equally often as 'appropriateness'. Acting politely thus equals acting appropriately equals acting according to the hearer's expectations.[1]

But how does a speaker get to know the expectations of the hearer? The answer lies in the fact that the norms that govern appropriateness are *social* norms. They are not individual norms held only by the hearer, but rather pertain to situations and cultures. Ide formulates it as follows:

> Whereas Brown and Levinson dealt with face wants, the discernment aspect of linguistic politeness is distinguished by its orientation toward the *wants of roles and settings.* (Ide 1989:231, my emphasis)

Or as Gu puts it, expectations do not only emanate from the hearer, but from *"[…] society, which endorses its normative constraints on each individual"* (Gu 1990:242). This social aspect is the gist of the norms encountered in all the theories (section 4.1). They are *cultural* scripts, *cultural* assumptions, *social* maxims, and so on. Contrary to Ide's claim in the previous quote, this is even the case in Brown & Levinson's theory,

---

[1] An exception to this is Watts' theory, where politeness is conceptualized as 'more-than-merely-appropriate' behavior – e.g. where Volition supersedes 'mere' Discernment, where the speaker voluntarily 'goes the extra mile' on behalf of the hearer. This exceptional status of Watts' theory as opposed to the others must be kept in mind throughout the rest of this discussion, but it will be attended to at a later point.

where face-wants are held by "every competent adult member" of a society (Brown & Levinson 1987:62), and the formula these individuals use to calculate the appropriate amount of politeness involves social factors like P, D and R. Moreover, in the 1987 reassessment of their theory, Brown & Levinson acknowledge that P, D, and R, as well as the notion of 'face' (which was first thought of as universal), are subject to "cultural specification" (ibid.:13ff). In a very real sense then, Brown & Levinson's 'individual wants' are actually 'cultural wants' just like Ide's rules of Discernment.

Of course, the question then becomes one of the nature of cultural or social norms. For it is hard to imagine an abstract entity such as a society or a culture as having wants or endorsing constraints. Such abstract entities may work well *theoretically* – may do a good job as concepts within the theoretical model of the world – but need some kind of operational specification to be of any *practical* value. Without further specification they are only of value as concepts among concepts, *within the world of the theory*. If they are to say something valuable about the *real world*, in relation to real human beings, they need some further explanation of how exactly they relate to human lives. The ontology of the society-individual connection needs to be laid out in detail. Without it we are left with a gap between the abstract level of the collective where the norms and rules reside, and the level of concrete individual behaviour which is explained by those norms and rules.

4.2.2 Sharedness

This gap between the cultural and the individual is currently left largely undiscussed; it is taken for granted. For example, in Blum-Kulka's theory the cultural-individual connection is captured by the notion of 'cultural script'. As cultural entities that cause the individual to behave in a specific way, cultural scripts are at the same time cultural and individual – in the speaker's head. They are the link between a culture and its members in that they are the guide to cultural order for individual members. Because they are at the same time cultural and individual, the link between both levels becomes immediate, not requiring further explanation – the scripts themselves *are* the explanation.

Lakoff's rules too are the individual embodiment of 'cultural ways of acting':

> [T]here are three basic strategies of politeness. Every culture adopts one as its dominant mode. If members of cultures with different assumptions are in conversation, each may unknowingly insult or confuse the other by utilizing the wrong system. (Lakoff 1990:35)

When 'the culture' adopts some strategy as its dominant mode, its members will use it. And when there is no specific dominant strategy, people do not know how to act, as becomes clear from Lakoff's discussion of diachronic change in politeness systems:

> During the thirteenth century various stylistic modalities were in flux in Europe. People were beginning to develop a notion of privacy: they began building houses with separate rooms, wearing more constraining and concealing clothing. About this time too, I believe, last names were being devised and used. All of these work toward a Distancing form of rapport. So we can infer from this sort of evidence that European society during this era was shifting from a target of Camaraderie to one of Distance. We would expect in such a period of flux to find more discomfort than usual among people as they realized their old internalized rule-systems were inappropriate but did not know yet what was expected of them in the new. (Lakoff 1979:74)

When people do not know the rules, they feel discomfort. People do not just know how to act, they need to be told.

But who does the telling? Where do the rules and scripts (or 'cultural assumptions', 'maxims', 'general terms of the CC', 'social norms' etc.) come from? In most cases the analysis does not address this question, causing the reasoning to become circular. For example, when Lakoff notes that in recent decennia, the west coast of the United States (notably California) has undergone a change from Distance to Camaraderie, she obviously does so on the basis of the observation of west coast residents' behaviour. The culture is said to change because people's behaviour changes. But at the same time, that change of behaviour is explained through a change in the culture, as people behave in a certain way because of internalized 'cultural rules'. So the 'culture', which is actually the (a posteriori) result of the observation of behaviour, is at the same time posited as the (a priori) causal factor for that behaviour – the explanation of why people behave in a certain way. The discomfort felt by thirteenth-century people resulted from individual change lagging behind cultural change, their behaviour not yet being adapted to an altered system of cultural norms.

So how exactly do concepts such as cultural scripts or rules provide the link between the culture and the individual? How do they succeed in being at the same time cultural and individual? How do they fulfil their function of bridging the gap between both levels? What processes are involved? For simply positing the concepts themselves as the explanatory factor without further clarification isn't enough; it merely causes the link to become 'immediate' and therefore untraceable – or (at least seemingly) no longer requiring to be traced out explicitly, the easy way out unfortunately adopted by many publications.

The answer to these questions is as simple as it is short. The concepts are ascribed a special characteristic: *sharedness*. All the members of a culture or society are claimed to have a shared knowledge of the rules, maxims, scripts, etc. This notion of sharedness occurs throughout the entire field of theories, either explicitly or as an implicit presupposition. Lakoff's rules are said to be rules that *"[...] all fluent speakers of a language use without conscious reflection: rules that are ingrained in the mind"* (Lakoff 1990:24). Leech considers the values his conversational principles and maxims bring into the theory to be *"[...] ones we suppose (...) are operative in society"* (Leech 1983:10) – not just in some people but in all of them, in society in general. In other cases sharedness is left implicit, as when Gu talks about "the Chinese conception of politeness" – the conception of 'the' Chinese – or in Fraser & Nolen's notion of a conversational contract – a unique text subscribed to by both speaker and hearer. In the latter, the general terms of the contract are relative to institutions or cultures – known to all their members.

In still other cases it may involve the notion of convention, as in Watts' theory where politeness is an *"[...] explicitly marked, conventionally interpretable subset of politic behavior"* (Watts 1989a:136) – while politic behaviour is "socioculturally determined" (ibid.:135), i.e. also (implicitly) shared. Conventions are also present in Blum-Kulka's theory where:

> [o]n the one hand appraisals of politeness will be motivated by cultural determinants of face wants and variable degrees of linguistic conventionalisation. On the other hand, they will be affected by culturally coloured definitions of the situation (Blum-Kulka 1992:275)

as well as in Ide's case, where the "rules of politeness" are said to be a subset of "social conventions" according to which members of a society behave (Ide 1989:230). Arndt & Janney's concept of 'social politeness' also involves conventions, while 'tact' relies on 'cultural assumptions' – ways of viewing the world common to all members of a culture. Finally, the notion of sharedness is perhaps most colourfully epitomized by Brown & Levinson's Model Person, a unified human being who has certain characteristics that *"[...] all competent adult members of a society have (and know each other to have)"* (Brown & Levinson 1987:61). The Model Person thus almost becomes the physical embodiment of sharedness.

Sharedness is such a fundamental requirement for the models of politeness considered in this investigation, that without it they simply couldn't exist. This fact, which is only rarely acknowledged (e.g. by Becker 1982:25), is most clear in the case of Brown & Levinson. For if concepts such as face, imposition, the formula and its P, D and R terms were not shared, speakers could never be certain of what would constitute a polite and appropriate strategy in any situation, and thus could never be sure which strategy would be successful or even acceptable to their addressees. Mitigation, face-redress and politeness would cease to be predictable phenomena, and there would be nothing for speakers to calculate – at least nothing valuable, since the success of the outcome of the calculations could never be guaranteed. In short, without sharedness predictability would disappear, and politeness could no longer be modelled. In this light the assumption of a Model Person makes perfect logical sense because, as the embodiment of sharedness, it is the only guarantee that a predictive model will work – or even make sense.

Again however, sharedness by itself does not suffice as an explanatory tool: merely saying that norms are shared does not really explain how the connection between culture and individual actually works. The link is still immediate: the norms are at the same time cultural as well as individual. How they come to have and are able to fulfil this dual role is still left unexplained. At best such a claim merely leads the question to become rephrased. For if scripts, rules and the like are claimed to be shared, then one must explain how they come to be shared. How do they find their way into each individual's head?

In general, two hints are provided, but unfortunately they mostly remain hints, without much thorough analysis to back them up. Lakoff, immediately after the above quoted discussion of European thirteenth-century change from Camaraderie to Distance, points to the importance of popular prescriptive literature – etiquette books. She claims that, although such books can be found at any time in history, in periods of change they are more plentiful and more important, as people in their behavioural quandary turn to such books for guidance on how to act properly. The fact that they can also be found outside of periods of change is explained by the claim that *"[t]here will always be some residual insecurity about the correct formulas for achieving the idealized and conventional mode of rapport"* (Lakoff 1979:74). In this view, cultural conventions would be learned and copied from books. But cultures do not write books, people do. So the abstract culture behind cultural rules would then actually be the writers of those books. They tell people how to act, they determine the rules, they are the culture. Obviously this would be a rather naive perspective, and it would probably be argued that the writers of etiquette books do not actually invent the rules, but rather describe or chronicle the mores of their time and culture in order to spread them throughout society. But in that case etiquette books can no longer fulfil their explanatory role for how the rules come to be shared, as the reasoning would become circular. The only way in which the argument stands is when the writers of etiquette books are indeed attributed the status of cultural leaders who invent the rules. But then again, not all members of a culture can be expected to have read their books. And what about cultures without a strong tradition of etiquette books? Some other means of explanation must be found.

This leads to the second hint politeness literature provides: socialization. Lakoff's rules are described as rules *"learned effortlessly in infancy"* (Lakoff 1990:24). Watts also refers to the importance of socialization, more specifically in connection with politic behaviour. Following Bernstein (1971), Watts defines socialization as "the process whereby a child acquires a specific cultural identity and his or her responses to such an identity" and argues that it plays an important role in the development of politic behaviour. He claims that:

> Hill et al.'s [1986] definition of *wakimae* [Discernment] strongly suggests that it is a major component in the Japanese child's socialization, shaping her/his speech codes in accordance with the roles he or she is expected to play in various social groups. (Watts 1989a:133)

However, as neither Hill et al.'s definition of politeness (as *"[...] one of the constraints on human interaction, whose purpose is to consider others' feelings, establish levels of mutual comfort, and promote rapport"* Hill et al. 1986:349), nor the rest of their study ever mentions the factor 'socialization', we are somewhat left in the dark as to the actual thrust of Watts' reference, as well as to the specific role socialization is supposed to play in the development of politic behaviour.

A more detailed account can be found in Arndt & Janney:

> All people in a culture who wish to be regarded as normal must eventually learn to make roughly similar types of inferences about their experiences. The penalty for not doing this is social exclusion, being labeled abnormal, retarded, defective, or deviant [...]. Thus, growing up to become a normal member of a culture is largely a matter of learning how to perceive, think, and behave as others in the culture do. By interacting with other members of the culture in different situations throughout their lives, people acquire broad frameworks of

> common knowledge, experience, expectations, and beliefs that en-
> able them to be tactful [...]. Stored in the mind in the form of global
> assumptions, these frameworks consist of standard presuppositions
> about what the culture normatively defines as 'reality', or 'the way
> things are' in the world [...]
>
> Such frameworks are absolutely essential to tactful communication,
> because without them, as Mead [...] points out, people cannot think
> about their own projected behaviour from the perspective of the 'gen-
> eralised other' and imagine how it might be interpreted or what its
> consequences might be. (Arndt & Janney 1992:30-31)

From early childhood on people interact in various situations with a variety of addressees, and from these multiple contacts they develop cultural
assumptions, i.e. group-based notions of reality, and a notion of a 'generalized other' which enables them to project and predict the effect of their
communicative contributions. These combine in the development of notions of 'normality' and 'tact' (politeness): what it is to be tactful and when
it is required.

Evidence for the role of socialization in regard to the sharedness of
politeness norms would have to be found in studies of politeness acquisition. However, as I have already outlined in regard to the study by Snow
et al. (1990, see above, section 2.3), such studies are usually not of much
help, as they fail to provide any really conclusive evidence that what is
transmitted from parents to children are the norms and rules proposed by
the theoretical model. If such a theoretical model (*in casu* Brown &
Levinson's) is to be derived from Snow et al.'s data, it can only be done by
making the same assumptions and presuppositions made by Brown &
Levinson. The study actually uses Brown & Levinson's model as the perspective from which children's discourse is analyzed, and thus sharedness
is a priori *assumed* just as in the theoretical model.

The same goes for most other developmental studies of politeness.
The epistemological reasoning behind Kwarciak's argument for using
children's speech for discovering politeness universals speaks for itself:

> Linguistic politeness in adulthood is influenced by numerous vari-
> ables, such as personality, lifestyle, or cross-cultural impact. In contrast,
> the same skill at early ages seems to be virtually isolated from the
> above influences. Further, the simplicity of the child's social world in
> middle childhood makes it almost transparent for research purposes.
> Finally, early linguistic politeness is highly limited by developmental
> constraints on cognition, so it seems to include only the hard core of
> the fully mature system of polite communication. In other words, we

can find in it those strategies that are considered the most important
by the society, and therefore taught to children first. (Kwarciak
1993:53-54)

The societal sharedness of the politeness system is taken for granted, even
though it is admitted that in adulthood factors such as personality and
lifestyle will "distort" it (ibid.:64). In fact, the isolation of those individual
factors as external influences on an otherwise pure politeness system reinforces and even depends on the a priori assumption of a societally shared
system. Sharedness is not an object of research, it is an assumption.
Kwarciak goes even further, and claims that studying children's politeness systems will ultimately reveal universals of politeness, which implies
a universally shared core politeness system.

Other studies use a similarly assumptive approach, in that they take a
theoretical notion of politeness (or simply use the term 'politeness' in a
taken-for-granted way) and simply apply it to children's discourse. Because all the subject children's behaviour is thus interpreted using one
unique set of norms/rules, the sharedness of those rules is not only presupposed, but even implemented methodologically. The research questions
can mostly be paraphrased as 'How well do children age x perform?',
'When (and why) do they start using mitigated forms, hints, etc?', 'When
do they start differentiating requests in accordance with interlocutor status, age, etc.?', and so on.[2] Although they do provide correlational data
between age and level of communicative competence – defined in terms
of a system of norms – such studies never actually question the sharedness
of those norms, nor examine the mechanisms of its emergence.

Of course there are exceptions. Ervin-Tripp (1982) briefly mentions
adult modelling as a factor – and immediately adds that this would probably lead to *"a good deal of social variation"* (Ervin-Tripp 1982:242).[3]
Becker (1982:29-30), who concentrates on the acquisition of appropriate request forms, is more elaborate and mentions three mechanisms:
the association of others' requests with their intended listeners and situations of use, trial and error and explicit training. These same strategies

---

[2] Examples of such studies are Axia & Baroni (1985), Baroni & Axia (1989),
Becker (1988), Becker & Smenner (1986), Ervin-Tripp (1982), Gleason (1980),
Ervin-Tripp, Guo, Lampert (1990), Garton & Pratt (1990), Nakamura (1996),
Nippold, Leonard, Anastopoulos (1982), Walper & Valtin (1992).
[3] Other studies that are not restricted to the correlation of age with competence,
but nevertheless also take sharedness for granted are, e.g. Becker (1982), Clancy
(1986), Demuth (1986), Gordon & Ervin-Tripp (1984).

("modelling in the home and preschool", "correction in society", and "instruction in the school system") have been proposed more recently by Nakamura (1996:246). Although these mechanisms may indeed accurately depict children's learning processes, they do not in themselves explain how and why sharedness would arise. They can all exist in a non-shared environment, and do not necessarily make any positive contribution to the emergence of sharedness. Learning to associate Others' requests with their intended listeners and situations of use can only cater for a shared request system provided those Others already share such a request system. Analogously, trial-and-error learning would require sharedness in the addressees of the trials, while explicit training presupposes sharedness in the trainers/teachers.

So in the end, sharedness remains an a priori assumption rather than an a posteriori observed fact. It could even be argued that there are strong indications *against* the empirical validity of sharedness. True, a notion such as 'cultural assumptions' may make sense in the light of *"[...] broad frameworks of common knowledge, experience, expectations, and beliefs [...] standard presuppositions about what the culture normatively defines as 'reality', or 'the way things are' in the world"* (Arndt & Janney 1992:30), that is, when physical-technical aspects of the world are involved. In order to operate effectively in society it is necessary to recognize a car when you see one, to know that it is an inanimate object (it won't bite, for instance) used for transportation, that it needs gas to fulfil that task, etc.; or to know what a table or a chair is and what they are used for, and so on. But when we are talking about the evaluation by a particular hearer of a particular speaker's utterance in a particular situation as (im)polite (for this is ultimately what politeness is all about in everyday reality), things cease to be all that obvious. As discussed previously (section 2.1.2), the empirical data themselves mostly witness variation rather than sharedness. People are never unanimous in their evaluations or rankings of (im)politeness or (in)appropriateness. What is more, the very fact that impoliteness and inappropriateness are conceivable and do occur seems to indicate that notions of politeness vary. Even in Japanese society, which is qualified by some as "extremely homogeneous" (Clancy 1986:216), Nakamura acknowledges the abundance of variability:

> Politeness levels vary greatly from person to person, as well as according to factors such as situation, gender, dialect, and age.
> [...]
> While many people are criticized for impolite speech, others, such as department store employees, are often criticized for being excessively

polite[…].
[…]
Opinion polls have revealed that more young people are having difficulty using *keigo*, and that many people feel the system should be
simplified. (Nakamura 1996:247)

However, none these observations lead to a variability-based approach.
Because sharedness is a theoretical assumption – prior to observations
instead of deriving from them – it guides the interpretation of data, and
thus observations of variability are also explained within a sharedness-
based framework. The two are made compatible by interpreting variability
as systematic, not individual but bound to fixed or determinable social
characteristics such as gender, age, situation, etc. In this way variability
remains predictable, and thus theoretically controllable – it can be incorporated without the need to revise the foundations of the theory. In spite
of internal (systematic) variability, the idea of a unique system of politeness (and thus sharedness) remains intact. Note from Nakamura's quote
that this assumption apparently also underlies commonsense notions of
politeness, as opinion polls show that people "have difficulty" using "the
system" and feel that it should be simplified, which not only testifies to
the commonsense assumption of a unique and shared system, but also –
and perhaps even primarily – to the fact that people feel such a system
should exist, i.e. that notions of politeness *ought to be* shared.

This combination of empirical variability with theoretical sharedness
leads to sometimes dual-sounding positions. For instance, on one and the
same page we can find the following statements:

Any study of polite language in Japanese would reveal enormous differences in usage according to various factors, such as gender, age,
dialect, educational background, context (e.g. topic of conversation,
formality of setting), and degree of familiarity. […] Verbal politeness
in Japanese involves two dimensions, namely: (1) formality, which
reflects the psychological and/or social distance between participants,
and (2) honorific and humble language, which indicates respect and
deference. The system of polite language in Japanese […].
Speakers of a given language must have more than mere linguistic
competence. To use language effectively, they must undergo language
socialization and develop communicative competence […] All languages have pragmatic rules, and politeness is an integral part of
pragmatic competence. A speaker with a fluent command of a variety
of politeness styles is capable of communicating effectively in a wide
range of social roles. […].

> In order to comprehend and produce polite language, children must
> first learn the linguistic forms of politeness, and second, they must
> understand the pragmatic rules that govern each socio-interactional
> context [...]. Children's appropriate use of polite language is depend-
> ent on their language acquisition [...] (Nakamura 1996:235)

On the one hand, variability is observed to be "enormous"; witness the
number of social factors adduced to explain this amount of variability
(with "such as" indicating that the list is not exhaustive). Nevertheless,
this enormous variability is interpreted as systematic, because based on a
shared system of pragmatic politeness rules which are learned in childhood and can be used appropriately or inappropriately. The system of
politeness evaluations remains fixed and determinable, which allows
Nakamura to conclude:

> Although Japan has become less hierarchical and more democratic,
> sociolinguistic errors involving inappropriate use of *keigo* tend to trig-
> ger an instantaneous negative reaction in the listener. (ibid.248)

Note how the claimed "instantaneous" reaction of the hearer links up with
what was said earlier about the conceptual bias of politeness models towards speaker behaviour, and the ensuing Pavlovian character of the
hearer's evaluation. And while the conceptual bias was seen to render the
interpretation of impoliteness problematic, the assumption of sharedness
can now be seen to make impoliteness even more mysterious. If speakers
and hearers share the same system of rules, then impoliteness could only
be a willingly performed act to antagonize the hearer, which mere intuition immediately contradicts, and would render examples such as that cited
in Arndt & Janney (section 2.2.8) uninterpretable.

4.2.3 Norm-ality

Sharedness introduces another way in which norms manifest themselves
in the theoretical models: through the notion of 'normality' and the 'normal'. As the politeness system is *"ingrained in the mind, learned effortlessly
in infancy"* (Lakoff 1990:24) and shared by all members of a society or
culture, any normal human being can be supposed to have internalized it.
Indeed, Arndt & Janney's cultural assumptions are notions of reality *"[a]ll
people in a culture who wish to be regarded as normal"* (Arndt & Janney
1992:30) must acquire. Not doing so results in *"social exclusion, being
labeled abnormal, retarded, defective, or deviant"* (ibid.:30). Thus,
"[j]uvenile, mad, incapacitated persons" are excluded from Brown &

Levinson's model – albeit only *"partially"* and in a footnote (Brown & Levinson 1987:285, footnote 7). But as these form only a marginal minority, Lakoff's politeness rules can safely be claimed to describe *"normal behavior"* within a particular society (Lakoff 1979:69).

As there are certain characteristics an individual must display in order to qualify as a 'normal' person, the notion of 'normality' clearly involves a standard or norm against which behaviour can be evaluated. Besides this moral evaluative aspect (with deviation being cast in pathological terms and involving some kind of exclusion from the group), normality also has a quantitative aspect. The characteristics that define normality are not random, but depend on the (perceived) typical characteristics of members of a particular group – i.e. of the majority. The moral evaluative side thus has a numerical corollary: it is the kind of behaviour *"most of us" "ordinarily"* exhibit (Lakoff 1977:89; Fraser & Nolen 1981:94). Within a framework based on sharedness, this majority can theoretically even be expected to comprise 100% of the population, with as only exceptions 'pathological' cases (Brown & Levinson's "mad" and "incapacitated") or people who are not yet "mature" (Brown & Levinson's "juvenile").

As a result, sharedness and normality provide the link back to hearer expectations. If the 'norm-al' behaviour for the majority of people in situation S is to display behaviour B, then obviously hearers can expect any speaker to perform accordingly. Sharedness ensures that the speaker is able to predict the hearer's expectations and perform appropriately. And because expected events are unsurprising and very often go by us unnoticed, politeness is associated with the 'unmarked' in a number of theories. This is explicitly the case in Fraser & Nolen, Blum-Kulka, Ide's Discernment and Watts' politic behaviour, but on an implicit level the association could be made for most of the other theories as well.

Finally, the combination of appropriateness, sharedness, expectations and normality with the conceptual bias towards polite behaviour results in a view where the majority of people are generally polite to each other – politeness is the norm in everyday interaction. Again, this conclusion is explicitly drawn by only a few researchers (Arndt & Janney, Fraser & Nolen, and arguably Brown & Levinson, see above, section 4.1) , but it will be clear that it is slumbering beneath the surface of all of the theories, as it would be a natural and logical conclusion from their conceptual underpinnings. The only exception is Watts' framework where politic behaviour is the norm, while politeness (being 'more than merely politic behaviour') constitutes an extra effort on the part of the speaker beyond the norm.

Although polite behaviour as the norm is a direct consequence of the quantitative aspect of normality – being a characteristic of the majority – it is also linked to the qualitative aspect. Both aspects are closely connected, as appears from the following quote in which Lakoff makes a case for the introspective over the empirical method of examining rule violations:

> [...]we might listen to tapes, or quiz informants, for years before we encounter some kinds of possible politeness-rule violations. Most of us, in most situations, are too well-bred to violate these rules: we know what trouble we'd get into if we did. (Lakoff 1977:89)

The norm is quantitative in that "most of us" follow the rules while rule violations are *"cases that normally don't occur"* (ibid.:89), and it is qualitative in that rule violation would be evaluated negatively and incur sanctions. The former is caused by the latter: people follow the rules because not doing so would incur sanctions.

4.2.4 Summary

In traditional politeness theories, norms and normativity have a number of different but interconnected aspects. On the one hand notions such as 'appropriateness' and 'normality' have a moral evaluative aspect, associated with 'good' and 'proper' behaviour, and via these with 'having good breeding'. As such, the commonsense association of 'polite' with a positive evaluation and 'impolite' with a negative evaluation are directly incorporated into the conceptual model. The theories thus again mimic commonsense thinking in anchoring the positive–negative dimension to (in)appropriateness via concepts designed to picture the moral value system of a society, such as scripts, rules, etc. On the other hand, norms also have a purely numerical aspect: again through 'normality' (now in the sense of what happens 'usually' or 'generally'), but 'expectations', 'conventions' and the 'unmarked' also capture this side.

Both sides are connected in that people generally follow the rules because they know about the moral evaluations involved, and want to avoid the sanctions associated with impoliteness. They are able to accomplish this because norms are not individual but shared by all. They belong to the level of society or culture, they are part of the 'sociolinguistic system' of which politeness is a subsystem (Hill et al. 1986:351). However, sharedness does not imply that everybody behaves in the same manner. The notion of a 'system' allows observations of variability to be incorporated into the theory in the form of systematic variability, with parameters such as gender, age, status (power), distance, etc. Variability is thus not random, but rather part of the system, which brings us to the connection between theoretical conceptualization and empirical observation.

4.3 Empirical norms

The moral evaluative aspect of norms can readily be found in empirical data (section 2.1.1): the association of politeness with 'good (ill) breed-ing' or 'having (no) manners', as well as the pains most parents go through in order to teach their children 'how to behave' (e.g. Becker 1988, Gleason 1980) need no further comment. The quantitative aspect of norms on the other hand is not equally obvious. Informants are never unanimous in their ratings of politeness, in their answers to DCTs and questionnaires, or even in their definitions of what politeness actually is and in which situa-tions it applies (Blum-Kulka 1990, 1992; Ide 1992, as discussed in section 2.1.2). This is reflected in the terminology used by the theories, with terms such as 'most (of us)', 'mostly', 'generally', or 'usually' – Brown & Levinson and Lakoff are the only ones who explicitly include 'all' mem-bers of a society. Further acknowledgement of individual variation can be found, for example when Blum-Kulka reports *"sharp interpersonal dif-ferences in defining performable speech acts; things one speaker finds easy to say or ask, others would not even attempt" (Blum-Kulka 1992:274)* So how are data that attest to widespread variability reconciled with theoretical models based on sharedness? Overall, three different strate-gies are applied.

4.3.1 Statistical analysis
The first strategy is methodological, and consists of what I will rather loosely call 'statistical analysis' in data processing. At the risk of over-simplifying matters, this practice can be summarized as follows. Sociolinguistics as the study of language from a soci(et)al perspective is concerned with language on the supra-individual level. It is not so much concerned with what any particular individual does, but rather with what groups of individuals do. As the goal is to arrive at interpretations that pertain to the group as a whole, widespread variability is an obstacle for sociolinguistic investigators, in that in the extreme case it would lead to a separate theory for each individual studied. The variety of answers must therefore in some way be reduced. To put it differently, in order to be able to interpret the empirical results as behaviour emanating from the group, the variety of behaviours must in some way or other be combined into one group-behaviour. The result of such an operation must be inter-pretable as one behaviour.

The statistical method is the perfect tool for this job as it produces behavioural averages. Instead of having to deal with – say – 100 different politeness rankings of utterances, one can calculate the average ranking position of each utterance to arrive at one average ranking produced by the group as a whole (Fraser & Nolen (1981) use this methodology in examining the notion of 'deference', see section 2.2.7). Analogously, a fruitful method in (intercultural) comparisons is to calculate percentages: of respondents who answered A to question Q, or who used linguistic form F in situation S, or of occurrences of form F in speech act X in situation S, etc. – the possibilities are virtually unlimited. Ide et al. (1992) and Hill et al. (1986) rely on it, it is a preferred analytical technique in the Cross Cultural Speech Act Realization Project (Blum-Kulka et al. 1989; Kasper & Blum-Kulka 1993b), and can be found in many other comparative studies (Aronsson & Sätterlund-Larsson 1987; Chen 1993; Berk-Seligson 1988; Garcia 1993; Sifianou 1992a, to name but a few). In more theoretically oriented studies these techniques are mirrored by the tendency to qualify theoretical claims by 'averaging' terms such as 'usually', 'normally', 'mostly', 'most people', etc.

The statistical strategy is often combined with the equally averaging methodological practice of classificatory coding. This consists in grouping together different forms as different realizations of the same basic form or 'form-category'. For instance, in order to obtain sufficiently comparable data in cross-cultural research, different (language-specific) utterance forms can (and arguably even have to) be coded or classified as belonging to one and the same utterance category. Instead of having to work with the forms themselves, the researcher can then work with the form-categories. 'Request', 'directive' or 'hint' can be such categories; or within the category of 'request', Sifianou (1992a:158ff) identifies such linguistic forms as 'intensifiers', 'cajolers', 'attention-getters', 'fillers', etc. When one respondent says 'it's cold in here' while another asks 'is the heating on?' and still another remarks 'I should have brought a sweater', these different utterances can be considered as one and the same request strategy using the category of 'hints'. So although in reality the respondents acted differently, as far as the researcher is concerned they displayed the same behaviour. Even large-scale categorizations such as Brown & Levinson's distinction between positive and negative politeness can be regarded as such classificatory coding categories.

My purpose here is not to contest the scientific validity or epistemological worth of statistical analysis and classificatory coding. In cross-linguistic research they may well be necessary in order to produce comparable data. I only want to point out that both methodological practices have a particular influence on the theoretical interpretation of empirical data.[4] Both have the effect (and indeed the purpose) of reducing surface variability so as to facilitate theoretical interpretation of the data. In this sense the data are simplified. Instead of having to account for the fact that one respondent produced utterance U_1 while another used utterance U_2, the researcher now need only account for the occurrence of utterance-category C_U to which both U_1 and U_2 are said to belong. Instead of facing two different data, the researcher now only needs to deal with one datum. The effect is even clearer in the case of statistical averaging.

This may perhaps best be illustrated by means of a hypothetical example.[5] Suppose we want to examine the concept of politeness in a particular group of people by means of a rating experiment. We construct a number of situations, and have one of the participants in those situations say a certain phrase at a certain moment. Then we ask the respondents to rate the utterance in terms of politeness, say on a scale from 1 to 7, with 1 meaning 'very polite', 7 'very impolite', and 4 being the 'neutral' point (not polite, nor impolite). Now suppose we get the ratings shown in Figure 6 for utterance U in situation S from our 20 informants.

This would result in an average rating of 3.15. Thus U would be considered 'rather polite': on the 'polite' side of the polite–impolite continuum, but not in an extreme position. In a norm-based theory this would imply the construction of a norm N that would capture the 'rather polite'-ness of U taking account of the characteristics of the situation. What such an analysis would miss, however, is the fact that although the average rating may well be 3.15, in reality U is rated across the whole spectrum from 1 to 7, and that there are 6 respondents (30% of total) that find U 'impolite' in situation S, while another 2 (10%) find U 'neither polite nor impolite'. The net effect is that, although an interpretation in terms of norm N may

---

[4] The following analysis will (over)simplify things considerably, and therefore not do proper justice to the subtleties and refinements that have been built into statistical analysis over the years of its existence and use. To repeat, it is absolutely not my purpose – nor within my league of competence – to present a fine-pointed critique of statistical analysis techniques. My only purpose is to illustrate the general effect they have on the scientific representation and interpretation of real-world complexity, particularly within the field of sociolinguistic politeness research.

[5] A hypothetical example is constructed (1) in order to have an example where the effect to be illustrated is more obvious, and (2) because most publications do not present their actual data, only the 'averaged' results, so the former are simply not accessible.

well make sense in light of the average rating, it does so *only* for that average rating. In reality it accounts for the answers of only 4 respondents (20%). The obvious but important fact that in reality people do not agree on the (im)politeness of U in situation S, with ratings running the whole gamut from 'very polite' to 'very impolite', is not at all represented in the averaged result, nor in the norm-based interpretation. Consequently an interpretation based on a single norm does not seem to hold its ground, as it involves a misrepresentation of reality.

Figure 6. Hypothetical rating experiment

Respondent	Rating
1	1
2	7
3	5
4	4
5	3
6	2
7	2
8	1
9	1
10	5
11	3
12	3
13	4
14	6
15	5
16	1
17	1
18	3
19	1
20	5

This effect becomes even more pronounced in a more extreme (though perhaps unlikely) situation. If half the respondents provided a rating of 7 while the other half produced a rating of 1, an average rating of 4 would be the result. Although such a rating would be right for the whole group, in reality it would represent no one person's true rating. In fact, the fundamentally oppositional structure of the group would be completely lost, and a norm-based interpretation would totally miss the point as it would lead to a norm no one actually upholds. Also consider that a rating of 4 might just as well be produced by a population where one half rated 6 and the other half 2; or where one half rated 5, and the other 3; or a third of the population rated 1, another third 4, and the remainder 7; and so on and so forth. The average does not say a great deal about the underlying reality that produced it. Although at first sight the average seems to say something sensible about the group *as a whole* – where the totality of its members are considered – in reality it does not. For example in the first case, with ratings of 1 and 7, the average would tell us that utterance U is considered '*neither* polite, *nor* impolite' by the group as a whole, while in reality the group would find U '*either* very polite, *or* very impolite' – depending on who you ask. The net total (average) result might be the same, but both cases actually involve quite different situations.

Although admittedly such an extreme situation would hardly ever occur – and if it did, it would take a truly dim-witted researcher not to notice the basically oppositional nature of the responses – the line of reasoning holds true for any situation without total unanimity among the respondents. No matter how small the variability involved, the calculated average always deviates from the reality it aims to represent. There is always a gap between the raw and the processed data which involves a misrepresentation. And no matter how slight the latter may be in absolute numbers, a norm based on a statistical average cannot account for the underlying residual variation, since norms cannot explain their own violation. Even if 99% of the population is unanimous and their behaviour can be captured by some norm, any really adequate theory must also be able to account for the remaining 1% not covered by the norm. Until now, however, theoretical frameworks of politeness have tended to neglect that fact – and that portion of the population.

As the approaches under consideration are *socio*linguistic, they are interested in the behaviour of the group more than in that of particular individuals. The statistical approach comes more or less naturally to them because it provides an image of what the group as a whole is doing: it can picture behavioural trends within the group. However, groups as such do not act, only their individual members do. So in the end even the most extremely 'socio'-oriented framework needs to say something about individual behaviour. After moving from the individual to the group level, they need a return path that explains how individual behaviour is related to the claims made about the group as a whole. In the approaches under study this is accomplished by norm-based theoretical models. This can be depicted as in Figure 7.

Norms are called upon to explain how individuals come to produce the average behaviour observed for the group as a whole. Unfortunately, something is lost in the process. The variability that was averaged out on the way from the individual to the group level is not reintroduced on the way back. Instead, the quantitative and qualitative aspects of norms, together with the notion of sharedness, only cater for the calculated behavioural averages, and so the original empirical variability remains lost in the resulting theoretical models.

Figure 7. The relationship between statistical processing and norm-based modelling

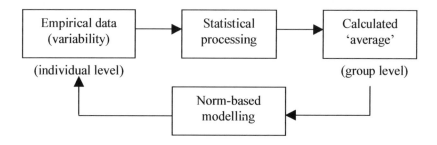

4.3.2 Systematic variability and variable systems

Or does it? For at first sight the theoretical models do seem to allow for a great deal of variability. Through the introduction of 'social variables' or 'social parameters' that differentiate speakers, hearers and situational aspects, the same utterance U is no longer invariably polite or impolite, but its evaluation depends on specific configurations of the parameters involved. U might be polite when uttered by speaker S_1 to hearer H_1 in situational context C_1, but not when uttered by a different speaker S_2, or to a different hearer H_2 in the same situation C_1 or to the same hearer H_1 in a different situation C_2, and so on. Brown & Levinson's P and D are such differentiating parameters: a different power- or distance-relationship between speaker and hearer may turn a perfectly polite utterance into an extremely impolite insult, and vice versa. Fraser & Nolen's 'specific terms' of the CC – power and role of speaker and hearer, institutional factors – fulfil the same role. Ide's notion of Discernment aims to capture exactly the way in which a speaker needs to assess such situational and relational aspects in order to determine which linguistic choices would be polite or appropriate for a particular occasion. And although Leech's theory is about 'absolute' (or inherent) politeness, he does acknowledge the existence of 'relative' politeness, i.e. *"politeness relative to context and situation"* (Leech 1983:102).

But although social parameters cater for some amount of variability, there is still a problem. Because of the conceptual bias towards speech production, the variability introduced by social parameters is also variability of production: it differentiates only between when and what can politely be *said by whom*. It pertains only to what speakers can and cannot do; social parameters do not allow for variability in the hearer's judgement. When the parameters deem utterance U by speaker S to hearer H in situational context C to be polite, then *any* hearer will make that same evaluation. The variability introduced by social parameters is systematic, it is part of the system of politeness, and that system itself remains shared between the members of a group. Social parameters do not lead to a situation where utterance U by speaker S to hearer H in situational context C is evaluated as 'very polite' by evaluator E_1, as 'reasonably polite' by E_2, as 'not polite nor impolite' by E_3 and as 'impolite' by E_4.

Unfortunately this is exactly the kind of variability observed in empirical data. Although according to the theories all hearers should make the same judgements of (im)politeness when contextual factors are known, in practice we find that they do not. Note that no amount of fine-tuning through the postulation of additional social parameters can ever remedy this situation, as the additional variability will remain of the systematic kind. As long as the fundamental notion of a unique and shared system remains operational, it will make sure that hearers are consistent (or even unanimous) in their evaluations. A similar problem arises from the hearer's judgement of an utterance as 'impolite', while the speaker meant it to be (and thus would evaluate it as) 'polite'. Although Fraser & Nolen acknowledge the plausibility of such an occurrence (Fraser & Nolen 1981:96), within current models (including their own) this is not really a theoretical possibility owing to the combination of sharedness and the conceptual bias.

The only way in which empirical variability can be accounted for without sacrificing the group-based interpretation would be to argue that the system is not shared among all members but can differ for different 'subgroups'. Lakoff seems to be headed in that direction when she allows for intergenerational variation. This variation is not of the systematic kind, for then it would resemble an age parameter which would stipulate that, for example, it is polite for people of age X to say U, but impolite for people of age Y (on which all members would agree). Lakoff's intergenerational variation is of a different kind. Here is what she says about changes in the use of the word 'fun', which used to be a noun only, but is becoming more and more popular as an adjective:

> Now decide on how you feel about each of the next three examples. Are they grammatical? Are they 'right'? Would you say them? Have you ever heard any of them?

Bob sure knows how to throw fun parties.
This party is fun, but Mary's was even funner.
This is the funnest party I've ever been at.

Monitor your reactions closely, but guard them carefully: they reveal
your age. The older you are, the more conservative you are likely to
be about these sentences. Younger people, teenagers especially, tend
to accept all of them without question. Older people, those over fifty
or so, like none of them. People in between might like the first of the
last set of examples, but not the latter two, or the first but not the
third. What's going on? This little corner of the grammar of English is
currently in flux. (Lakoff 1990:26)

Although it is not about politeness, this quote is relevant because Lakoff
claims that grammar, just like politeness, consists of a system of rules
which people apply in order to arrive at judgements of grammaticality:
*"In order to tell which strings of words are grammatical sentences of a
language and which are not, speakers refer (unconsciously) to the rules I
have just discussed."* (ibid.:27). Technically speaking, judgements of politeness and grammaticality are not that far apart. So if different people
within a group or culture can differ in their judgements of grammaticality,
the same can be expected for (im)politeness. And indeed, Lakoff acknowledges this possibility:

> More common, both cross- and intraculturally, are confusions that
> arise because participants, while implicitly in agreement that polite-
> ness is appropriate to the discourse, have different definitions of how
> to be polite. This discrepancy is possible because there are three ba-
> sic strategies of politeness. Every culture adopts one as its dominant
> mode. If members of cultures with different assumptions are in con-
> versation, each may unknowingly insult or confuse the other by
> utilizing the wrong system. (Furthermore, cultures, *as well as indi-
> viduals*, have different ideas about what is likely to produce conflict
> or unpleasant confrontation, and will therefore resort to politeness
> strategies under different conditions). (ibid.:35, my emphasis)

So politeness judgements can differ intraculturally because participants
have different definitions of how or when to be polite, which is exactly
the kind of empirical variability discussed in the previous section. Although this intriguing point would certainly deserve further elaboration,
the rest of Lakoff's exposé is all about cultural systems and intercultural
misunderstandings only. These two sentences are the only occasions where

intragroup differences with regard to politeness are mentioned at all.

This is not really surprising when we take a closer look at what the existence of such variable systems of politeness would entail. What does it mean for the system itself to be variable? Judging from Lakoff's discussion of intergenerational differences, it would at least mean that the population of a culture could be subdivided into a number of smaller groups (generations), each having different systems. But even within these groups Lakoff only talks of 'tendencies', so rather than a few broad 'generations', maybe many more 'age-groups' could be distinguished. The question then arises of how far one could push such a distinction, of how 'fine' the age-differences involved can become?

And what of her claim that *individuals* can have different ideas about what is likely to produce conflict and hence about when to be polite? Would individual variability entail that every individual has a different system? But then what is the point of an analysis structured in terms of a cultural system that is supposed to be shared, and which is posited as the very basis of the theories of politeness? As sharedness would disappear, so would predictability, which is the cornerstone of a system-based scientific analysis. If speakers can no longer predict hearers' evaluations, politeness loses its effectiveness and thus its very reason for existence. Speakers would have to learn about the particular politeness system of each different hearer before they could ever be polite with any degree of effectiveness.

And just think of the multitude of other factors besides age that could be imagined as influences on linguistic judgement. To stick with the 'fun' example, why not include conservatism versus open-mindedness with respect to linguistic change, where one could equally construct an infinitely fine continuum?[6] In the end, it is not really surprising to find only a slight

---

[6] But this of course would no longer be a valid 'external' influencing factor, as the group-defining characteristic would involve the very linguistic judgement that is being examined. Indeed, how would one determine a person's conservatism in regard to linguistic change other than by that person's reaction to linguistic changes, such as the adjectival use of 'fun'? The reasoning would become circular and the observed correlation devoid of any real explanatory value. Occasionally this kind of circular analysis can be found in the literature however, as for example when Bates & Silvern (1977, as quoted in Kwarciak 1993:59) found a 'strong correlation' between children's production of linguistic politeness and their 'social adjustment' as rated by their teachers. A similar method was used by Wood & Gardner (1980, as quoted in Becker 1982:13, Becker & Smenner 1986:540, and Ervin-Tripp et al. 1990:315) who had teachers rate their

mention of this kind of variability in Lakoff's and others' publications: if pursued far enough, it would destroy the very basis on which their theories are built.

4.3.3 Determining who knows best

A third and final way in which empirical variability is handled is by simply deciding 'who is right'. We have already encountered examples of this strategy in other contexts above, but it is useful to repeat and examine them more closely here. The strategy comes down to claiming that the scientist is somehow 'right', and if other people think differently, they must be 'wrong'. Leech for example practises a mild form of this 'who knows best' game when he states that:

> There is an unfortunate association of the term ['politeness'] with superficially 'nice', but ultimately insincere, forms of human behaviour, and it is therefore tempting to write off politeness (at least in some cultural environments) as being a trivial and dispensable factor which is no more than a 'garnish' on the serious use of language. In pointing out the importance of the PP for the explaining of other principles (the CP and the IP) I have tried to show otherwise. What tends to confuse the issue, I think, is a failure to distinguish between absolute politeness and relative politeness. (Leech 1983:83)

As Leech's theory posits politeness as being involved in the mechanisms of understanding – on the same level as Grice's CP – and therefore as a serious business, he needs to deal with views that claim otherwise, that relegate politeness to the status of 'icing on the cake of real communication', an insincere and therefore trivial 'garnish' on language. Leech argues that the proponents of such a view are wrong and bases this position on the distinction between absolute and relative politeness – between 'inher-

---

pupils in terms of dominance vs. submissiveness, and then examined these pupils' linguistic behaviour towards one another. Rather unsurprisingly, their findings *"showed that the dominant speakers gave most orders and were least polite, and that they were by far the most successful in gaining compliance"* (Ervin-Tripp et al. 1990:315). It must be admitted that Ervin-Tripp et al. – as a rare exception – do report a fishy smell as they remark in parentheses that there is 'some' circularity involved, since the teachers' ratings *"may come from observation of success in eliciting compliance"* (ibid.:321) I would say it lies within the very definition of a 'dominant' person to be someone who orders others around and is successful at it.

ent' politeness and politeness 'relative to context or situation'. This distinction can at the same time also be used to reconcile the theory with empirical variability:

> For example, in Japan, the scale of politeness is exploited differently by women than by men, and (apparently) more by people in the western part of the country than by people in the eastern part of the country. It is on the basis of such group norms that we judge individual people as being 'polite' or 'impolite' in particular speech situations [...]. Relative politeness is therefore variable on many dimensions, according to the standard or set of standards under scrutiny. General pragmatics may reasonably confine its attention to politeness in the absolute sense. (ibid.:84)

The general-local distinction thus allows the researcher to claim that if people disagree with the theory in their (im)politeness evaluations, this is due to the distinction between relative and absolute politeness. Their evaluation is local and therefore of no concern (and is not a threat) to the theory's position. Furthermore, the definition of absolute politeness as 'inherent' conveniently gives it a more 'basic' status than relative politeness which is 'basic politeness plus local influences'.

Although Leech employs rather a mild form of this strategy (it could be argued that his claim amounts to the observation that the concerns of the theory and those of ordinary speakers merely 'differ'[7]), some more serious and less benign forms can also be found. Fraser's (1990:220ff) 'social-norm view' category of politeness perspectives is said to reflect the understanding of politeness generally embraced by the public within the English-speaking world, which is illustrated by quotes from historical and latter-day etiquette manuals. This view of politeness is then somewhat abruptly dismissed by saying that *"it is safe to say that the social-norm approach has few adherents among current researchers"* (ibid.:221). The remainder of the paper is entirely devoted to those scientific perspectives, with the social-norm view left aside as some kind of archaic viewpoint not worthy of any in-depth discussion. Although admittedly Fraser's paper is primarily intended as an overview of *scientific* rather than commonsense perspectives on politeness, this treatment does tell us something about how some researchers envision the relationship between scientific and

---

[7] Although it still has a definite and distinct 'theory knows best' thrust to it, as ultimately people's behaviour is explained by the theory's evaluations of politeness, regardless of what the participants themselves might think.

commonsense notions, especially in the light of what Fraser & Nolen say
about empirical methods in their study of deference:

> [...] although speakers believe that they understood deference and
> can recognize it, it is very clear that one cannot follow the linguistic
> tradition and appeal directly to the intuitions of the native speaker to
> sort out the degree of deference associated with particular expres-
> sions. To be sure, there would be general agreement that the use of
> 'You ought to do that right now' as a suggestion is far less deferential
> than 'I suggest that you do that fairly soon', but the use of such
> intuitions quickly breaks down on the more subtle cases, and judges
> are inconsistent. (Fraser & Nolen 1981:93)

The variability discussed by Fraser & Nolen closely resembles the kind
of variability encountered in empirical investigations of politeness: different judges produce different evaluations. But rather than treating this
variability *as variability*, it is interpreted as *inconsistency* and the data are
dismissed as a valid source of information on the notion of deference. The
researchers aim for a view of deference as a system, in an approach that is
conceptually biased towards the speaker and the production of behaviour –
note the association of deference with speakers' linguistic choices in the
quote. As we have seen, such a view does not accommodate hearer variability very well because of its intra-theoretical predictiveness, so when
the data do not fit the explanatory framework, the researchers dismiss the
data rather than dismissing the framework.

The same strategy is applied by Blum-Kulka in her investigation of
politeness in family discourse. When informants were asked to provide
examples of discourse in their own family that would be amenable to judgements of politeness, Blum-Kulka observes that:

> [i]n several cases, the examples stopped short of family discourse.
> 'Politeness is irrelevant when it comes to the family', said one in-
> formant. 'One should be polite with strangers, not with friends and
> family', said another. A few informants voiced contradictory views:
> 'politeness is very important in the family'; 'all family members should
> be polite to each other'. A second theme in the interviews was the
> assessment of the Israeli system of politeness. Here again, informants
> disagreed: some found the system satisfactory, others found it lacking
> in comparison with other cultures they have had a chance to observe.
> (Blum-Kulka 1990:260)

As Blum-Kulka is also looking for a system-approach (she refers to "the

Israeli system of politeness" in the singular), such wide disagreement does not fit the explanatory framework. This incompatibility is solved by claiming that:

> contrary to the credo of some of our informants, politeness considerations *do* figure strongly in families' ways of speaking. Hence in essence my argument is that family discourse *is polite*, but it enacts its politeness in culturally and situationally specific ways. (ibid.:261, original emphasis)

So again, instead of acknowledging the variability present in the data and designing a framework that will accommodate it, the data that do not agree with the framework are simply dismissed. Note the use of typographic stress to emphasize the contrast between her own claims and those of some of the informants, indicating that her strategy is not an unconscious and unintended methodological slip, but a fully conscious deliberate course of action.

All in all, this third strategy of coping with non-systematic variability is the least elaborated but the most straightforward: if the theory clashes with the data, then the data must be wrong – or rather the informants that produce the data must be wrong. Ordinary people are not to be trusted in their assessments of reality, so data should not be taken at face value. They should be approached with the necessary caution, and researchers should be ready to pass them by as they may not always provide an accurate picture of what reality is 'really' like. Nevertheless, as only some of the informants produce inaccurate assessments, there must also be some that *can* be trusted and relied upon for analysis. So according to the theories some people are 'right' and some people are 'wrong'. The question then of course is how can such a position be justified scientifically? How is this situation incorporated and explained? The answer is found in considerations of 'competence'.

4.3.4 Competence

The notion of competence has been used by linguists (in the Chomskyan tradition) as well as sociolinguists (such as Hymes and Gumperz). Although definitions of the concept differ widely,[8] it can generally be said to

---

[8] As the present account will not fall back on any specific definition of competence, and only a few aspects of its meaning are important for the present argument, a full-fledged exegesis of the notion will not be presented. For a more in-depth discussion see Figeroa (1994).

refer to 'knowledge a language user needs in order to be able to use language', whether this knowledge is seen as primarily a mental propensity (as in Chomsky's notion) or more as an ability based in and on practice (as in Hymes' interpretation). In commonsense terms, competence also has the meaning of a 'differential ability', that is, the fact that some people are more skilled at some tasks than others – a competent bricklayer not only knows how to lay bricks but also does it well in comparison with others who are not so good at it.

Although the notion of competence is hardly ever explicitly discussed by politeness theories, it provides a way of combining theoretical constructs based on shared cultural norms with empirical (hearer-)variability. Evidence for its possible use can be found in Werkhofer's (1992) discussion of the 'modern' versus 'traditional' views of politeness. Whereas in the modern view politeness is interpreted in individualistic and strategic terms (as in the Gricean approaches), the traditional view sees politeness as essentially governed by social forces (as in approaches where sociological variables are predominant). As will be clear from my argumentation up to now, these two views should be regarded as different dimensions of politeness, as both are present in each of the theoretical perspectives – albeit in roles of variable importance. In this light, Werkhofer's distinction represents the field of tension between the individual and the social dimensions of politeness.

Werkhofer argues for a theoretical conceptualization that would successfully unite both views. He sees politeness as a 'medium' that individuals can employ for their strategic aims. But because of its social and historical dimension, this medium also transcends the individual, and as such is endowed with a power of its own. Although individuals may use it strategically, they *"[...] will not be able to master the medium completely"* (Werkhofer 1992:193-194). Because of the complexity of any fully-fledged politeness system, the number of social identities that may be involved, and the complexities of the acquisition process, the user might not be able to gain a full knowledge of it, and *"incomplete mastery and/or knowledge of the system may induce the user to do things (s)he is not completely aware of and would, if (s)he were aware of them, probably not want to do"* (ibid.:195). Thus, within a culturally shared system hearer variability can be explained in terms of competence. People will differ in their evaluations of politeness for the simple reason that not all of them have a full and complete knowledge of the system.

Although the idea is mostly not directly discussed by the theories in question, it is implicitly present in different ways. For one thing, it would explain and justify the 'who knows best' strategy. Because the theories aim to capture the system in its fully-fledged complexity, their findings are bound to differ from the evaluations of at least a number of people. It also explains Fraser & Nolen's (1981:93) distrust of informants' metalinguistic talk about notions such as 'deference' as input for the conceptualization of such notions. And it is explicitly present in Brown & Levinson's Model Person, who unites all 'competent' members of a society/culture.

The idea is also compatible with the association of the system with 'normality' in its quantitative sense. The system explains what 'most' people 'normally' do – as not everyone is equally proficient, exceptions may occur. At the same time, the idea further clarifies and develops the association of politeness with a 'good upbringing', as becomes clear from Lakoff's discussion of the relation between linguistic expertise and social success:

> In a meritocracy such as ours, we believe that those who best demonstrate the ability to think and persuade should have the lion's share of power. [...] People who say things right, who plead their cases well, will be listened to and their suggestions acted upon. They will make the money, win the offices, find love, get all the goodies their society has to give. [...] Those whose linguistic powers are less potent fall by the wayside. [...] A great deal rests on the speaker's ability to use standard language and to tailor utterances to the physical and social context in which they occur: to know the rules of the culture. Those properties do not have as much to do with intelligence or benevolence as they do with having had a comfortable upbringing and a good education. (Lakoff 1990:296)

So, a 'good' upbringing consists of being properly taught the rules of the culture. And as the politeness system also consists of such cultural rules, being polite is a matter of 'proper' behaviour both in its technical sense (appropriate according to the rules of the sociocultural system) and in its moral sense (well-mannered). In this way Ide's claim that people with a "good upbringing" observe the politeness rules more strictly (Ide 1982:377), or Lakoff's claim that "most of us" are too "well-bred" to violate the rules (Lakoff 1977:89) become almost tautological, as the sociolinguistic and the moral systems overlap or even coincide. The specific implications of this overlap between the 'scientific' sociolinguistic system and the moral system will be discussed more fully in a later section.

The idea of variable competence could also explain the need for popular prescriptive literature on politeness – etiquette manuals. Not all people are equally proficient in politeness, and many (if not most, following Werkhofer's claim that full mastery of the system is a near impossibility) could be 'educated' further to perfect their skills. So there is a real need for such works, which explains their overall popularity. Coulmas (1992) reports on a 1981-82 survey by the Japanese National Language Research Institute which revealed that no fewer than 86% of the subjects felt they had less than adequate skills in using honorific language.

Finally, variable competence could even justify the observed practice of confining the theoretical analysis to the level of the cultural system, and not going from the cultural level back to that of individual behaviour. For obviously, if individuals are variably competent in using the system, their behaviour can only be a weak version of the cultural system. And because the latter is what politeness is really all about, it deserves the bulk of attention. Note that this practice is consonant with the Chomskyan attention to the 'ideal' competence system and its concomitant lack of focus on actual performance, or Saussure's emphasis on 'langue' versus 'parole'.

So it seems that the notion of (variable) competence can solve a number of problems identified in the predominant conceptualizations of politeness. However, it is not without its own problems. For if individuals cannot be expected to gain complete mastery of the system, the system would not work very well. As speakers could never be certain of whether a hearer has the same level of competence as themselves, they would have a difficult job deciding which strategy would be successful. And if they find that their strategy does not work, they can never be sure whether this is because of their own or the hearer's incompetence. For faced with an incompetent hearer even a fully competent politeness strategy would fail to have its desired effect. Analogously, a strategy may well be successful because it is used by an incompetent speaker to address an equally incompetent hearer. In the end it would be very hard, if not impossible, to ever find out who is competent and who is not. No one could ever be certain about their own level of proficiency because a valid touchstone for polite behaviour would be difficult to find – most people being (at least susceptible to the doubt of being) at least partly incompetent. In fact, no one could ever be sure about anyone's proficiency in the system.

Of course one could argue that this is where etiquette manuals come in, as they are authoritative works on the subject. But then again, the question remains where their writers get their proficiency. As the system is social in nature and origin, people cannot simply invent the rules. So the writers of the manuals must also learn what the system 'really' is from looking at the reality of interaction. But if people cannot be trusted because one may always be observing an incompetent interlocutor, the writers could never be certain they had learned anything 'true' about the system. And even if the possibility of gaining proficiency in the system did exist, there would be absolutely no point in trying to achieve this. For in everyday interaction few people if any could be expected to have full mastery of the system – or even be equally proficient as oneself – so proficiency would not constitute a social gain. It could never or only very rarely be put to good use, for if it were used to an incompetent user, it would most probably not have its desired effect – and may even have the opposite effect.

And if ordinary people can never be sure of gaining 'true' knowledge of the system, how can scientific theory? As a direct (and for sociolinguists rather annoying) consequence of the introduction of variable competence, the system would necessarily always remain elusive: since no one is fully proficient in it, there can never be any 'objective' experiential criteria for determining its characteristics or 'rules'. Because the majority of respondents could well (and may even be expected to) be 'wrong', such a system could never be adequately described, and it would be inherently indeterminable. If 86% of the Japanese feel they do not have an adequate proficiency in honorific language, what sense does an empirical investigation make? In the face of that much 'incompetence', does it still make sense to maintain that there is a system at all, as the world apparently turns on happily without people knowing about it, and without it playing any significant role in society?

4.3.5 Summary
Empirical data manifest a kind of variability that is not consistent with the notion of a shared system of norms, and none of the strategies called upon are able to deal with it in a sufficiently effective way. Although statistical analysis can 'smoothen the wrinkles' in the data enough to make variability practically invisible, it cannot make it go away. Any adequate theoretical framework still needs a return path from the averages back to the actual data that produced them. Systematic variability (increasing the systematic complexity of the theoretical model) simply produces the wrong kind of variability. While a more complex model may *look* better suited to accommodate variability, it still takes hearer judgements for granted and is thus unable to cope with variability in that area. The 'who knows best' strategy of siding with one or the other evaluative camp, claiming that this is the 'right' position while the others are 'wrong', obviously still leaves the question of how some can come to be right and others wrong when the system is supposed to be shared. And the answer to that question – competence – is not really up to its task either, as it introduces

more problems for a shared-system approach than it actually solves.

Although informants generally do agree that politeness is a normative phenomenon where speakers' behaviour is evaluated against a (shared) system of norms, these norms do not readily reveal themselves in actual empirical practice. So much variability is encountered that special methodological practices are called upon to reduce it to manageable levels, and to extract averages which can then be used as indications of the norms that are assumed to exist. The norms do not directly emanate from the data, they must be produced. Nevertheless, the commonsense conceptualization in terms of norms is retained, and as those norms need specific methodological practices in order to be found, they can be said to be *prior* to the empirical findings. They determine the valid empirical methodologies, of which the findings are the *result*. So although theoretical and commonsense models share the same ontology, neither of them seems to square with empirical reality. At the very least, that reality needs to be moulded to some extent in order to be interpretable by means of the models.

4.4   Culture

Ultimately, empirical hearer variability is left largely unexplained. There is always a certain amount of residual variability, consisting of those who are 'wrong', or of those whose notions fall outside the statistical average. The only point at which hearer variability is theoretically recognized and successfully accounted for is at the level of culture, it seems. So we should take a closer look at this notion to examine exactly how successful a concept it is.

4.4.1 Culture in theory
Culture is a notion that is often used, though seldom explicated to any great extent. It surfaces in each of the theoretical frameworks, as it is commonly accepted throughout the field that politeness differs 'from culture to culture'. Even essentially universalistic frameworks such as Brown & Levinson's include elaborate provisions to account for intercultural differences (1987:242ff). According to Brown & Levinson these differences can involve the general level of the weightiness (W_x) as determined by the sum of P, D and R; the composition of W_x, i.e. the differential assessment of P, D and R; the extent to which all or some acts are considered FTAs; the composition of the sets of members to which positive politeness is appropriate; and the distribution of strategies over the most prominent dyadic relationships.

Intercultural differences are not of the systematic kind, they do not just fine-tune an interculturally shared system. Rather they alter the basic parameters of the system, so that the system as a whole changes between cultures. A similar utterance uttered by a similar speaker to a similar hearer in a similar situation (as far as intercultural similarity can be determined and attained, of course) will be evaluated differently by evaluators from different cultures. So cultural variation is of the variable systems kind described in section 4.3.2.

Note however that this is only partially true. For Brown & Levinson's P, D, R and W_x factors, as well as FTAs, positive and negative face, and their associated politeness strategies are still claimed to be interculturally shared. Although their evaluations may differ, their role remains the same. Every human being has 'face'; cultures only differ in when and how face can be threatened or redressed. Likewise, each culture has the notion of an FTA; the difference lies in what utterances qualify as FTAs. So the ingredients of the politeness system remain constant, only the recipe differs. This is not only the case in purely universalistic frameworks such as Brown & Levinson's, but can also be found in more culture-relativistic frameworks, although there the shared components may be of a more abstract or vague nature. According to Ide, for example, the fact that politeness is made up of a Volition (conscious voluntary) and a Discernment (unconscious obligatory) part holds across all cultures; only the relative importance of these dimensions differs. Then again, the constituents of the dimensions seem to be constant, with honorifics belonging to Discernment, and what Brown & Levinson would call positive politeness belonging to Volition.

Although elements that are shared and elements that differ interculturally can be found in each and every theory, a detailed exegesis of this aspect of the frameworks will not be made, as it is of no consequence for the present argument. The point of interest here is that all theories to some extent incorporate the notion of a 'variable system' which can cater for hearer variability, and that this variability is associated with the notion of 'culture'. The system is thus essentially cultural in nature, since within a culture, sharedness remains intact. This raises the question of the nature and scope of a culture, and of the nature of cultural variation.

Vague culture
The first observation in this respect is that its scope is not defined very accurately to say the least. In Brown & Levinson's discussion of 'cultural variation' (Brown & Levinson 1987:242ff), the terms 'culture', 'society' and 'group' are used interchangeably. Sometimes the term 'subculture' is

also encountered, although it is not clear how it relates to the other three. A quick scan of the discussion of the relationship between their universal theory and culture-specific facts (ibid.:242-255, section 7.2) reveals a variety of terms associated with 'cultural variation', both abstract (terms for collectivities of people in general) as well as concrete (terms denoting specific collectivities). As for abstract terms, besides the already mentioned 'culture', 'society', 'group' and 'subculture', we also find 'subcultures within societies', 'some particular population in general, whether a group or a social category' and 'social population'. As for concrete collectivities, we find geo-political entities ('Westerners', 'Western cultures'); ethnic entities ('the Mbuti Pygmies'); political entities ('the USA', 'England', 'India'); geographical entities ('Java'); geographical parts of political entities ('western USA'); social classes in political entities ('different social classes in England'), in geo-political entities ('upper-class and lower class in some Western societies', 'middle-class Europeans', 'middle-class subcultures' in 'Western culture'), in a geographical region of a political entity ('higher castes in South India'), or in a geographical part of a larger geographical area in a political entity ('castes in a region of South India'); ethnic groups in a city ('New York Blacks'); gender ('women', 'men', 'Iatmul men', 'Iatmul women'); languages ('English' 'Swedish', 'French', 'Tzeltal'); languages within a geo-political entity ('European languages'), or within a historical timeframe ('nineteenth-century Russian'). All these abstract and specific collectivities can be subsumed under the single heading of 'culture', as becomes clear from the introductory statements of section 7.2 where Brown & Levinson specify its subject matter as:

> Here we ask, in what ways do our claims for pan-cultural strategies of language use fit the culture-specific facts [...]? (ibid.:242)

To find such a wide array of variously defined cultural groups within such a confined space may be exceptional, but it does set the tone for what we can find throughout the politeness theories and the whole field of related sociolinguistic literature. A short, non-exhaustive categorization of culture-defining characteristics reveals the following:

Language: Culture is practically defined in terms of language in Leech, in Ide and Matsumoto (Japanese), Gu ('modern Chinese', more specifically *"the language used by the mass media and taught at schools and to foreign learners"* Gu 1990:237), Blum-Kulka (Hebrew vs. English – 1982; 1987), Fraser ('the English-speaking world'), and Arndt & Janney (American English).

It can also be found in Wierzbicka, in claims such as: *"Cultural norms reflected in speech acts differ not only from one language to another, but also from one regional and social variety to another."* (Wierzbicka 1985:146). Olshtain (1989) talks of 'cross-cultural differences' and 'cross-cultural variance', while her data derive from 'Canadian French, German, Hebrew, and Argentinean Spanish'. Wolfson et al. provide a nice example by producing the following statement:

> Yet a *cross-linguistic* study of apologies may well reveal that the notions of offense and obligation are *culture specific*, and must, therefore, become an object of study in themselves. In examining data collected from speakers of different *cultural* backgrounds, we must keep in mind that situations, which elicit apologies in one *language* could easily fail to do so in another. (Wolfson et al. 1989:180, my emphasis)

Finally, the Cross-Cultural Speech Act Realization Patterns project (Blum-Kulka & Olshtain 1984; Blum-Kulka et al. 1989; Kasper & Blum-Kulka 1993b) and all the studies that have derived from it focus on eight languages: Australian English, American English, British English, Canadian French, Danish, German, Hebrew and Russian.

Speech community: Lakoff & Tannen (1979) introduce an abstract term not encountered so far, namely 'speech community', which is also used interchangeably with 'culture'. Meier does the same when discussing universality, but adds language and society:

> Each *speech community* has means to communicate deference, mitigation, directness, and indirectness, etc. It dare not be assumed, however, that these means will find functional equivalence across *languages* and *cultures*. The folk notion of one *culture* being 'more or less polite' than another can be ascribed to one *language* using linguistic forms, for example, that are associated with a different meaning in a comparable context in another *speech community*.
> Politeness can be said to be universal only in the sense that every *society* has some sort of norms for appropriate behavior[...](Meier 1995:388, my emphasis)

The term can also be found in Blum-Kulka & Sheffer (1993:198), while Leech uses the related term 'language community' (1983:84).

Ethnic group: Often particular languages are associated with particular ethnic groups, i.e. social collectivities not associated with political boundaries. Rhodes, for example, studies Ojibwa, a language spoken by *"an American Indian group of the upper Great Lakes region"* (Rhodes 1989:249) while Nwoye studies Igbo, a language *"spoken by the Igbo people of South-eastern Nigeria"* (Nwoye 1989:259). In other cases the overlap is not complete, as in studies of Black English (Labov 1972) or as when Brown studies politeness in Tenejapa, which is characterized as:

> a peasant Mayan community in the Chiapas highlands of southern Mexico, about 20 miles from the town of San Cristóbal de la Casas. It is a corporate community of Tzeltal-speaking Indians, in a populous rural area where there are many other Indian communities of Tzeltal or Tzotzil speakers, each of which maintains a strong ethnic identity distinguishing it from the others and from the dominant Ladino (Mexican national) culture. (Brown 1990:126)

(Geo-)political boundaries: Examples include Blum-Kulka's investigation of the 'Israeli' notion of politeness, and her intercultural work on Americans vs. Israeli vs. American-Israeli (Israeli immigrants in the USA – Blum-Kulka 1990, Blum-Kulka & Sheffer 1993). Gu's 'Chinese culture' and Ide's 'Japanese culture' also have an associative link with the Chinese and Japanese nations. The 'British' vs. 'Swiss' are studied by Watts (1989a, 1992b), who also uses terms such as 'American and Swedish cultural frameworks', 'a European/North American cultural framework' (Watts 1989a), or 'Western European or North American cultures' (Watts 1992a). German vs. American vs. Japanese culture is covered by Lakoff (1979), while she also claims that whereas Distance is the characteristic politeness strategy for 'Europe', Deference is characteristic for 'Asian societies', and as for Camaraderie, the USA can be divided into Eastern and Western (more specifically 'California(n)') parts.

Religion: Although perhaps of minor importance, religion is sometimes mentioned – if perhaps only indirectly – as a cultural factor. Blum-Kulka (1990, 1992; Blum-Kulka & Sheffer 1993) has done some research involving 'Jewish families', while Krummer (1992) also refers to religion when he traces Thai modesty to Buddhism.

Social class: Social class is another possible determinant of politeness systems. Historically, the notion of politeness can be retraced to 'courtly' language, and thus behavioural norms of 'the members of the court' (Burke 1993; Ehlich 1992). Mostly social class is combined with other factors, so for concrete examples I refer to the other sections (Blum-Kulka

& Sheffer 1993; Brown & Levinson 1987; Lakoff 1977). Ide (1982:377) notes that "lower-class people" tend to observe the Japanese rules of politeness "less strictly".

Historical-temporal dimension: Culture seems also to have a distinct temporal dimension. We have already seen how Burke (1993) discusses politeness in these terms. After claiming that in terms of good manners *"different cultures have their own ideals"* (ibid.:94) and that it is the anthropologist's or sociolinguist's task to *"discover what these ideals were or are"* (ibid.:95), he embarks on a discussion of such ideals in 'classical and medieval traditions', 'sixteenth-century Italy', 'seventeenth-century France', and 'eighteenth-century Britain'. Note the superposition of the temporal dimension on political boundaries. Other historical studies of politeness share a similar *modus operandi*. Sell, in his study of politeness and literary texts, attaches the temporal dimension to linguistic characteristics ('English-language cultures') as well as political characteristics (*"What, for instance, did 'prudence' mean in eighteenth-century England?"* – Sell 1992:109). Ehlich (1992) combines it with geo-political notions ('the Ancient Orient', 'the Ancient Near East', 'Ancient Israel', 'Ancient Greece and Rome'), with social class ('the members of the court' in 'the high Middle Ages'), or social class in combination with religion ('the secular upper classes in the Middle Ages'). Neuendorff also combines temporal with political characteristics in claiming that *"the action-patterns on which concrete actions of politeness are based differ from country to country as well as in the course of time"* (Neuendorff 1987:52). Watts (1992a) contrasts modern scientific approaches of politeness to the characteristics of the notion in 'eighteenth-century England'. Finally, Lakoff claims that Distance politeness *"has been our standard form of politeness for about a millennium"* and *"has been characteristic of the middle and upper classes in most of Europe for a very long time"* (Lakoff 1990:35, 37), while in thirteenth-century Europe politeness changed from a Camaraderie to a Distance model (Lakoff 1979:74). The relevant timeframe is not necessarily equated with a particular century, however. Keshavarz (1988) studies forms of address in 'post-revolutionary Iranian Persian', while Gu's 'modern Chinese' is situated in *"New China, that is, China since the founding of the People's Republic in 1949"* (Gu 1990:239). Finally, the relevant timeframe can be as short as one generation. Lakoff mentions intergenerational differences with regard to grammaticality evaluations, while Ide (1982:377) mentions the possibility of intergenerational differences in politeness behaviour and expectations, with older people expecting stricter observance of Japanese politeness rules than younger people.

As becomes clear from these examples, the defining characteristics of 'culture' are often if not mostly combined into more or less complex constellations. The list is all but exhaustive, and can be extended with practically any parameter deemed socially relevant. One needs only to think of Leech's 'schoolboy' ethics (1983:10, see section 2.2.3) to see that 'culture' can have a greatly variable scope. Yahya-Othman (1994), for example, studies politeness in the 'Swahili culture' or 'Swahili society', which is described as 'native speakers of Kiswahili, specifically in Zanzibar town, on the island of Unguja'. Lakoff conflates nationality, profession and social class, when she discusses the operation of 'Rule 1' in *"our society (American academic middle-class)"* (Lakoff 1977:89). Finally, Blum-Kulka & Sheffer apply almost all of the afore-mentioned social characteristics in the composition of their respondent database, adding 'education' and 'religious observance':

> The 24 families studied are all native-born, *middle- and upper-middle-class Jewish* families, with two to three school-age children. [...] The selection criteria were: (a) *college education* for both parents, (b) *professional occupation* for both parents, (c) European *family origin* for both parents, (d) being *religiously nonobservant*, (e) being *native-born Israeli or American*[...] (Blum Kulka & Sheffer 1993:198, my emphasis)

In their theoretical discussion this group is described as a 'speech community', while the aim of the study is to capture 'cross-cultural diversity' through the search for 'cultural differences'.

It must be emphasized, however, that culture is not *explicitly* theoretically defined in terms of the particular social characteristics used in each investigation. It is seldom explicitly maintained that people who fit some set of specific characteristics form a culture. Rather, the two are unquestioningly juxtaposed. Whereas in the theoretical discussion terms such as 'culture', 'society', 'cultural differences' or 'cultural variability' are used, when it comes to the empirical part of the investigation – or in non-empirical studies, when it comes to providing examples – one encounters phrases such as 'in language X' or 'among the Y'. The link is implicit. In fact, the notion of 'culture' is never theoretically examined or even discussed to any depth at all. It is used rather loosely, with its meaning simply taken as self-evident. Sometimes the different notions are explicitly distinguished from one another, as when Leech claims that the CP and PP *"[...] operate variably in different cultures or language communities, in*

different social situations, among different classes, etc." (Leech 1983:10).
Clearly, it would seem, a social class or a language are not 'cultures'. But
it would neither seem completely nonsensical to claim that upper and
lower classes exhibit 'cultural differences'. And this is exactly what happens in the literature: the differences found between speakers of different
languages, between different social classes, societies and so on, are all
labelled 'cultural differences'.

So in terms of their operational value or role within the theoretical
model, those notions can be and are used interchangeably. In Leech's
theory, for example, they are all subsumed under the notion of 'local'
constraints on language use, and so they all have the same theoretical
function: they are the limits of operation of the CP and PP. Analogously,
in all the other theories they form the level of abstraction at which the
system operates, and thus on which the norms, scripts, rules, etc. are assumed to be shared. Just as norms, scripts and rules were collectively
discussed under the notion of 'norms', so too societies, language communities and so forth, can all be discussed under the notion of 'culture'
because they share the same theoretical and operational status.

'Culture' thus becomes a very productive notion. It can be used to talk
about almost any kind of group, from the very small and local ('Tenejapa')
to the immensely large ('Western culture'), from the general ('Americans')
to the specific ('American west coast academic middle-class white males
over forty'). But this flexibility of the notion is at the same time its greatest weakness: it can denote just about anything, so its use is always vague.
What does it mean to speak of 'different cultures'? Where does one culture end and the other begin? With what precision can a culture be located?
These are not trivial questions considering the ontological role of the notion as the social level at which systems are shared.

Homogeneous culture

Regardless of their actual delimitation, cultures are by definition internally homogeneous – at least as far as politeness is concerned – because
they are the level on which the politeness system is shared. If behaviour
can be explained through cultural scripts in the heads of speakers, or rules
learned effortlessly in infancy, then all members of a culture can be supposed to exhibit the same or at least similar behaviour. Note that this is not
contradicted by the existence of systematic variability, as this kind of
variability is system-internal. No matter how complex the system may be,
it is still assumed to be shared throughout the culture.

As a consequence, the notion of culture cannot explain hearer variability below the intercultural level. A possible solution would seem to lie

in subdividing cultures into subcultures of various sorts. The fact that the notion of 'subculture' is sometimes encountered, and that various social characteristics such as social class, religion, gender or age are posited as cultural factors, indicates that many a theory has taken this route. However, as already discussed in section 4.3.2 regarding Lakoff's inter-generational variability, if this method were asked to explain all observed intracultural (hearer) variability, the system-based approach would eventually annihilate itself, and this may be one of the main reasons why there is so little in-depth theoretical discussion of notions such as 'culture', 'society', 'social class' and the like. For these notions are only useful as long as they remain vague and undefined, and as long as their theoretical implications are left unexamined. As such they are perfect partners for statistical averages: in all their vagueness 'cultures' seem tailor-made to account for the 'average' behaviour of a 'group'. However, they cannot be called upon to lead the way from the averages back to the underlying variability that produced those averages lest they annihilate themselves and destroy the very basis of the model that summoned them.

Indeed, upon closer inspection it would seem that cultures *are* in fact averages of some sort, or at least that is the only role in which they can really make any sense. Take any number of people who have something in common – let's say they are from the same country X – ask them to rate an utterance in terms of politeness, then either calculate an average of some sort or see what the majority of respondents have answered, and the result can rightly be said to say something about the culture of that group as a whole. Pick out any specific inhabitant of X, however, and his or her answer might very well be the opposite of the observed cultural average. Thus, although culture may be useful as an *abstract descriptive* notion, as an a posteriori derivative of the observation of behaviour across a whole group, it is not per se also able to function as a *concrete explanatory* notion, as an a priori causal factor for individual behaviour. Unfortunately, this is the very function it is asked to perform in current theories of politeness, through notions such as cultural norms, scripts, rules and the like.

Sampled culture

The fact that cultural norms can only explain 'average' (i.e. truly 'cultural') behaviour and that they lead to internally homogeneous cultures when used as an explanatory tool has a peculiar methodological effect. If cultures are homogeneous it is no longer necessary to perform the gargantuan task of querying all the Japanese or the Israelis. Instead, it suffices to take a relatively small sample to gather adequate information about Japanese or Israeli culture. One can take 8 Jewish-Israeli, 8 Jewish-American, and 8 Jewish-American Israeli immigrant families to find information about Israeli and American culture and any differences between them (Blum-Kulka 1990). And if one wants to be really careful to take any subcultures within the larger culture into account, one can interview 52 Israeli families about their concepts of politeness, making sure that they represent:

> [...] a wide spectrum of Israeli society. Families varied in terms of parents' ages (from early twenties to late fifties), socio-economic status (lower to upper middle class) and degree of religious observance. (Blum-Kulka 1992:256)

The working assumption thus seems to be that social class, age and religion are determinant characteristics of (sub-)culture, so that people with the same age, socio-economic status or degree of religious observance will have the same or very similar concepts of politeness. The size of samples used in politeness research varies between several hundred respondents, as in Ide (1992), to only a few per culture, as in Watts (1989a), who examines interaction in one British and one Swiss-German family. Watts does acknowledge that his data base is 'small and restricted', and admits that *"generalizations derived from empirical evidence can hardly be given on such a slender data base"* (ibid.:148), yet this does not prevent him from deriving rather elaborate conclusions about differences between the 'Swiss German cultural framework' and the 'British cultural framework'.

It is not my intention here to criticize sociolinguistic investigators for working with data samples rather than whole populations, as the latter would constitute a quite difficult if not entirely impossible empirical endeavour. I simply want to point out that sampling always involves the assumption of homogeneity at some level – the idea that people with the same social characteristics will have the same opinions and notions. A such, sampling is legitimized by, and itself also reinforces the legitimacy of, the theoretical notion of a shared culture.

Polite culture
The notion of 'culture' as it is currently used in scientific thinking is invariably equated with the positive rather than the negative aspects of a society – again, at least as far as politeness is concerned. This results from (1) the definition of politeness as belonging to the level of '(a) culture', (2) the conceptual bias of politeness towards the polite end of the continuum, and (3) the association of politeness with appropriateness. As a result, only polite behaviour can ever be culturally appropriate, while

impoliteness is somehow non-cultural in nature. The possibility and existence of impoliteness is never denied by the frameworks; it is readily
admitted that it occurs – either by accident or misunderstanding, or willingly and consciously – or that principles of politeness can be exploited in
order to deceive the hearer. Only, impoliteness and deception themselves
will never be explained in terms of cultural norms. The rules always and
only tell people how to be well-mannered, never how to be ill-mannered.
Apparently people have to find out about the latter by themselves, as culture is not going to tell them.

This may seem trivial at first sight but ceases to be when one considers
that norms and rules are explanatory factors for human behaviour. The
rules are ingrained in the mind and people rely on them in order to make
sense of other people's behaviour, as well as to determine how to act themselves. In this sense they are the very basis of social interaction, the fabric
of social community. As norms can only explain polite behaviour, culture
becomes polite behaviour only, while impoliteness is relegated to a phenomenon outside culture. Polite behaviour is part of the culture, impolite
behaviour is not. Remember how informants' complaints about impoliteness in Israeli public contexts were explained by Blum-Kulka as a lack of
cultural scripts. As a result, Israeli culture is a culture of polite people. If
people are not polite, there must be a gap in the cultural system. The same
phenomenon can be observed in any of the other theories. The cultural
norms always spell out to people how to be polite, never how to be impolite. As a pleasant bonus, cultures are certain to be 'good', 'positive' entities
where people are polite to one another, pay each other due respect and are
generally warm and friendly. In other words, cultures are good places to
live, and well worth being a member of.

The connection between culture and good manners becomes explicit
in several instances. Ide maintains that *"people with a good upbringing
observe the rules more strictly"* (Ide 1982:377), while Lakoff claims that
*"a culture has implicitly in its collective mind a concept of how a good
human being should behave: a target for its members to aim at and judge
themselves"* (Lakoff 1979:69), and that *"[m]ost of us, in most situations, are too well-bred to violate these rules: we know what trouble
we'd get into if we did"* (Lakoff 1977:89). So the qualitative aspect of
norms, together with the conceptual bias towards polite behaviour and the
association of the politeness system with the level of culture all work to
further enhance the positive definition of 'culture'. Culture is about good
upbringing, good breeding and good human beings in general. Culture is
not only a quantitative, but also an 'ethically correct' entity.

4.4.2 Culture in practice

The most important characteristics of the notion of 'culture' as employed in theories of politeness are its vagueness and its transformation from an observational into an explanatory notion. As the latter proceeds via the notion of sharedness, this notion too has a fuzzy scope. The net result is a rather ramshackle construction which looks solid from the outside, and is highly adaptable to cover all different kinds of observations, but is best not asked to carry too much practical explanatory burden. This can be illustrated by means of a few examples of how culture is applied in practice.

After defining polite behaviour in terms of cultural expectations for appropriate behaviour relative to social situations and role-relationships, Blum-Kulka claims that it is predominantly deviations from these cultural norms that will arouse attention, since appropriate behaviour is largely taken for granted and therefore goes unnoticed most of the time. Such deviations from 'normal' politeness (either too much or too little) may trigger conversational implicatures:

> Minimally, participants in an exchange will just notice if undue effort is being invested in 'being polite'; maximally, they will attribute to the speaker a hidden agenda of some sort. For example, a wife might interpret her husband's extremely polite behavior to her mother as a sure indicator of his dislike for his mother-in-law; within any given role-relationship 'unusual' politeness, by a child to a parent, say, or between spouses or friends, might be suspected as an attempt at manipulation. (Blum-Kulka 1992:276)

Since the husband's politeness to his mother-in-law deviates from the cultural norm for this relationship, his wife interprets it as conveying dislike for her mother. She can do this because the norms are shared between husband and wife. But if norms are cultural, sharedness must be extended to cover all members of the same culture. As this can reasonably be assumed to include the mother-in-law, she too can be expected to notice the deviation and make the same inferences as her daughter. So the husband ends up conveying dislike for his mother-in-law not only to his wife, but also to her mother. What is more, as they all share the same norms he must be aware of this! So if he *wants* to convey dislike, why not do so directly instead of going through the trouble of applying inappropriate politeness? After all, the net effect would be the same.

The traditional answer to this question would argue that the husband can always deny the inferences, and claim that his actual intention was literal: to convey politeness. But then again, if appropriate politeness is a matter of cultural norms, the application of inappropriate politeness would only lead the wife's mother to infer that her son-in-law is culturally incompetent, or at least not very well-mannered. So the latter's defence would amount to claiming cultural incompetence. And again, as all this is 'cultural', he actually knows this, so he consciously opts for a strategy that conveys information he actually wants to hide, with as his only escape route a claim for incompetence or ill-manneredness.

The only way in which he can really hide his dislike from his mother-in-law and get away with it is to apply the *right* amount of politeness. In that case, his mother-in-law would suspect nothing (or at least he could deny any suspicion successfully), and his wife, well, if he dislikes her mother she will know anyhow from private conversations, and will simply interpret his politeness as insincere. So the explanatory power of 'culture' is not very great in this example. On the contrary, it actually hinders an adequate account. For the explanation to hold – and even for the example to work at all – the theoretical construction of cultural norms must be abandoned.

Another example of how the vagueness of the notion of culture can blur an explanation that relies on it can be found in Lakoff (1990:163ff). As part of a discussion of the notion of 'culture clash', Lakoff recounts a scene from a Californian courtroom hearing in which a young man of Asian descent, "probably a Hmong tribesman", stands trial for having kidnapped a young woman whom he wanted to marry. Among the Hmong this is the traditional way of proposing marriage. The girl in question is held incommunicada until all parties come to an agreement: either the girl and her family agree to the marriage, or the whole thing is called off. Apparently this is what the man, who "evidently" was "a relative newcomer" to the United States, had done, but the girl or her family "had objected and taken legal steps to voice that objection". The defendant does not speak English, and communicates through an interpreter. The judge presiding over the case is reported to say "'You call it courtship, we call it kidnapping. Don't let it happen again. I will tolerate one culture clash, no more. Do you understand?'" The defendant nods to signal his compliance. Here are some quotes from Lakoff's further discussion of the incident:

> From the young man's perspective, things have become surreal. He is in a strange place, like nothing he has ever seen, nothing he can imagine. (It is unlikely his tribe back home had formal courtrooms like this one.) People are speaking a language he cannot understand; all he knows is that he is in trouble, big trouble. [...] He has been told to

wear his best clothing (or a passable suit has been found for him) – more signs that something portentous and strange is in the works. But he doesn't have the language to get his questions answered, doesn't even know how to form them, or doesn't dare.

[...]

Then how can we imagine a translation of the judge's English into Hmong? And how can what the interpreter says possibly be meaningful – in any way equivalent to the judge's intention – to the defendant? The judge is wise and caring, but helpless because of the constraints imposed on him by the legal system and the language barrier.

[...]

Culture clash, a phrase intelligible to most Americans, presupposes a society conversant with the idea of multiple cultures coexisting uneasily. What sense would it make, even without the language difficulty, to a man just recently torn from a society that knows only itself and its own ways? Do the words *culture* and *clash* exist in Hmong? And if they do, does the literal translation convey a meaning anything like that of the original? The defendant nods at the judge, but does he comprehend what he was told? Even if he knows he'd *better not do it again*, does he fully understand what 'it' was, or why he shouldn't? And how to translate 'you call it courtship, we call it kidnapping' into the language of a culture in which courtship *is* kidnapping? (ibid.:164-164, original emphasis)

Three remarks can be made about how 'culture' is used in this example, that show that it is not a straightforward, objective or scientific notion.

First of all, 'culture' does not have the same explanatory weight for Americans as opposed to Hmong. It is an overwhelming factor in the Hmong's behaviour, who is pictured as a 'cultural dope' whose actions are completely determined by his culture. He comes from a culture "that only knows itself and its own ways" – then how and why did he wind up in the United States? – and cannot cross the cultural barrier easily. American culture does not 'know only itself'; on the contrary, the judge can easily cross the cultural divide, and understands the defendant's actions from the Hmong as well as from the American perspective. As for the Hmong man, however, doubt is expressed as to whether he understands anything at all of what happens to him. How can he understand the American difference between kidnapping and courtship, as in his culture courtship is kidnapping? The absurdity of this question becomes obvious when the roles are reversed: How can the judge understand that among the Hmong kidnapping is courtship when in his own culture it is a felony?

A second remark is that the Hmong man and his culture are treated rather patronizingly. Although he presumably came to the United States through his own choice, he is reported to be completely bewildered and frightened. Everything is strange and surreal to him, like *"nothing he can imagine"*, as if his understanding and imagination were also limited. A "passable suit has been found for him"; apparently he cannot do this by himself (of course not, he doesn't have a clue where he is or what anything around him means). His grasp of the situation is paraphrased in childlike terms: he understands "he is in trouble, big trouble", or that "he'd better not do it again". The judge is never portrayed in such terms; his understanding is fully mature and covers all complexities of the situation.

Finally, this underestimation of the 'cultural Other' also appears from the explanation of the court case as a "culture clash". Apparently the girl's cultural background is not known, as she may be *"a more assimilated member of the same group or a member of a different culture with other marital traditions"* (ibid.:164). If she were also Hmong, it is hard to see where the culture clash lies, as she and her family must have known the man's intentions. Characterizing her as "more assimilated" to American culture is overly simplistic: as if she had suddenly forgotten all about Hmong culture, or as if her assimilation had caused her to see courtship the American way and to regard Hmong courtship customs as a felony. On the other hand, if the girl were from a different culture, the man will have known this. It is hard to imagine they had had no prior contact at all, with the man just grabbing a girl that looks suitable. Moreover, in Hmong courtship the man holds his future bride incommunicada "until an agreement is reached", which implies contacting the family and divulging marital intentions to them and to the girl. So again they must have known what was going on. In either case the cultural interpretation is too feeble to present an adequate explanation. Unless truly dim-witted, the man must have known American and Hmong courtship customs differ. Perhaps he had already tried the American way without success, and decided to use a stronger argument by going at it the Hmong way, but the family didn't give in and retorted by filing suit against him. In any case, it is certain that they didn't agree with the marriage proposal, or they would have arranged a marriage instead of a court case. Either they severely disliked the man and immediately pressed charges, or the man wouldn't take no for an answer and adamantly refused to let the girl go, turning the courtship into a real kidnapping.

Whatever their reasons, in none of these cases is the lawsuit the simple result of a culture clash. If the judge was able to understand the man's non-malicious intentions, the girl and her family can be expected to also have been able to do so – after all, they were smart enough to understand how to use the American legal system. A more plausible explanation would be one that avoids simplistic reasoning and regards the Hmong as human beings on a par with Americans. This means that they are able to see and understand cultural differences and react to them in a compassionate or aggressive way. Instead of being dominated by their cultural way of seeing things, the cultural Others can be seen to creatively exploit the situation, using the legal system and Hmong courtship customs as arguments in a dispute.

Whatever the precise nature of the case may have been, the cultural explanation by itself seems a rather simplistic one. Of course, this does not deny the existence of cultural differences. Clearly the Hmong have a quite different courtship tradition from Americans, and such differences may well be labelled 'cultural'. It is another thing, however, to attempt to turn those observational facts into explanatory concepts, as is done in politeness theorizing. As I have tried to show, trying to explain behaviour by means of the notion of 'culture' involves a very real danger of (over)simplifying reality to the point of turning active, creative human beings into 'cultural dopes'.

4.4.3 Culture in difficulty
So in the practice of reasoning and exemplifying, the notion of 'culture' tends to become rather blurred. If the seemingly *ad-hoc* uses of the term are taken seriously, the notion either annihilates itself, or it annihilates the conceptualizations it is asked to defend. A notion that can simultaneously denote any group of people based on any (combination of) characteristic(s) loses its operational value. On the other hand, if the notion were fully adjusted to the amount of empirical variability encountered, cultures would become so small that the notion of shared norms would lose its explanatory value and fail the explanatory role it is currently asked to fulfil.

Moreover, the assumed predominance of the cultural level presents the danger of reducing individual behaviour to the simple manifestation of cultural concepts. A few examples have shown how this may lead to rather simplistic explanations which do not hold very well under close scrutiny. Not insignificantly, cultural Others are more likely to fall prey to such simplifying practices than cultural peers. Together with the observation that culture is often called upon to account for positive aspects of behaviour but never for negative aspects, this leads to the conclusion that the notion is at best a non-neutral concept, and at worst a stigmatizing one.

4.5 Science and normativity

Norms are predominant in both commonsense and scientific conceptualizations. The question that must now be addressed is how theoretical and commonsense norms relate to each other. As appears from the foregoing discussion, the theories mostly seem to mimic commonsense normativity. In constructing a system of norms as the basis of politeness, they simply retain the normative nature of commonsense politeness in their conceptualizations. But what exactly is this 'normativity' of commonsense politeness? Politeness always involves an evaluative act where behaviour is judged in terms of (in)appropriateness, in terms of '(im)proper', 'well(/ill)-mannered' conduct. As such, it involves a distinction between 'right' and 'wrong', and thus constitutes a moral judgement, where the evaluator imposes a moral order on the evaluated by means of which he or she condemns or commends. This is especially clear when parents teach their children 'how to behave'. They encourage or discourage behaviour because it is 'good' or 'bad' respectively, where good and bad take the shape of 'polite/impolite', 'nice/not nice', etc. In this sense commonsense politeness has a clearly prescriptive edge: it has to do with what 'should (not)'.

4.5.1 Neutral theories

If an ordinary speaker's evaluation of (im)politeness involves a moral judgement, what does this mean for the theoretical perspectives? Clearly they too are involved in determining the (im)politeness of behaviour, as a large portion of their effort consists in laying out the norms and rules for polite behaviour. Are they also passing moral judgements? As discussed in section 4.1, most theories would claim not. Although some researchers such as Leech and Lakoff feel the need to explicitly deny any morally prescriptive side to their conceptualizations, in most frameworks the issue is left implicit. On the explicit level, two arguments against prescriptivism are deployed. One involves the distinction between ethical and linguistic-technical principles, the other the distinction between prescription and description.

Ethical vs. technical principles

The first argument holds that the norms of scientific conceptualizations are not moral or ethical in character, but represent linguistic-technical principles. Leech and Lakoff use this argument explicitly, but it is arguably also implicitly present in any of the Gricean approaches, as well as in frameworks that translate norms into technical concepts such as scripts, rules, etc. Leech's argument goes as follows. Although in everyday interaction principles such as the CP or the PP and their associated maxims would be interpreted as ethical norms, in scientific theory they become technical principles that explain how communication works, for example how speakers can 'mean more than they say' and be understood as such. The argument hinges on Leech's distinction between general and local principles: whereas locally the CP may be an ethical principle, as a general principle it is not. As discussed in section 2.2.3, besides sphere of application – general principles belonging to science and local principles to everyday life – the distinction also involves the role of contextual factors. Local principles take full account of contextual conditions, while general principles are valid in abstraction from those conditions – in the sense of 'without considering', 'regardless of' or 'leaving unspecified'. Being involved with general principles only, the theory thus claims to look at language without specifying or considering local social conditions (culture, situation, speaker and hearer, etc).

And this is where the argument runs into trouble. For in real life conversations are of course always and necessarily embedded in specific local conditions. As one can safely say that language exists only in (and for the purpose of) real life, claiming there is a general side to language, that language can be investigated in abstraction from local context is a contradiction in terms. Whereas isolated sentences may well be studied in abstraction from any context[9] – for example in terms of their logical structure – this is no longer possible when the field of investigation is extended to incorporate stretches of conversational interaction between speakers, especially when the investigation considers the inferential or assumptive processes of the interactants, which is exactly what Leech's theory does. In those cases interactants can no longer be imagined in abstraction from context, as the occurrence of specific inferences and assumptions always and necessarily depends on specific contextual circumstances.

Let me illustrate this with an example Leech adduces to exemplify the workings of the CP:

---

[9] Which of course is not entirely true, as sentences 'in abstraction from any context' only appear in certain specific contexts, namely those of scientific investigation and description.

(5)   A: When is Aunt Rose's birthday?
         B: It's sometime in April.
(Leech 1983:30)

Leech says about B's utterance that, although its direct sense is a proposition to the effect that Aunt Rose's birthday occurs in April, A will derive the additional meaning that 'B does not know the exact date of the birthday'. This additional piece of information is arrived at by means of the maxims of the CP. The inferential process goes roughly as follows. A notices that B does not provide the right amount of information in answer to his or her question – the exact date of the birthday. B has thus violated the maxim of Quantity. However, since A has no particular reason to suspect B of being deliberately uncooperative, he or she will assume that B's answer is motivated by some other maxim. This could be the maxim of Quality: if B does not know the exact date of the birthday, providing an exact date would amount to telling a lie, to a breach of the maxim of Quality. Therefore, in order to uphold the maxim of Quality, B must breach the maxim of Quantity. This line of reasoning can be summarized as 'assuming that B is being cooperative, if B does not specify an exact date, this means he or she does not know the exact date'.

Although this looks good at first glance, it is only a partial and highly locally biased explication. For whether or not A will arrive at the inference that 'B does not know the exact date' depends on the specific local circumstances under which the conversation occurs. If A is marking birthday dates of friends and family on a calendar or in an agenda, the inference is most likely to result, as an exact date is then required. But one could just as easily think of circumstances in which it would not occur at all. Imagine the conversation takes place on September 20, and that it is embedded in the following exchange:

(6)   A: I have this feeling that we've forgotten to send someone a
            birthday card.
            Isn't there someone in the family whose birthday is in
            early September?
         B: Not as far as I know.
         A: When is Aunt Rose's birthday?
         B: It's sometime in April.

B's utterance 'sometime in April' in (6) could now be heard as standing in contrast to 'in early September', which would render the assumption that 'B does not know exactly' irrelevant. The main effect on A would be reassurance that his or her fear is unfounded, which would make any inference about whether or not B knows the exact date unnecessary and thus highly unlikely to occur. Other circumstances in which the inference would not occur include cases where A knows or suspects that B does know the exact date but is unwilling to provide it for some reason. And as those cases involve A assuming that B is uncooperative rather that cooperative, it could very well be argued that the inference of 'additional meaning' in such cases requires an Uncooperative Principle (UP). The CP thus enables the inference of additional meaning only in some cases, while in others a UP would be required – or none, when no additional information has to be inferred beyond what is literally said. Consequently, the CP is no longer a general principle without which communicative understanding would break down, but rather a highly local principle, only valid for those cases in which cooperativity can indeed be assumed. Furthermore, as the analysis depends on the assumption that A and B operate according to the CP, the CP is not so much an assumption of A and B, but first and foremost of the researcher. Thus claiming that it is the general or normal case goes way beyond description, and does indeed involve a moral stance.

In short, because Leech's analysis must assume that the interactants make specific interpretations in order to make sense of concrete stretches of interaction, it must necessarily also assume specific (local) conditions. The analysis is therefore only valid in cases where those local conditions actually occur, and does not in any way represent the general case. The fact that the researcher picks out one specific case (cooperativity) and promotes it to general status involves a moral choice, as it amounts to saying that communication is basically a cooperative endeavour while in reality it often is not.[10]

Description vs. prescription

Leech seems to be aware of this, as he admits that the CP and PP do introduce certain values into the scientific analysis (ibid.:10; see also above, section 4.1). But he claims this does not present a problem *"so long as the values we consider are ones we suppose, on empirical grounds, to be operative in society, rather than ones we impose on society"* (ibid.:10). This brings us to the second argument deployed to fend off accusations of prescriptiveness: the theories merely *describe* the norms, they do not *prescribe* them. This argument can be found in most theories, as it is implicitly

---

[10] For the same point made by means of different examples, see Kandiah (1991).

present in the theoretical claim that the norms or rules posited by the theory describe what is 'generally', 'normally', or 'usually' the case for 'most' people in a culture. As Lakoff phrases it: *"We are not, as everyone should know by now, setting up prescriptive rules for the way people are supposed to behave [...]. We are describing what we see [...]"* (Lakoff 1977:86). Unfortunately, this claim is – again – not as innocent as it looks.

On the one hand, it has already been argued that empirical reality shows much more variability than is attested to by the theoretical conceptualizations. Informants are seldom unanimous, and some of them sometimes disagree completely with the norms statistically derived from the data. On the other hand, it has also been argued that the social level on which the norms are supposed to be shared, is extremely vague; it can denote all kinds and sizes of groups, and even involve continuous characteristics such as age. So when claims are made about 'the' Japanese, Chinese, Israeli, American or Western norms of politeness, it is far from clear whether – and far from plausible that – these norms truly hold for all the Japanese, Chinese, etc. A third factor to be considered is the existence and popularity of etiquette manuals which, as discussed above (section 2.2.6), point towards variability more than sharedness. So although the norms proposed by the theories may well be operative in society to some extent, they are apparently not operative for the totality of the population. A choice is being made between possibly conflicting norms – remember Blum-Kulka's claim that, contrary to what some of her informants say, dinnertime interaction *is* polite.

But even if the norms were to be consensually held throughout society, this would not automatically make the theories immune to the accusation of prescriptiveness. As Cameron (1995:3-11) explains, the distinction between descriptiveness and prescriptiveness is itself not unproblematic. Only think about the fact that descriptive works *par excellence* such as dictionaries are often used as normative sources of authority on how particular words should be used. The same can be said about the rules laid down in grammatical works: they not only describe what *is*, but also and primarily how things *should be*. The mere fact that dictionaries and grammars are used for language teaching and learning precludes a non-normative character, for in this role they serve a prescriptive purpose: they make sure that what the language *is* (according to the descriptions of the work) is also what the language *will be* for the student.

And if this is true for word meaning and grammar – aspects of language not readily associated with norms – it is all the more true for plainly normative aspects such as politeness. Scientific theories admittedly do not have the same practical role in everyday life as grammars and dictionaries, and thus do not have the same practical impact on everyday language use. Popular etiquette manuals rather serve this function, and their precepts are readily acknowledged to be prescriptive, both by their readers and by scientists. Yet scientists do exactly the same thing: they lay down the rules of politeness, they stipulate what politeness is and 'how to do it'.

Of course they are not always as specific as etiquette manuals. Fraser & Nolen and Watts hardly make any claims about the (im)politeness of specific utterances. But the reasoning still holds. For unlike in matters of physics – where the scientist's descriptive efforts can hardly be argued to dictate the laws of nature to the universe – in social and ethical matters, the dividing line between description and prescription is not only blurred, but disappears altogether. If someone says 'saying "thank you" to the shop assistant who helps you is polite', he or she is not only describing his or her norms of politeness, he or she is at the same time also taking an ethical stance, outlining norms against which people are judged. He or she is in effect saying: here is what I prescribe as 'proper behaviour'.

The reification of politeness

Besides the explicit arguments against prescriptivism in the previous two sections, a third one can be identified, although this is not a real 'argument' as it is never explicitly used as such by the theories. It is implicit in the sense that it is part of the conceptualization of politeness itself, or better: it is an ontological implication of that conceptualization. The notion of politeness as a 'shared system of norms' situated on the level of 'culture/society', which operates through 'social variables' that determine what is (im)polite for a given speaker/hearer combination in a given situation, and in which speakers can be more or less proficient, establishes what I will call the 'reification' of politeness. Politeness is regarded as a unique and objective system that exists 'out there' in reality, that can be discovered, manipulated and examined just as a physical object can. This view actually forms the basis of the description vs. prescription argument, as the latter already presupposes the status of politeness as an object that can be described neutrally, i.e. non-ethically involved.

The reification of politeness is so deeply ingrained in the theoretical frameworks that it can be found in almost any aspect. If politeness is not relative to the individual, it does not depend on his or her evaluation, which results in the powerless hearer and the loss of the evaluative moment. Politeness becomes an absolute characteristic of language use, which leads to the conceptual bias towards behavioural production, while it also establishes the sociocultural system of norms as an object to be discovered and learned about by individuals. The latter entails that people can be 'wrong' in their evaluations, which finds its way into the notion of competence, and leads to the conceptualization of impoliteness as misunderstanding or incompetence, and to certain methodological choices and practices – distrust of intuitive knowledge, the need for statistical empirical methods. It also provides a convenient way in which discrepancies between the evaluations of the theory and those of ordinary speakers can be explained and justified. Finally, an absolute and objective system can also be unambiguously described, leading to a general preoccupation with spelling out the norms, with determining the rules for 'how to be polite'. At the same time it also allows this practice to be an ethically neutral endeavour, as the scientist who describes an objective system is of course not him- or herself prescribing the rules contained within it.

4.5.2 Normative theories

So not only are the arguments adduced in order to escape normativity and prescriptivism not very effective, they only hold ground in the context of a reified notion of politeness, which results in a number of conceptual characteristics and methodological practices that were argued throughout the preceding chapters to be highly problematic. Consequently the question asked in the introduction to this chapter must be answered affirmatively: the commonsense normativity of politeness is unquestioningly retained in the theoretical conceptualization. In everyday interaction, judgements of (im)politeness are passed as if there do indeed exist absolutely valid norms (shared by the whole community) that form the grounds on which judgements are made. If a child were to ask why he or she has to say 'thank you' or 'please', the answer would probably not be 'because I say so', but rather some general statement like 'because it is polite (nice)' or, as one mother was reported to do in Snow et al. (1990:302, quoted above, section 2.3), by explaining that this is how the world works – by positing some kind of behavioural law. This idea of absolute norms and behavioural laws is simply retained in the theoretical models – translated into various kinds of linguistic principles – even though empirical data need substantial modification before such norms can actually be found.

As a result, the theories end up laying out the norms of politeness, stipulating 'how to be polite', and in doing so cannot escape the normative prescriptivism that is associated with such practices in everyday reality. As such, the scientist becomes a moral judge, an arbitrator of what is 'appropriate', 'good' or 'correct'. Even if the reified notion of politeness is accepted, the scientist still cannot escape laying claim to objective knowledge in the form of absolute competence in his or her description of the system of politeness. So in Nakamura's statement that:

> [e]xcessive use of these forms [beautification honorifics] by women, especially mothers and preschool teachers [...] has recently been the target of much public criticism [...]. Some women, in their effort to sound refined and polite, overuse beautification honorifics, using incorrect forms. (Nakamura 1996:244-245)

the scientist is actually claiming to be able to identify the right amount of beautification honorifics as well as the correct forms to be used – contrary to mothers and preschool teachers who can be wrong in their judgement of such matters. In the light of the normativity of commonsense politeness, this claim to perfect competence actually becomes a claim to moral authority. Analogously, the theoretical perspectives become normative endeavours when they produce evaluations of politeness and claim to do so in an objective, definitive and authoritative way.

In the light of empirical variability, this moral involvement of the models entails that they take sides in the ongoing moral debate that is everyday life: they choose one particular moral position and promote it to absolute or at least cultural status. Their side may be that of the statistically 'average' respondent, their point of view that of the 'majority' of society, they nevertheless remain particular points of view, which in practice leads to the silencing or even exclusion of other positions – all performed with scientific authority. Let me explain this by means of an example. In Kienpointner's (1997) as well as Culpeper's (1996) studies of impoliteness, the interactional practice of ritualized banter, reported by Labov (1972) as widespread among New York black adolescents, is classified as a form of impoliteness – mock impoliteness. However, in section 2.1.1 it was argued that this language practice is not regarded as impoliteness at all by the participants – on the contrary, it is reported to enhance solidarity. It would seem obvious that a clear line needs to exist between banter and insult, between banter and impoliteness, in order for such a practice to be effective. So where does the qualification of 'impoliteness' derive from? Such language use might indeed be regarded as impoliteness if it occurred between members of the white majority of New York, or perhaps between scientists. Although labelling such behaviour 'impoliteness' may arguably not constitute a moral condemnation by the researcher (indeed, it is *mock* impoliteness), it clearly does represent a morally involved point of reference. As the descriptive term derives from the ethical reality of the researcher (or the white majority), this description does not involve objective standards, but rather is embedded in the sociocultural, moral-ethical reality of everyday life. It is guided by standards outside the social group that is being described. Note that the same process is involved in stereotyping, where one group's standards are imposed on another – so that from an American point of view, the Chinese may seem 'modest' or even 'humble', while the Chinese may regard Americans as 'boisterous' or even 'aggressive' (Young 1994).

So in choosing one particular standard the researcher is siding with a particular party in the moral struggle over the definition of reality. But as one always needs *some* point of reference, perhaps this cannot be avoided. Indeed, if ritualized banter were described as 'sounding', this would also involve a particular viewpoint: that of the New York black adolescents themselves. But as this involves the standards of the group to be described, moral imposition could perhaps be avoided by confining oneself to strictly emic descriptions. However, with regard to politeness, I would argue that this merely shifts the problem to a smaller (intra-group) plane, where one would still be confronted with considerable variability of standards. Although based on empirical research, Blum-Kulka's claims about politeness in Israeli family interaction still disregard the opinion of some of her informants.

It may not even be a matter of groups at all, as can be observed from Kienpointner's discussion of 'sociable rudeness', a form of impoliteness that *"[...] is based on the fact that certain subgroups of a speech community can have a positive attitude towards rudeness"* (Kienpointner 1997:268). Although it can also enhance group solidarity, sociable rudeness is not the same as ritualized banter, as appears from Schiffrin's (1984) research, which as reported in Kienpointner:

> [...] found that Jewish couples tended to use strategies of communication which would be experienced as aggressive, non-cooperative behavior by other groups of the Anglo-Saxon speech community: preference for disagreement, increased volume, rapid tempo, persistent attempts to get the floor (Schiffrin 1984:318). Yet, the speakers interviewed by Schiffrin seemed to enjoy this conversational style as a means to enhance sociability. [...] Of course, Schiffrin also found that 'cooperation between speakers and support of speaker's selves, may not be too deeply buried beneath the surface forms of competition and threats to speakers' selves (1984:324). This is an important fact because otherwise it could be argued that this conversational style is only judged to be rude from an out-group perspective. (Kienpointner 1997:268)

In other words, and in more general terms:

> [t]he subgroups of a speech community which engage in sociable rudeness agree to experience their own behavior as at least slightly aggressive. (ibid.:268)

This aggressiveness is why – as Schiffrin claims – the interactants' support for one another must remain clear at all times. They only experience this form of rudeness as 'sociable' when it is clear that it is not 'true' rudeness or aggression. But on the other hand, this also means that as long as mutual support *is* assured, interactants will not experience each other's behaviour as truly 'rude' (although they may find it aggressive or competitive). So as long as mutual supportiveness is assured, i.e. *within the interactional context of what Kienpointner calls 'sociable rudeness'*, rudeness is not the evaluation actually made. Again, describing this behaviour as 'rudeness' or 'impoliteness' implies an outsider viewpoint, not in the sense of an 'out-group' – the same interactants would also make the evaluation of rudeness in different interactional contexts – but one of interactional context.

But even if one is rigorous enough to confine the analysis to the strictly emic viewpoint, including only those interactants that agree with a certain description of behaviour, and only those specific interactional contexts in which the description is actually made, one still ends up with a description of behaviour from a particular viewpoint, i.e. the scientist still ends up taking the viewpoint of a particular hearer. So it seems that the problem of moral involvement of descriptions of politeness simply cannot be avoided. It is not a problem of numbers, it is a problem of principle. (Im)politeness is inherently a matter of moral evaluation, so whenever anyone (everyday speaker or scientist alike) uses those terms to describe someone else's behaviour, morality inevitably rears its head.

Terms such as 'polite' and 'impolite' can never really be said to merely describe behaviour, since their use always involves a moral evaluation and thus a morally involved position. It may not necessarily constitute a conscious condemnation of the other's behaviour, but it cannot escape the implication of some(one's) standard being used for evaluation. That is, of course, only if one insists on using those terms 'descriptively'. I will come back to that later.

4.5.3 What's wrong with normativity?

If moral involvement is practically inevitable, perhaps instead of trying to avoid it we might just as well embrace it. Normativity might be held in check by being conscious of its presence. If we cannot but make a choice, we should at least make it knowingly and responsibly. But then the problem still remains of *what* choice to make, which position to take in the description of everyday moral-ethical reality? If our words will always constitute a 'voice', we will not only always speak *for someone*, but also *against* someone, albeit at best only through neglect. All the more so as our 'descriptions' have 'scientific' authority. Could we really carry that burden?

At least some think we can. In a re-analysis of a job interview from Gumperz' film *Crosstalk* (Gumperz et al. 1979), Kandiah (1991) interprets Grice's Cooperative Principle in explicitly moral terms. In the interview, Mr Sandhu, an Indian immigrant to England with a university educational background, is applying for a full-time job as a librarian at a college named Middleton College. Since he came to England, Mr Sandhu has spent 14 years in manual jobs and as a bus conductor. Having obtained a professional librarian's qualification and sending out 150 applications, he has recently acquired a position looking after materials in a training resource centre. However, as this is only a temporary position which is about to expire soon, Mr Sandhu has sent out another 50 job applications, resulting in 2 job interviews, the second of which is the one at Middleton College. Mr Sandhu does not succeed in getting the job, however. It is an uneasy interview, in which neither party is very cooperative. Mr Sandhu's answers are interpreted as 'uncooperative' and 'evasive' by the interviewers, who gradually become more and more impatient and unsympathetic towards the applicant. In the end it looks as if they are searching for a reason not to hire him. Kandiah disagrees with Gumperz' analysis of the interview as an instance of communicative breakdown due to intercultural misunderstanding, i.e. a linguistic-technical communicative failure. Kandiah convincingly demonstrates that such an analysis would be inadequate and unrealistic, as it ends up treating the interactants as 'cultural dopes' rather than as creative and intelligent human beings – in an argument similar to the above rejection of Lakoff's analysis of the Hmong courtroom case (section 4.4.2). He nevertheless acknowledges that the job interview does constitute an interactional 'failure' of some kind, and argues that an adequate theory should be able to capture this. His own effort turns to Grice's Cooperative Principle. After arguing that it cannot be considered a linguistic-technical principle on the basis that (1) it only accounts for a part of empirical reality, namely interactions in which participants are indeed being cooperative, (2) that uncooperative interactions do not constitute technical communication failures at all in that in such cases the interactants clearly do 'understand' each other and (3) that such interactions can be accounted for without reference to the CP, Kandiah concludes that its validity must therefore be sought elsewhere, and so:

> [...] we eventually arrive at the realization that the most plausible
> source of the validity of the principle lies, in fact, in something which
> is far larger than the theory itself and which in a sense may be consid-
> ered to be outside it, namely morality – issues of right and wrong, of
> justice, of equality, of the integrity of the individual person, etc. The
> violation of the cooperative principle in the job interview marks the
> exchange as a failure because this violation reflects a larger violation
> by the participants of each other, a failure of understanding in a fun-
> damental moral sense. (Kandiah 1991:370)

This interpretation fully embraces the values which, as Leech acknowledged, the CP brings into the analysis, and even makes them the *leitmotiv*
of the scientific investigation. In Kandiah's interpretation, the CP is converted from a linguistic-technical into a fundamentally moral principle.
But the analysis does not stop at acknowledging the moral nature of the
CP. It is not enough to simply acknowledge the morality involved in language use and then try to find a way around it. Morality should itself
become the basis of the scientific account, and the analysis should be one
in terms of *"[...] issues of right and wrong, of justice, of equality, of the
integrity of the individual person, etc., all of those various issues that may
be brought together under the more encompassing label 'ideology'"*
(ibid.:370-371). Because no analysis can ever escape moral involvement
in describing social reality (as reality itself is essentially moral), any claim
to objectivity actually imposes a rigid moral order on the otherwise fluid
moral reality it describes. A specific momentary state of the moral order is
captured and promoted to objective fact. The fixed moral order resulting
from such a description effectively denies the nature of social reality
as a moral struggle. What is more, this depiction of social reality as a
fixed state:

> implicitly makes a case for the preservation of the status quo, some-
> thing which the underdogs have always tended to find as biased and
> unreasonable as the top dogs have tended to find objective and ra-
> tional. (ibid.:372)

Scientific objectivity thus becomes the implicit promotion of the status
quo, which amounts to a reactionary moral stance.

As already argued in section 2.1.1, the 'moral struggle' aspect is highly
important in politeness, both at the macro- and micro-social level. Should
we then follow Kandiah's example and embrace the moral involvement of
our analyses by taking an explicit moral standpoint? I would argue against

such a position, as scientific research would become a moral investigation involved in approving and condemning, an explicitly prescriptive endeavour not different from that of etiquette manuals (except perhaps in popularity). And as will be clear from the discussion so far, this would amount to doing explicitly what I have criticized the frameworks for doing implicitly. Besides, an explicit moral standpoint is not an analytical requirement, it is not necessary in order to be able to understand what is going on in interaction. It suffices to acknowledge and take account of the moral aspect in order to see the social struggle character of any situation. A full understanding of Mr Sandhu's job interview can be attained by simply bringing aspects such as race, power and discrimination into view; it is not necessary to also *condemn* the situation as a moral failure, as Kandiah does. Although the researcher is of course entitled to a moral position – as long as he or she is explicit about it – such a condemnation by itself does not teach us anything about what the interactants are actually doing, about the social mechanisms behind linguistic reality.

In this light, a politeness theory that mimics the interactants' behaviour and tries to make scientifically grounded moral judgements becomes rather a pointless exercise. Just as in Bourdieu's example (see above, section 2.1.2), where a definition of 'ethnic identity' in socially and politically involved terms loses sight of the argumentative nature of the notion and of the social world altogether (as it accepts the objective reality of the concept and loses sight of the fact that it is a discursive reification), so too an account of politeness in morally involved terms implies the reification of a morally argumentative notion – and position – into an objective reality. So rather than letting moral issues inform our research efforts, we should turn them into an object of study. Although we should embrace normativity by letting it into the analysis, we should guard against becoming involved in the normative reality we are studying. The same suggestion is made by Cameron (1995) in an investigation of 'verbal hygiene' – a notion that covers all kinds of prescriptive practices involving language use. Although her study does not cover politeness, it would obviously fit in nicely as a form of verbal hygiene. Cameron argues that prescriptivism can be avoided by not attempting to arbitrate between different prescriptive positions, but rather to *"pose searching questions about who prescribes for whom, what they prescribe, how, and for what purposes."* (Cameron 1995:11). So if we really want to 'describe' politeness, we should study it as a form of prescription: what it does, how, when and for whom. Only by describing existing voices *as voices* can we avoid becoming ourselves a voice in the moral struggle that is society.

4.6 Summary

In this chapter I have examined the notions of norms, normativity and as a corollary, culture. Although the term is not always used explicitly, 'norms' in one form or another can be found in all the perspectives. The common-sense idea that politeness is a matter of socially shared norms is retained in the scientific models, where those norms are translated into social/cultural principles that guide language behaviour. Norms are thus not relative to the individual, but become absolute, objective entities operating on the level of society/culture. Politeness is seen as a system of such absolute norms that needs to be internalized by the individual through socialization.

Shared norms do not readily manifest themselves in empirical research, where variability seems rather to be the norm. In order to be able to extract norms from empirical data, those data first need to be processed. Various statistical methods are called upon, all leading to 'averages' that can be translated more readily into norms. Any remaining variability is handled in one of three ways: by introducing social parameters that cater for increased systematic variability, by interpreting it in terms of (in)-competence or simply by declaring it to be 'wrong'. Of these methods only the notion of competence can cope with non-systematic hearer variability, but then only at the cost of destroying the fundamental notion of a 'shared system' of politeness.

As sharedness manifests itself on the level of 'culture', this notion was also examined more closely. The analysis revealed a highly versatile concept, but one that is never rigidly defined, and thus too vague to be of practical value. Although its vagueness squares well with the idea of 'average' group-related norms, it does not perform well as an explanatory concept, at best hindering an adequate account of interaction, at worst leading to the reduction of human beings as mere manifestations of cultural characteristics.

The particular way in which the theories handle the normativity of politeness leads them to become morally involved in the world they attempt to describe. Although various arguments are used to avoid prescriptivism, these are not very effective and only hold in the light of a reified notion of politeness with all its associated problems. The only way in which normativity can be adequately tackled without reverting to prescriptive accounts is by making it the object of research. But this in turn precludes traditional descriptions of politeness that spell out the norms of a particular society, leading instead to the study of politeness as a factor in the moral debate of social life.

Chapter 5: Social and psychological issues

This chapter will bring together a number of different observations made throughout the analysis, about the implications of various aspects of the theoretical models for speaker and hearer and for the nature of social reality. I will argue that they combine to form a coherent social-psychological model underlying all of the frameworks. The questions addressed in this chapter thus concern the images of man and society that are implicitly projected by the politeness models. These images are not necessarily also explicitly endorsed by the theories, but rather result from the conceptual choices made in their interpretations of politeness.

5.1 The social

In a critical review of sociolinguistics, Williams (1992) identifies a structural functionalist undercurrent in most contemporary sociolinguistic research traditions. With this qualification Williams refers to the work of Talcott Parsons (e.g. 1966, 1967, 1968 [1937], 1968 [1951], 1970, 1971), an influential American sociologist whose ideas on the nature of society, which go back to those of Weber and Durkheim, have spread to other fields of scientific thinking. Although Parsons is never mentioned by any of the politeness theories under discussion, many characteristic traits of Parsonian Structural Functionalism can be recognized in their conceptual make-up. As such Parsons' social model functions as an implicit default social theory (or *doxa* in Bourdieu's terms – 1977:164) for current politeness research, manifest in aspects that are not necessarily explicitly discussed, but taken as self-evident.

Because Parsons' ideas are sufficiently well-known, and a full-blown exegesis of Structural Functionalism would lie beyond the scope of the present study, only those points relevant to politeness theory will be discussed. So at the risk of grossly oversimplifying Parsons' ideas, let us take a look at how they relate to what has been argued so far about politeness theory.

5.1.1 The Parsonian normative order

The starting point of Parsons' social model is his theory of human action, which comprises four basic 'action systems', each referring to distinct aspects of human reality: the behavioural system (human physical-anatomical characteristics, physical needs, etc), the personality system (psychological aspects such as aggression, affection, etc), the social system (human collectivities on various levels of generality) and the cultural system (symbolic aspects of human interaction such as values, beliefs, etc). Although distinct, these systems are closely interrelated, with each one incorporating aspects of all of the others. For example, the personality system is related to the physical system in that personal goals are a function of physical aspects such as the need for food or the urge to procreate, while psychological aspects also determine how physical needs are expressed or gratified. The personality system is also connected to the social system, with social structure providing opportunities for the satisfaction of personal goals, while the make-up of social structure in turn is determined by the nature of those goals. Finally, the personality system also interacts with the cultural system in that cultural beliefs are both 'answers to' and 'channels for the satisfaction of' psychological needs. However, regardless of these close mutual relationships each system always retains its distinct nature, and cannot be reduced to – or completely explained by – any or all of the others.

The cybernetic hierarchy

In terms of 'behavioural control' the four systems stand in a distinctive unidirectional relationship: they form a 'cybernetic hierarchy' (Parsons 1966: 9,14) in which the cultural system occupies the highest position, followed by the social, personality and behavioural systems respectively. Although mechanisms of cybernetic control operate from the bottom up as well as from the top down, both types of control are of a totally different nature. The bottom-up influence is conditional, and thus a rather passive force: each lower order system defines the limits within which higher order systems must remain. Psychological drives are geared to the satisfaction of physical needs, social systems must contain mechanisms that satisfy physical needs, etc. The top-down influence on the other hand is a regulative and more active factor. Higher order systems organize, structure and give meaning to the lower ranking systems. Cultural beliefs and values determine the actual structure of social systems, which in turn organize the fulfilment of psychological and physical needs.

These differential control mechanisms result in an overall top-down influence: higher systems influence lower systems more actively than vice versa. In combination with the distinctive nature of each system, this leads to a view where social reality is not only a reality *sui generis*, independent of the individual level (Parsons 1971:7), but also takes precedence over the individual – because the latter occupies a lower position. In the Parsonian world social reality controls individual behaviour, and culture is "*not conceived of as constituted by an aggregate of individuals, nor by*

individuals themselves, but rather by an atemporal and symbolic organi-
sation of ideas, values and norms" (Williams 1992:48).

Culture and society

As part of the social system, 'society' is distinguished from other social
systems in being *"[...] characterized by the highest level of self-*
sufficiency relative to its environments, including other social systems"
(Parsons 1971:8). Self-sufficiency should be interpreted in terms of 'stability of interchange relationships' with other social systems, and the
ability to control these relationships so as to successfully cope with 'dis-
turbances', or to shape them favourably according to society's own goals.

Besides being stable and self-sufficient, Parsonian society is also rather
vague. According to the above definition, modern multinational industrial corporations (which in Parsonian parlance are also 'social systems')
would qualify as 'societies', given their ability to survive, their power to
ward off threats or shape their environments according to their own wishes,
and their relative independence of politically defined societies. This does
not seem to be Parsons' intention, however, as he only includes 'political'
societies. But then again, he mentions political collectivities on various
levels of generality, spanning the whole range from small kinship-defined
groups over ethnic-territorial groups to large exclusively politically defined nations. Sometimes even broader terms such as 'medieval society'
or 'European society' are used, while the importance of religious differences is also mentioned (Parsons 1966, 1971).

Cultural systems are equally vague, with references to "Christian culture", "the secular culture of the Renaissance", "modern secular culture"
or "Western Christendom", (1971:29, 30, 52, 141). In definitional terms,
as 'organized patterns of ideas, values and norms' their delimitation is not
very clear either. Just like societies, it is unclear precisely *when* a given
cluster of norms or ideas qualifies as a fully-fledged cultural system – the
kinds and number of ideas/norms that need to be involved, the nature and
tightness of their clustering or the scale of the population throughout which
they are spread.

Social structure

On the supra-individual level, Parsonian society thus consists of a cultural and a social component.[1] Whereas the cultural refers to the abstract

---

[1] The personality and behavioural systems also include supra-individual aspects, as the latter refers to *species-specific* human physical characteristics
and the former includes references to *generally human* (psychological)

ideational world – the organization of ideas – the social component refers to the concrete 'physical' organization of society. Social structure comprises the 'implementation' (ibid.:8) of the ideational cultural system in social reality through a system of concrete social relations. And as culture occupies the highest position in the cybernetic hierarchy, social structure becomes the "realization" or "institutionalization" of the cultural value-system (ibid.:13).

Social structure manifests itself on two 'levels'. On the one hand society is made up of a number of different social systems, each with their own characteristics and relationships to one another. Examples are the family, economic organizations or political systems. On the other hand this structure of groups translates into a system of social relationships between individual members of those groups, in the form of 'social roles' with associated statuses. For example, within the educational system, individuals may be teachers, students, principals, etc., while these same persons are fathers, mothers, sons, sisters, etc. in the family system. Social roles are therefore the central connection between the supra-individual and the individual level, as they implement the social and cultural systems in the individuals making up that system.

This is accomplished via normative 'expectations': cultural values linked to social roles create behavioural expectations ('norms') about what an individual in a particular social role should (not) do. And so social roles also engender patterns of evaluation, as an individual's 'performance' can be measured against role-expectations. Norms on the one hand provide the necessary legitimacy for the social structure by means of their reference to values (Parsons 1966:11), while at the same time also reinforcing those values by implementing them as a practical aspect of everyday (inter)action. As such they lie at the heart of the whole system of society:

> [t]he core of a society, as a system, is the patterned normative order through which the life of a population is collectively organized. As an order, it contains values and differentiated and particularized norms and rules, all of which require cultural references in order to be meaningful and legitimate. (ibid.:10)

---

characteristics. However, as they are more directly relevant to the individual level – their influence on the supra-individual level being of the conditional kind – they can be regarded as primarily 'individual'.

Consensus

For the Parsonian normative order to function properly, a general consensus over the relevant norms is required. Without it, norms would no longer be able to perform their regulative function for the social community – they would lose their ability to provide unity and cohesion. The independent nature of social reality coupled with its high position in the cybernetic hierarchy imply that this consensus is both 'real' and 'imposed'. It is a real consensus in that it involves people thinking about things in the same way – as opposed to a working consensus in which people may think about things quite differently but where in the practice of interaction these differences lead to the establishment of a practical *modus vivendi*. It is also an imposed consensus, because culture as an independent system is an a priori factor structuring individual behaviour. Culture is an empirically "objective" system that needs to be learned about by each individual (Parsons 1966:6) where 'learning' is to be understood as *"[...] the incorporation of cultural pattern elements into the action-systems of individual actors"* (Parsons 1968 [1951]:16).

Although the Parsonian order does allow for a certain amount of individual variability (primarily because of differences in learning abilities/ possibilities and differential exposure to cultural elements), this variability is a matter of different *degrees* of sharedness, and does not affect the basic premise of a 'real' cultural consensus. Individual variability arises because different individuals may have incorporated different elements or areas of the total cultural system, or because different individuals have incorporated the same elements or areas to different degrees.

What is more, the 'basic condition' of a 'stable' interaction system (society) is one of sharedness, where in the practice of interaction the actor's conformity-deviation balance tends to coincide with his or her gratification-deprivation balance (ibid.:38) – so that conformity with cultural values leads to favourable reactions of Alter and thus to gratification for Ego. This mechanism leads to a situation of extensive integration between the cultural and personality systems, which is a prerequisite for a society's self-sufficiency and survival (Parsons 1966:10; 1971:9). So although sharedness may not be total or absolute, it does by definition apply to the majority of the population.

Functionalism

Functionalism refers to the fact that all of the action systems form a cohesive, functionally integrated whole: society – which can thus be regarded as the 'ultimate' social action system. As an independent system, society has its own goals and path of evolution. In the Parsonian world, this goal is stability: internally society strives towards social order, externally towards continuance. The different subsystems all contribute to these goals, all playing a functional role in maintaining the societal system. For example, the cultural system provides the values and norms that legitimize the societal system, while the social systems provide the structure through which these values are implemented – the mechanisms of socialization, of social control and enforcement, etc. Such functional relationships run in all possible directions, and between all of the action systems. For example, cultural norms and values must also cater for the exigencies of the personality system (address social and psychological needs) and the behavioural organism (address physical needs) and must remain in tune with existing social institutions; the different social systems must be in line with cultural values, while also providing the individual with rewards for conformity with cultural norms through the gratification of psychological needs (social esteem) and/or physical needs (decent housing, food, etc.); and so on around the matrix of logical possibilities. In short, all subsystems of a society must work together to form a coherent, self-sufficient system that can ensure its existence in space as well as through time.

However, as it is the (autonomous) social system which strives for stability, and not its individual members, the rules and norms of the system do not 'come naturally' to those individuals. On the contrary, the individual needs to be socialized into the system and continually motivated to maintain conformity with the norms, either through gratification (positive stimulus) or social control (negative stimulus or deprivation). The individual's natural, spontaneous behaviour does not conform to the norms:

> [...] the orientations which an actor implements in his complementary interaction in roles, are not inborn but have to be acquired through learning. We may then say that before he has learned a given role-orientation he clearly tends to act in ways which would upset the equilibrium of interaction in his incumbency of the role in question. (Parsons 1968 [1951]:205)

A stable and structured social system is not something that arises naturally out of human interaction, but rather depends on mechanisms for learning the rules of interaction, as well as mechanisms to motivate people to keep on following those rules. Without such rules and mechanisms of enforcement, people would tend to destroy the system.

Evolution and change
In a view where societies strive towards internal and external stability, the

conceptualization of change becomes more or less problematic, especially in a top-down interpretation where the social/cultural is higher on the cybernetic ladder than the individual. As Parsons himself says, owing to the nature of the model, the continuance of the social equilibrium is a theoretical presupposition, and therefore non-problematic (ibid.:481). However, change is not simply excluded from Parsonian theory. As a brief glance at history will confirm, it would be impossible for any self-respecting social theory to claim – even implicitly – that societies are static entities. The question then becomes one of how evolution and change can be incorporated in a model based on consensus and stability.

The conceptual make-up of the Parsonian model has repercussions for both the nature and the possible causes of social change. Because the conceptual focus is on the state of equilibrium, change mostly involves the evolution from one (initial) state of equilibrium to another (terminal) equilibrium (ibid.:483). However, the equilibrium itself can also incorporate an element of change. Such systems where change is 'institutionalized' – exemplified by scientific investigation (ibid.:491) – are said to involve a 'moving' rather than a 'static' equilibrium.[2]

As for the causes of change, in a top-down cybernetic system individual human beings cannot bring about cultural change, so the burden of evolution comes to fall on culture – on the system – itself. According to Parsons, there can be multiple causal factors:

> [t]he impetus to a process of change may perfectly well originate in the development of a cultural configuration, such as a development of science, or of religious ideas. It may also perfectly well originate in a change in the genetic constitution of the population, or a shift in the physical environment such as the exhaustion of a strategic resource. […] Another very important possibility lies in the progressive increase of strains in one strategic area of the social structure which are finally resolved by a structural reorganization of the system. (ibid.:493)

Note how the causal factors mentioned are all supra-individual or impersonal, not only the non-man-made, 'physical' factors such as resource depletion or genetic changes, but also the man-made factors, which are stripped of their 'individual-human' aspects: change can result from "a

---

[2] It must be noted that other research, notably Kuhn (1962), would suggest scientific investigation fits the first category more than the second, i.e. as a system where change occurs as a movement from one state of equilibrium to another.

development" of "science" or "religious ideas", or of "strains" in "the social structure". These processes are somehow inherent in the system itself, and their nature is likened to the principle of entropy in classical mechanics (ibid.:501). They are not the result of active contributions by individual human beings, at least not in any causal sense; individuals are involved only in the rather passive role of learners, as the objects rather than the subjects of social change:

> Such changes may, even over the span of active adult life, be considerable, so that the expectations of an early period must be considerably readjusted to meet the requirements of a later one. Here again the process can be successful only through the operation of learning mechanisms in the context of socialization, of further role-specification of orientations. (ibid.:242-243)

Exactly how cultural configurations or religious or scientific ideas come to change, or exactly how these changes spread and lead to altered role expectations is never addressed. The discussion is confined to what happens after a change has taken place. For example (ibid.:505ff), a change in the scientific or technological field is said to have repercussions on the role-structure of society (new occupational roles emerge and old ones become obsolete), on the organizational structure as a whole (increasing division of labour leads to more elaborate and thus more formalized organizational structures), on the power structure (with, for example, new resources becoming of strategic importance), on the cultural (technology becoming an expressive symbol of status) and religious fields (science coming to 'explain' phenomena that were previously the domain of religion) and so on and so forth.

5.1.2 The polite order

From the various observations made throughout the previous chapters, it will be clear that the Parsonian model fits the politeness theories like a glove, both in its broad and general worldview as well as in many of its details. The idea of culture/society as an independent system in a cybernetic hierarchy where the supra-individual precedes the individual is common to all of the theories. Invariably culture/society is endowed with the causal power to lay down the norms according to which individuals should behave. Concepts such as cultural rules or scripts, posited as explanations of individual behaviour, are the tools through which this control is implemented. These 'norms' are the pivotal concepts between the abstract cultural level and the level of concrete individual behaviour, and are connected with social structure through the notion of social roles. As they are shared throughout the culture/society, they ensure the cohesion and smooth functioning of the societal system.

Since most of the correspondences between the Parsonian and the politeness models should be all too obvious from the discussion so far, it would be a tedious exercise to spell them out in detail, as it would amount to little more than a repetition of points already argued. But the Parsonian model also contains some characteristics that have not yet received attention in the discussion of politeness, and also provides a few points of contact that allow observations or arguments made about politeness to be placed in a new perspective.

The cultural rule

Because the Parsonian normative order is ruled by the abstract cultural system through social norms, it provides a logical link between the basic conceptual tools of politeness theory – cultural norms – and its methodological practice of averaging out individual variability. In the Parsonian perspective, the individual *needs* to be calculated out of social reality in favour of cultural averages, as only the latter can cater for the cybernetic hegemony of the social level. The methodology and central conceptual tools are thus closely interrelated, as they reinforce and legitimize one another.

Besides in ontological importance, the cultural/social in politeness theory also matches its Parsonian peer in vagueness, both in definition and in practical application. In both models the notions of culture and society are at the same time theoretically under-defined and operationally overloaded, so that they become highly flexible explanatory tools. It is curious, though, that even in a highly elaborated social theory such as Parsons', notions that are so central to the model should remain so vague. Although this vagueness does a perfect job as long as the discussion remains abstract and theoretical, it runs into trouble as soon as the concepts need to be exemplified. I would argue that we are not dealing here with a lack of scientific rigor or accuracy on behalf of politeness or Parsonian theory, but rather that vagueness is an inherent characteristic of concepts such as culture and society. Both are highly generalizing notions and thus necessarily pass by concrete detail and individual variability, whereas exemplification always involves a confrontation with the detail, variability and individuality of social reality. The two simply do not mix easily.

Social structure

Social structure, the Parsonian link between the cultural and the individual, can also be found in politeness theory, where it fulfils exactly the same role. Brown & Levinson's P and D parameters are a clear example, since they derive directly from the social relationships in which individuals find themselves. And as P and D are merely a specific realization of 'systematic variability' (section 4.3.2), any other form of systematic variability in the cultural system of politeness can also be regarded as representing Parsonian social structure. Like social structure, systematic variability culminates in the construction of social roles. Although sometimes only in the rather crude form of social parameters such as power and distance, social roles are crucial in politeness theory, in that they determine the rights and obligations of interactants – what is (im)polite for whom.

The centrality of social roles is especially manifest in empirical investigations of politeness and related sociolinguistic research. For example, in DCTs, role-play experiments and questionnaires, subjects are invariably asked to picture themselves in interactional encounters with 'a police officer', 'a professor', 'a fellow student', 'a stranger', 'a neighbour', 'a waiter', 'a close friend', etc. Sometimes the subjects are even asked to picture *themselves* in a particular social role, as in Takahashi & Beebe (1993) where the respondents – Americans and Japanese of unspecified walks of life – are asked to imagine themselves as 'a beginning graduate student', 'a student', 'a student in a sociology class', 'a teacher trainer', 'a professor in a history course', 'a corporation employee', 'a middle manager in a large corporation', 'a corporate executive' and 'a corporation president'. This methodological practice demonstrates the assumption of a clear-cut, imaginable correlation between social role and the enactment of sociocultural communicative norms (namely politeness norms). The fact that in real life the respondents do not occupy the roles they are asked to imagine themselves in, is not regarded as problematic and does not invalidate the data. Neither do the researchers qualify their research as an investigation of the *perception* of social roles. The data are taken to provide accurate information about the actual social roles in question. Roles are therefore not dependent on the humans fulfilling them, and accurate knowledge of them does not require actual experience – it is quite likely that most of the respondents are not 'corporation presidents', do not personally know anyone who is, and have never been in or even remotely near the office of one.

Although admittedly in the practice of interpreting the data such highly specific roles are mostly abstracted into general oppositional distinctions such as high/low power, large/small social distance, etc., and the experiment does not lead to role-specific conclusions (genre 'corporation presidents are X'), the fact remains that these specific roles are used as input to generate data, and that for the power and distance data to be anywhere near correct, the respondents are required and assumed to have a pretty good idea of what it means to be a corporation president.

Social norms

Because of its emphasis on norms – or norm-like concepts – the politeness system fits in snugly at the very core of Parsonian social theory. It can be envisioned as one of the normative systems that form the connection between the cultural and social systems, as one of the patterns of evaluation and expectation that make up the social roles which secure the fit between the two systems, and thus as one aspect of how the societal normative order is practically realized. The fact that in Parsonian terms the politeness system is located on the pivotal point between culture and social structure correlates nicely with the politeness theories' lack of analytical distinction between 'culture' and 'society/social structure', with 'culture' as the umbrella term for anything 'social'. This pivotal position would seem to imply that politeness is *both* a cultural *and* a social phenomenon. And as in Parsonian theory 'culture' occupies the cybernetically highest position, the social system could be regarded as an 'expression' of cultural values, which would more or less justify mixing both factors together.

Social consensus

But norms can only fulfil their cybernetic task of implementing cultural values if they are supported by a general consensus. Parsonian consensus arises out of the internalization of the elements of the cultural system (ideas, values and norms) into the personality system, which leads to integration between the cultural and personality systems. It is exactly here that central concepts such as Blum-Kulka's cultural scripts or Lakoff's rules fit in. They were seen to be at the same time cultural as well as individual/mental entities – they are part of culture as well as being 'in the heads' of speakers. This ambiguous status can now be explained in the light of the interplay between the different action systems. As each of the action systems contains elements of each of the others, the personality system will also contain elements from the cultural system, i.e. there are points at which the cultural and personality systems so to speak intersect. Concepts such as scripts and rules can be interpreted as the *loci* of such intersections, which explains their ambivalent identity. They are both 'how' and 'where' cultural norms are internalized by the individual; they are the mental vehicles for the process of internalization and thus the embodiment of the social consensus.

Parsons' explanation of why internalization should take place also strikingly resembles claims made by the politeness theories. Compare his explanation in terms of the conformity-deviation balance coinciding with the actor's gratification-deprivation balance (that is, the actor conforms to cultural norms because it is the most 'efficient' thing to do, because it leads to gratification while deviation leads to deprivation) with, for example, Brown & Levinson's contention that:

> [i]n general, people cooperate (and assume each other's cooperation) in maintaining face in interaction, such cooperation being based on the mutual vulnerability of face. That is, normally everyone's face depends on everyone else's being maintained, and since people can be expected to defend their faces if threatened, and in defending their own to threaten others' faces, it is in general in every participant's best interest to maintain each others' face [...] (Brown & Levinson 1987:61)

Since both the 'content' of face – the kind of wants involved and their possible objects – as well as the norms for how to maintain it are determined by the culture, the cultural conformity-deviation balance indeed coincides with the gratification-deprivation balance of the actor. People adhere to cultural norms because it is in their best interest to do so: maintaining someone else's face eventually leads to gratification of one's own (social) needs. By extension, whenever politeness is seen as a 'way to get things (done)' the gratification-deprivation argument applies, as politeness is then directly related to gratification for the actor. This includes the widespread notion of politeness as conflict-avoidance, as well as the general association of politeness with positive evaluation and social approval.

Apart from the *locus* of the integration of the cultural and personality systems, and the mechanisms of *how* and *why* it develops and is maintained, another point of overlap between Parsonian and politeness theory concerns the question of *when* this integration takes place, of when and how the individual becomes a cultural being through the internalization of cultural norms. In Parsonian as well as in politeness theory, the answer refers to socialization, and is closely related to the mechanisms of how consensus is maintained. Where Lakoff remains rather vague in simply stating that her rules are 'learned effortlessly in infancy', Arndt & Janney are much more specific about exactly how the norms for being tactful are learned, explaining that *"[...] growing up to become a normal member of a culture is largely a matter of learning how to perceive, think, and behave as others in the culture do"*, and that the vast majority of people do so because *"[...] the penalty for not doing this is social exclusion, being labeled abnormal, retarded, defective, or deviant"* (Arndt & Janney

1992:30). The mechanism thus closely resembles the way in which the Parsonian social order is maintained: learning the social norms is met with social approval, deviance leads to social disapproval – possibly even exclusion. Again the conformity-deviation balance and the gratification-deprivation balance overlap. Socialization in Parsonian theory follows exactly the same path, as *"[s]uccessful socialization requires that social and cultural learning be strongly motivated through the engagement of the pleasure mechanisms of the organism."* (Parsons 1966:12).

However, just as in the Parsonian model, consensus does not come naturally to human beings. As politeness norms are imposed by the culture/society, socialization and social control mechanisms are required to ensure that people will learn about and maintain the norms. The natural propensity for human beings would be disruptive behaviour, i.e. impoliteness, which is confirmed by Blum-Kulka's interpretation of Israeli impoliteness in public contexts as a lack of cultural scripts in that area. When people are not guided by scripts, they revert to impoliteness.

Functional integration

The overlap between the culture's conformity-deviance balance and the actor's gratification-deprivation balance – assuring consensus and norm-compliance – in combination with the integration of politeness with social structure – in that it determines the rights and obligations of interactants in terms of their social status or role – leads to a view where politeness becomes a set of norms ensuring that people behave according to their place in the societal structure. The norms stipulate the appropriate behaviour for different social roles and relationships, and people will behave according to those norms because it is socially gratifying to do so: it is met with social approval, with request compliance, it avoids conflicts, and leads to smooth communication.

So politeness has a functional role in relation to the structural maintenance of society: it ensures its internal coherence, it ensures that everybody knows his or her place and remains within its confines. It has already been argued (see above, section 4.5.3) how a morally involved theory, together with a claim for scientific objectivity, may lead to a reactionary account of social and moral reality, promoting the social status quo. Now this claim can be placed more clearly in perspective. Because politeness can be interpreted as a normative instrument for the functional integration of the societal system, it is indeed involved in ensuring the stability and status quo of that system. The politeness norms make sure that those in powerful positions receive due respect and deference, while the powerless behave in appropriately powerless ways, so the system is involved in making sure that those in power remain in power.[3]

And this is not the result of some devious plan cooked up by those in power. On the contrary, the norms are 'objective' socio-cultural elements, they are 'given' to both the powerless and the powerful. The latter obey them just as much as the former do. They are an external force (in Gu's words, emanating from 'society', or in some other views an even more impersonal 'linguistic-technical principle') which stipulates the rights and obligations of all cultural members in respect of each other. In an extreme Parsonian interpretation, this functionally integrative force can even be argued to not only benefit the powerful, but also the powerless, as it contributes to the survival of the whole of society.

This social functionalist mechanism not only operates on the level of social structure, but equally applies to the cultural values and beliefs of society – promoting a cultural status quo – and even on the micro-social level. The latter is especially clear in Watts' notion of politic behaviour as geared to the maintenance of interpersonal equilibrium, where 'equilibrium' is understood in terms of an achieved interactional state/balance. Politeness as an 'enhanced' form of politic behaviour thus promotes the maintenance of the interactional status quo (Watts 1989a:144). Likewise, Fraser & Nolen's notion of a 'social contract' describes a fixed set of rights and obligations to which the conversational partners (have to) submit. Together with the definition of politeness as 'remaining within the terms of that contract' (and the observation that such behaviour is the norm rather than the exception), this also implies that politeness is geared towards maintaining an interactional status quo.

Social change

Because of the close fit between Parsonian and politeness theory in terms of social consensus and functional integration, social change becomes a similar phenomenon in both frameworks, as can be illustrated by Lakoff's (1979:74) description of thirteenth-century changes in European politeness customs (see also section 4.2.2). Just as in the Parsonian model, in Lakoff's interpretation change in the politeness system is a top-down phenomenon where cultural change precedes behavioural change – with an intermediate period of widespread unease when people realize their old norms are no longer valid, but do not yet know what the new ones are.

---

[3] At least in a symbolic hegemonic sense. I would not claim that it is an instrument of power equal to physical force.

Lakoff's vision further fits the Parsonian view in that changes in politeness result from (or at least correlate with) other changes on the social level, such as urbanization. Finally, politeness changes from one system (Camaraderie) to another (Distance), i.e. from one (stable) state of the system to another. The Parsonian notion of social evolution applies equally to the other frameworks. The very fact that politeness is conceived of as a status quo seeking system of social norms already implies a notion of change as movement between consecutive stages of equilibrium. This can be illustrated by Fraser & Nolen's notion of a Conversational Contract. In the economic world, the aim of a contract is the fixation of rights and obligations, so that one partner cannot inadvertently change them. If (one of) the partners want(s) to change some of the terms, they have to negotiate a new contract – which again lays down a fixed interactional order. So change consists in the movement from one contract, or one contractual state, to the next.

But because the social mechanisms involved in politeness normally lead to social stability, social change remains more or less problematic for the theories. The possibility of social change is of course never *denied*, but neither can it be easily *explained* or accounted for. The very concepts used to capture politeness resist the conceptualization of change: they do not by themselves lead to a worldview where change is a normal or natural phenomenon.[4] As change and evolution are not incorporated in the conceptualization, they are not organic properties of the social world that is depicted. In an extreme version, the Parsonian world becomes:

> a world devoid of developmental history, that experiences only consensus over values and norms, displays a high degree of integration among its components and displays only mechanisms which reproduce the status quo. [...]. Deviance and change are reduced to residual processes or to a kind of Durkheimian pathology. (Williams 1992:63)

Little wonder that such processes are never the object of much explicit theorizing and, if they receive any attention at all, are simply mentioned in a taken for granted kind of way.

---

[4] In a sense this is the same kind of problem as was identified in the discussion of the conceptual bias towards polite behaviour (section 3.4.1). The concepts adduced to explain polite behavior cannot of and by themselves explain impolite behavior, for which a whole new and different kind of theory would need to be constructed. Analogously, norms *qua norms* cannot by themselves account for change, since they are geared to do exactly the opposite: establish and maintain equilibrium.

5.1.3 Summary

The social worldview underlying the politeness theories has a distinctly Parsonian character, which is exemplified by a number of key notions: priority of the social over the individual, normative action, social consensus, functional integration and resistance to change. The similarities are many, and can be found in different aspects of the theories:

a) The most prominent resemblance lies in the construction of a 'cybernetic hierarchy', in which culture occupies the highest position and thus dominates the individual, who consequently more or less disappears from view.

b) Although theoretically construed as a (coherent) system, culture becomes rather a vague concept when it needs to be specified in operational terms, when such systems need to be identified in the real world.

c) The crucial link between the cultural, social and individual levels is embodied by the concept of 'social roles'. Individuals more or less 'enact' social roles – and thus also culture.

d) This link operates through the fact that social roles determine sets of social expectations, which in turn engender patterns of evaluation – in politeness terms: norms, scripts, rules, etc.

e) Politeness can thus be seen as one of the 'normative orders' that make up society, or as one of the mechanisms through which the Parsonian normative order of society is established and maintained. As such, politeness norms establish the link between culture, social structure and individual behaviour. They are the *locus* of the interconnection between those different levels.

f) Parsonian society requires and thus presupposes a far-reaching – although not complete and perfect – consensus among its constituent members. The same presupposition can be found in the politeness theories, where the perfection and completeness of the consensus was seen to be qualified through the notions of systematic variability and competence.

g) Consensus is established through socialization, and maintained through mechanisms involving the actor's gratification-deprivation balance. That balance is also involved in the process of socialization, and functions to encourage conformity with the social norms, while deviance is discouraged.

h) As such, politeness can be seen as a system, mechanism or force involved in the establishment and maintenance of the Parsonian functional integration of society. This is ultimately exemplified by what was labelled the 'status quo-seeking' nature of both the Parsonian and politeness worlds – which is where the notion of politeness as conflict-avoidance fits in.

i)   The latter also influences the conceptualization of social change and evolution. Owing to the top-down nature of the cybernetic hierarchy, change and evolution are social, and thus supra-individual, phenomena. And owing to the strong consensus-orientation of the theoretical models, change and evolution are seen as progressing in stages – from one state of equilibrium to another, rather than as a constant flux. In general, change is not a natural characteristic of the world, but is always a more or less painful process, involving stress, strain and a rupture of the social equilibrium.

5.2   The individual

After drawing the main outlines of the social system implicit in politeness theories, we can now ask what kind of individual such a system implies, that is, what kind of psychological model the theories presuppose. This issue was already touched upon at various points in the previous section, for example, when it was stated that in the Parsonian social model the individual is cybernetically dominated by the cultural and social systems, or when this top-down structure of society was seen to presuppose a far-reaching consensus among its constituent members. These were rather general remarks, however, and were only examined in terms of their social implications. Now we can explore them in terms of their consequences for the individual, while also looking for other clues as to the psychological presuppositions of the theories.

5.2.1 The Parsonian individual

From the Parsonian cybernetic structure with its emphasis on consensus, it would appear that individuals are strictly culturally determined, that they are dominated by their culture which determines their beliefs, values and behaviour. On the one hand this is true. Parsons explicitly claims that the individual is essentially powerless in relation to culture. Individuals cannot create or substantially change a cultural system; at most they can make a few marginal contributions to it (Parsons 1966:6). In the normal course of things they passively internalize its beliefs and values. Moreover, in an argument for the compatibility of his social model and Freud's psychological model, Parsons (1970:chapter 4) argues that contrary to Freud's own thesis, not only the Superego, but also the Ego and even part of the Id are essentially social/cultural constructs. Whereas in Freud's theory the Superego is – to put it simplistically – the warning finger of society watching over the Ego's handling of the Id's drives, Parsons claims that the latter two also result from the internalization of social/cultural values and behavioural patterns during socialization. Thus even a person's most basic wants and drives are to a certain extent culturally determined.

On the other hand it is not *entirely* true. Although the total person (Superego, Ego and Id) may show traces of a definite cultural input, Parsons is careful to avoid claims of total cultural determinism. The basic premises of his model already state that each of the action systems is analytically independent of the others, so that the individual, although definitely a cultural being, cannot be *reduced* to the culture. Moreover, although individuals share a common human genotype and cultural environment, they have a unique phenotype and their physical, social and cultural environment is in certain respects always unique. Sharedness will therefore be limited to 'broad features' of the culture, while a more detailed look will reveal so many differences that each individual is actually a 'unique variant' of this shared culture (Parsons 1966:7). So despite the emphasis on consensus and sharedness in the conceptualization of social and cultural systems, Parsons does acknowledge variability on the individual level. Let us take a closer look at the nature of this variability.

At first sight, Parsons' characterization of individuals as being 'unique variants of a culture' may seem to indicate a common pool of cultural values and beliefs, from which each member draws a slightly different sample. Simply put, in a culture consisting of elements a, b, c, d and e, person x has internalized a, b and e, but is not concerned with c and d, while person y is made up of a, c and d, but is not concerned with b and e, and so on. In this kind of world, the culture is still a unique, unequivocally determinable, coherent system, from which different individuals draw in different amounts without being concerned or even in touch with *all* of the culture's elements. Individual differences would thus be quantitative rather than qualitative. Person x holds value b, while c is not important to him or her, whereas person y has internalized c, but not b. The difference does not lie in that person x holds value b, while person y holds value *not-b*. X and y *complement* rather than *oppose* each other, their beliefs and values are not conflicting. But apparently this is not what Parsons has in mind, as appears from his discussion of socialization:

> The socialization function may be summed up as the development in individuals of the commitments and capacities which are essential prerequisites of their future role-performance. Commitments may be

broken down in turn into two components: commitment to the implementation of the broad values of society, and commitment to the
performance of a specific type of role within the structure of society.
Thus a person in a relatively humble occupation may be a 'solid citi-
zen' in the sense of commitment to honest work in that occupation,
without an intensive and sophisticated concern with the implementation of society's higher-level values. Or conversely, *someone else might
object to the anchorage of the feminine role in marriage and the
family* on the grounds that such anchorage keeps society's total talent
resources from being distributed equitably to business, government,
and so on. Capacities can also be broken down into two components,
the first being competence or the skill to perform the tasks involved
in the individual's roles, and the second being 'role-responsibility' or
the capacity to live up to other people's expectations of the interpersonal behavior appropriate to these roles. (Parsons 1970:130, my
emphasis)

Whereas the first part of this quote does indeed seem to indicate the above-
mentioned 'complementary' variability, the second (in italic) does not.
There it appears that individuals can not only differ in *which* values they
are concerned with (individuals being involved in different 'areas' of
the common culture) but that they can also have *conflicting* values
(individuals having *different* views about the *same* areas of the culture). And this is an entirely different kind of variability, which –
although its existence is intuitively obvious – has some serious implications for the notion of 'culture'.

For where could this value 'not-b' fit in? If it is maintained that cultures are coherent systems, then not-b would strictly speaking not belong
to the culture. This is all the more so if the requirement that cultures are
'systems in equilibrium' is added, as not-b would propose a definite challenge to b, bringing conflict and strain into the system. Technically
speaking, this strain/conflict would need to be resolved in some way for
culture to regain its normal stability – the culture would have to choose,
either between b and not-b, or some value 'f' which constitutes a compromise between b and not-b.

But if not-b does not belong to the culture, then what about the persons who uphold not-b? Would they need to be characterized as cultural
outsiders? Or in the light of the definition of socialization as the internalization of cultural values, would this mean that such a person is not
'well-socialized'? Or that he or she is 'ill-adjusted'? In an extreme phrasing maybe even a 'cultural failure'? All in all this option would result in
rather a strict definition of (the) culture, since people who hold values

that conflict with those along which the culture is defined must be excluded from it.

On the other hand, if not-b were allowed into the cultural system, this would evidently mean that conflict would also be allowed into the culture. But if conflict can be part of a culture, then the defining characteristics of coherence, cohesion, sharedness and equilibrium must be abandoned. Opposing values do not make for a coherent system (at least in the cultural area they are concerned with), so there is no longer a consensus but rather (latent) conflict, and any equilibrium will be a frail one at best, depending on whether or not the opponents try to gain ground for their values.

So the acknowledgement of the existence of conflicting values has two possible results. It either destroys the culture as a group – or at least severely restricts it scope – by excluding those who hold values that conflict with the defining values of the culture, or it destroys the scientific definition of the culture, since it introduces elements that do not square with fundamental notions such as sharedness, coherence, cohesion, and, to a lesser extent, equilibrium.

An apparent solution would seem to lie in defining culture as what the *majority* of a population thinks, which is also Parsons' own view. A person could then disagree with what the majority thinks without necessarily destroying the (notion of) culture. To stick with Parsons' own example, if in a particular society the majority of people are convinced that the feminine role is (or should be) anchored in the family rather than in economic life, then that belief/value is part of the culture of this society. And this remains true whether or not every member of the culture/society agrees with it. The fact that someone disagrees does not by itself alter the opinion of the majority, it merely places that person outside the majority. Only when a sufficient number of people alter their opinions could the culture be said to have changed. This view is further reinforced by linking it to social structure, which in the Parsonian world is the implementation of the cultural system, and thus the expression of cultural values. If a society contains structural elements (institutions, laws, etc.) that restrict the feminine role to the household, the majority of the population is taken to regard it as a social value. Obviously, the fact that some people would like to see women in the workplace does not by itself change the social structure and thus the culture of that society. Only if this group becomes so large that it is able to alter the social structure could the culture be said to have changed.

However appealing, this solution is not adequate, as the reliance on social structure splits up the notion of 'culture' into an 'ideational' (ideas, values, beliefs) and a 'material' (social structure) part. And this introduces at least two problems. On the one hand it presents a radical departure from Parsons' own definition of culture, which included only the ideational part. The inclusion of social structure in the definition of culture would blur the analytical distinction between the action systems, seriously upsetting the whole model of social action (if one is derived from the other, the distinction is *de facto* abandoned). It would also threaten the analytical independence of the systems, and would overturn the cybernetic hierarchy (where social structure is supposed to be lower than culture).

On the other hand, it poses practical analytical problems in that it is only applicable to 'ideal democratic' societies, because it assumes that social structure always matches the opinion of the majority. In reality the outcome of a democratic process is at best a compromise between the opinions of different factions, and as such often not really representative of any of the factions' values. And as social power is often not quantitatively, but economically or otherwise determined, the resulting social structure reflects the values of the more powerful more than those of the majority. Finally, not all the values and beliefs that live in a society are represented in the democratic decision-making process, so that the eventual outcome of this process may not even remotely be related to the opinions of non-represented parties. And for non-democratic societies – especially totalitarian regimes – the identification of ideational culture on the basis of material social structure may amount to a sheer absurdity.

In the light of all this, the 'majority' definition of culture does not adequately solve the problems introduced by allowing conflict(ing values) into a consensus-based definition of culture. Apart from destroying the theoretical foundations of the model it was intended to salvage, as well as being of little practical value because rather unrealistic, the 'majority' definition of culture also handles conflict by exclusion: it simply restricts the scope of the culture by excluding the very values and beliefs it was called upon to account for ('not-b').

In sum, a consensus model of society/culture is fundamentally and intrinsically in difficulty when it needs to handle conflicting values, as it always ends up excluding those values from the culture *strictu sensu*. In the light of the intuitive obviousness and omnipresence of conflicting values, it will be clear that 'culture' then becomes an essentially political notion: if cultures are coherent, consensual systems in (or striving for) equilibrium, the practical identification and delimitation of 'a (particular) culture' will always and necessarily involve acts of exclusion. One needs to choose between conflicting values in order to determine which ones belong to the culture and which ones will be excluded. And as abstract values only exist relative to the people that hold them, this act of choosing actually comes down to deciding who will be counted as a member of the culture, and who will be excluded; who will be regarded as 'central' (ascribed a 'defining' role), and who will be branded as 'marginal', 'outsiders' or even 'opponents' – from where it is only a small step towards notions such as 'threat' and 'enemies'.

The two kinds of variability identified above ('complementary' variability where differences concern different values, and 'conflictual' variability where differences concern the same value) refer back to the differentiation between 'systematic variability' and 'hearer variability' (section 4.3.2). Systematic variability is of the complementary kind, while 'hearer variability' is conflictual, as two people can differ in their evaluation of the same utterance by the same person in the same situation.[5] Although Parsonian theory acknowledges hearer variability and attempts to include it, it is not clear how it can be made to fit in with the consensus, harmony, stability and coherence of its social model. The two seem ill-matched, to put it mildly.

As the social model underlying politeness theory is basically Parsonian in nature, it faces the same problems. However, politeness theory seems to have taken a more radical stand on the issue. Although obviously hearer variability is observed in experimental data, it is simply ignored in all subsequent theorizing. It is either calculated out of view through statistical processing, ignored through concentrating only on what the majority does, or downright – and rather authoritatively – contradicted and dismissed as the deficient ideas of not-to-be-trusted ordinary speakers (sections 4.3.3 and 4.3.4). Politeness theories adamantly stick with the consensus model of society/culture, which results in the implicit depiction of a world populated by rather rigid and uniform individuals.

Again it must be stressed that the theories never *deny* the existence of individual variability. Only, whenever this is touched upon, it is done in a cursory fashion by one or two fleeting remarks, as a brief aside to the actual analysis which is devoted entirely to the development of a model based on consensus. Individuals that do not fit in are simply left out, their behaviour is not allowed to contribute to our understanding of politeness. At best it is explained away as 'deficient practice'. As such, current politeness theories only explain part of the observed behavioural spectrum. They construct theories into which not every individual fits, or at least

---

[5] For the theoretical framework, that is. Of course, different evaluations do not necessarily lead to conflict between the evaluators, but it does cause an internal 'conflict' for the consensus-model.

theories that do not take every individual equally seriously.

5.2.2 The polite individual

Besides being psychological characteristics in their own right, social uniformity – sharedness culminating in Brown & Levinson's Model Person – and the notion of a 'powerless hearer' who can only passively apply cultural norms (section 3.4.2), also lead to an 'objectivist' view of politeness, where social norms are reified as absolute(ly determinable) characteristics of situated linguistic practices (section 4.5.1). This objectivist perspective is not specific to politeness theory, but fits in with a long tradition of thought in linguistic and cultural/social thinking. It refers back to the historical process of scientific specialization which established different disciplines within the human sciences, each concentrating on one particular aspect of human 'being'. While the Saussurian tradition established language as a distinct phenomenon that could be studied in isolation, anthropology and sociology limited their focus to culture and social structure, and psychology concentrated on the individual. This evolution burdened scientific thinking with a fundamental conceptual separation between those different aspects of human being, establishing them as separate 'objects'. Even when it later on became clear that those aspects are actually interconnected and should be studied in relation to each other, the conceptual separation was often maintained in various 'integrative' initiatives such as (at least significant parts of) anthropological linguistics, linguistic anthropology or sociolinguistics. For example, the fundamental sociolinguistic question of 'how' language and culture, or language and society, are related to one another still presupposes that language, culture and society are different 'objects', self-contained entities that can be clearly delimited and described independently of one another.[6]

As Bourdieu (1977:24) remarks, the objectivist perspective (of language, culture and/or society) leads to a theory of "social practice as execution" where the individual does little more than execute the rules of culture, social structure or language. As the previous discussion has made clear, this equally applies to politeness conceptualized as a system of social/cultural/linguistic skills. Thus Bourdieu's remark makes clear that the politeness theories' social modelling does not draw a very flattering psychological picture of human kind, which is more or less reduced to an

---

[6] Moreover, the third aspect – individual psychology – is usually or mostly not (explicitly) touched upon in the answers provided to those questions. It is presumably left to be addressed by a further integrative discipline such as 'psychosociolinguistics'.

army of robots programmed by their culture with a number of evaluative algorithms. This rather grim psychological picture resulting from the objectivist point of view is further enhanced by the fact that sociolinguistics has traditionally been concerned with the social more than the individual aspects of language, and by the fact that the human sciences in general have never been all that interested in the idiosyncratic, but rather relish the common: *"Scientists have long seen their task as that of discerning principles that relate to as wide a range of phenomena as possible; 'universal laws' are generally accorded a privileged status, and the cachet diminishes with decreasing generality"* (Briggs 1997:452). Even psychology itself, the study of the individual *par excellence*, has long trodden the same path, searching for objective laws of behaviour, looking for what makes any (particular) individual into a (general) person rather than what makes any person into an individual (Shotter 1975, 1993). On an even larger plane of generality, the scientific endeavour *tout court* has always had a more or less 'natural' propensity towards the general rather than the particular. Hence it is not all that surprising to find politeness theory going in the same direction, neglecting or even ostensibly discarding the particular, the idiosyncratic and the individual in favour of the general, the common and the group.

Of course I would not argue that generalities and groups do not deserve our attention; quite the opposite. The problem identified here is that politeness theory tends to concentrate solely on the group, to the detriment of the individual. But as psychology is an intrinsic aspect of human being, it cannot simply be ignored, and so it *will* necessarily be addressed by any social and/or linguistic theory, even if on an entirely implicit level. Social/cultural theorizing always and necessarily contains presuppositions about the individuals making up the cultural/social groups under investigation. The problem thus lies in a lack of adequate psychological modelling on the part of the politeness theories, which end up with a social model that is not very hospitable to individuals.

The resulting implicit psychological model can be identified by three main characteristics. Firstly, the 'powerless hearer' implies a psychological model highly reminiscent of the mechanistic Stimulus-Response (S-R) model (Shotter 1975:chapter 4). Whenever a hearer is presented with a specific stimulus – a specific linguistic utterance made by a person with a particular social position, in a particular situation – he or she produces a specific response – a particular evaluation of that utterance in terms of (im)politeness. As the response consists of the mere recognition of the utterance's objective (im)politeness according to the cultural system's rules/scripts for evaluating utterances, the same stimulus-utterance will trigger the same response, the same evaluation each time. In an extreme phrasing, the hearer acts more or less like a Pavlovian dog, the only difference being that the stimuli and responses involved are more complex.

Secondly, the model has a definite cognitive bias, where behaviour is cognitively driven rather than cognition being behaviourally driven, or that the two would be in some way inseparably intertwined. The core of the politeness theories consists of cognitive concepts located in the minds of speakers and hearers (rules, scripts, norms, etc.), and their main aim is the quest for *"rules, laws or principles which determine people's behavior and which the [...] scientist [...] can discover"* (Shotter 1975:57). From a psychological point of view, this comes down to understanding *"'how the mind works' [...] by discovering the logical structure of the 'information' which, like a program, controls its operation"* (ibid.:58). A cognitive approach implies a view where action is the result of thought, i.e. where people think first, and then act on the basis of the outcome of their thinking. People first assess all aspects of the situational context, and on the basis of that information decide on the appropriate linguistic strategy. This is most notable in Brown & Levinson's framework, where politeness is defined as a form of rationality involving means-ends reasoning through the application of a formula.

Thirdly, in combination with the claim that politeness is the (qualitative and quantitative) norm, the cognitive aspect implies that the rationality involved must be one of social conformity. Social conformity is not the same as, nor a direct consequence of sharedness, since sharedness implies only that people will make the same evaluations and says nothing about whether or not people will use polite rather than impolite strategies. Whereas sharedness applies to the hearer (the evaluation of linguistic strategies), conformity refers to the speaker (the use of linguistic strategies). Because politeness consists of norms of appropriateness associated with social roles, being polite means acting according to one's place in the social structure. Being polite thus implies accepting and maintaining the existing social structure. And since politeness operates according to principles of rationality that lead to people being polite rather than impolite, it involves a rationality of social conformity, of the acceptance and maintenance of the existing social order. And in theories that interpret politeness as a linguistic-technical principle, social conformism arguably becomes a general linguistic principle which lies at the basis of how communication and understanding works – and thus becomes a prerequisite for successful and effective language use.

In sum, the psychological profile of individuals implicit in current politeness theorizing is one of social conformists whose cognitive structures and mechanisms drive them to execute the culture they are part of and over which they are powerless. This profile derives from basic methodological and (social-)theoretical choices identified in the earlier chapters of this discussion: (statistical) empirical abstraction, social/cultural predominance, the presupposition of sharedness/consensus implemented through the centrality of the social role concept, politeness as an objective characteristic of behaviour and the emphasis on synchronic 'systems'.

5.2.3 The cultural individual

The observed lack of psychological modelling in the politeness theories should be qualified somewhat. Concepts such as rules, scripts or norms in general can very well be regarded as psychological concepts, as they were argued to reside in speakers' heads. So the psychology in politeness theory is not all implicit. However, the problem with these concepts is that they do not derive from psychological modelling but rather from social modelling. They are primarily social concepts that are simply transposed into speakers' heads. The psychology involved is thus only secondary to the sociological theorizing: the individual is constructed from the position of (and largely to defend) the social/cultural model. Norms are both cultural and individual at the same time, so both levels are linked in a direct, one-to-one relationship. And as the social level is primary, the individual becomes a mere reflection of the social. The resulting psychology is rather simplistic, as individuals are mere embodiments of their culture and thus become 'mini-cultures', localized reflections of culture.

As a corollary to this notion of a 'cultural individual', the individual can be described almost entirely – or at least adequately – in social/cultural terms. This can be seen from the centrality of the social role concept. As far as politeness is concerned, people 'are' the social roles they occupy. The politeness system is entirely based on the association of appropriateness norms with social roles. The only individuality left comes in the form of either systematic variability or competence. But as systematic variability can be regarded as a more fine-tuned version of the social roles concept – with more social parameters creating a more diversified structure of roles – the only true individuality lies in the notion of competence. Unfortunately that notion is defined in terms of appropriate role-related behaviour, as 'acting in accordance with the cultural norms', so it can only account for individuality as a form of incompetence. So in the end a competent individual is not so much an individual but rather an ideal social/cultural being.

In this way, all the characteristics of the politeness social model work together to rob the individual of his or her individuality. True individuality is dismissed as incompetence and discarded as valid input for the theoretical model. As a direct consequence of the reification of politeness into an objective set of norms, politeness is not a matter of personal opinion, but of hard fact. In matters of politeness there is apparently no room for truly personal opinion.

Some scientists are aware of this rather harsh implicit psychological picture and feel the need to counter it:

> [...] linguistic rules are, perhaps, subcases of more far-reaching human behavioral rules. Linguistic competence is only one type of cognitive competence; proper non-linguistic behavior can be thought of as 'grammatical', aberrant non-linguistic behavior as *'d [read 'asterisked'[7]]; that is to say, non-linguistic human behavioral patterns can be reduced to the same formal sets of rules as linguistic patterns are: often they will share rules, as we hope to show here. *Hopefully this remark will not get the advocates of human freedom and theological free-will upset. We're not, as everyone should know by now, setting up prescriptive rules for the way people are supposed to behave*, any more than the rules in Chomsky's Syntactic Structures told people how to form nice sentences. We are describing what we see – reducing the apparent chaos of human interaction, linguistic and otherwise, to predictability. *This does not mean we can predict what you will do*, any more than knowing the rules of English syntax allows us to predict what you will say. *We graciously leave you your autonomy*; all we want to do is to understand, say, why word B follows word A in a sentence, why action A generally precedes action B in a non-linguistic transaction. This understanding comes in the form of rule-writing. (Lakoff 1977:86-87, my emphasis)

Unfortunately, just as in the argumentation against prescriptivism (see above, section 4.5.1) the denial is only nominal, as the arguments adduced do not hold ground on close scrutiny. Although it is true that the Chomskyan rules do not tell people how to form 'nice' sentences, and English syntax does not predict what people will say, the comparison between syntactic and politeness rules is simply not valid. Politeness rules *are* about how to form 'nice' ('proper') sentences: failing to do so is captured in terms of 'ill-breeding', or as 'ill-mannered', 'aberrant' behaviour. And the theory *does* aim to predict what people will say, witness claims

---

[7] Which refers to the practice within Generative Linguistics (and elsewhere) of marking ungrammatical sentences with an asterisk (*).

such as *"[...] the proper butler, ever maintaining Rule 1 aloofness, says 'Dinner is served', not 'You wanna eat'; the democratic American host, however, says 'let's eat'"* (ibid.:88-89).

The only real exception seems to be Fraser & Nolen's framework, where ultimately politeness *"[...] is totally in the hands (or ears) of the hearer"* (Fraser & Nolen 1981:96). However, since the bulk of the CC consists of general cultural, institutional and situational terms, and *"[i]n general, speakers operate within the terms of the conversational contract"* (ibid.:96), individual freedom is rather limited. So in spite of claims to the contrary, the emphasis on the social/cultural to the detriment of the individual leads to a world that is not a friendly place for individuals, with little room for personal opinion.

5.2.4 Summary

True to the Parsonian undercurrent, the theories' primarily social orientation leads them to largely disregard the individual and his or her psychological make-up. Their almost exclusive preoccupation with matters cultural leaves the psychological implications of their modelling unexamined. The net result is a rather simplistic implicit psychological picture, with a definite cognitive slant, emphasizing a rationality of social conformity, and some elements that are distinctively reminiscent of Stimulus-Response psychology. Together, these three characteristics indicate a cognitivist psychological foundation (Edwards 1997:chapter 2).

The social/cultural bias also introduces a largely social/cultural definition and delimitation of the individual. If the individual has any place at all in the models, it is in the capacity of a socio-structural location that fits in with the overall politeness-structural framework of systematic variability. In terms of politeness, people can at most be 'fathers', 'children', 'neighbours', 'friends', 'strangers', 'policemen', etc. Anything more individual is discarded as incompetence. The individual *qua individual*, as a unique person with a unique social history and a unique view of politeness, is not allowed into the theory.

5.3 The social and the individual

As appears from the preceding sections, the notions of the social and the individual are closely interrelated – in a relationship where the centre of gravity is located more towards the social/cultural side. After having discussed each side separately, a few remarks can be made concerning the implications of the combination of the cultural and individual notions we have encountered. Together with findings from the preceding chapters, in which a number of problematic areas of current politeness research were identified, these remarks will then be used as the basis for the development of an alternative conceptualization of politeness. Besides bringing individuals back into harmony with culture, this conceptualization should be able to avoid all of the identified problems associated with the Parsonian worldview.

5.3.1 Culture vs. the individual

In everyday reality, the individual intuitively seems much more important than the powerless, largely socially defined constellation of internalized norms and beliefs, without any real creative influence on the cultural world, that politeness theory presents to us. For one thing, it is obvious that the world is primarily made up of individual human beings. We all have separate bodies, and we always and only communicate with other individual human beings. Even our contacts with institutions are practically realized through individuals within those institutions, and the institutions themselves also only exist through the efforts and behaviour of individuals who found them, vote for them, manage them, work for them, represent them, use them, etc.[8] Thus ultimately the social/cultural relies on the individual for its existence, as it is individuals who perform the action through which societies and cultures arise. Although it may well be that no individual *qua individual* – in isolation – can make or break an entire culture/ society, it is equally true that cultures and societies *are* made or broken by *all individuals acting together*. So ultimately the social/cultural requires some more active and powerful notion of the individual for its explanation.

Empirical research invariably deals with individuals, who are the only tangible reality from which the social/cultural can be derived. As a statistical derivation, the social/cultural itself is a highly abstract datum. However, this does not mean that it does not exist, nor that it has no influence on the individual and is only marginal to our understanding of the world. It may be analytically interesting to study it in isolation, in order to get a picture of the 'average' behaviour within a group, or to find out what the majority of the population's behaviour looks like. But the legitimacy of abstract social derivation does not relieve us of the obligation to constantly stay aware of its proper status. We should always take the social/

---

[8] Of course, the emphasis placed on the individual here is not intended to deny the influence and power of institutions *as institutions*, it is only meant to bring the individual back into focus.

cultural for what it is: an a posteriori abstracted (analytical) construction.

As the embodiment of abstract culture, social norms are equally abstract entities: they are also the result of a posteriori analytical derivation. In practice they are not derived directly from individual behaviour, but rather from the abstract(ed) social average behaviour. In this sense norms are not empirically *found* at the individual level, rather they are *posited* as explanations for the social findings. Although they are proposed as explanatory concepts providing a return path from the social/cultural back to the individual level, their true epistemological status is *beyond* the abstract social/cultural average, even *further away* from the individual than this average.[9] In terms of the schema introduced in section 4.3.1, on the epistemological level the picture would look more like Figure 8.

Figure 8. Revised relationship between statistical processing and norm-based modelling

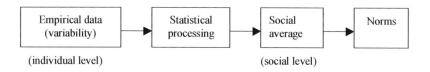

(individual level)   (social level)

So if in the explanatory process those norms are transposed back into the individual's head and posited as a behavioural driving force, the resulting individual is a purely social and equally abstract creature. He or she is *not* the same individual with which the analytical process began. And whereas their role as explanatory concepts posits norms as the link from the individual to the social level (explaining how individuals come to produce social behaviour), in reality they operate in the opposite direction: they function as a means to impose the abstract social average on the individual.

Because this path from the social to the individual is direct – with the calculated average being transformed into a norm which is then simply transposed into the individual's head – this leads to a rather simplistic image of both the individual and the culture. The notion of the individual is simplistic in that all individuals are supposed to have the same single

---

[9] Which is of course not to say that norms as such would not play any role on the individual level. The only point made here is that the specific norms identified in politeness theory are posited rather than found, being a derived abstraction from a variable empirical reality. In a later section I take a closer look at the meaning of norms on the individual level.

norm in their heads, which gets there by straightforward internalization. Each individual thus becomes a mini-culture, a direct and simple reflection of the same social average. Culture becomes an equally simplistic notion in that it is also reduced to that single calculated average norm. Referring back to the hypothetical rating experiment presented in section 4.3.1, the empirical reality of an amalgam of multiple and conflicting ratings is thus reduced to a consensus over one single rating. So in reality there seems to be more to individuals and cultures than politeness theorizing may lead to believe.

Consequently, when trying to say something about a group of people as a whole, we must be very cautious about keeping any general or average findings in their proper perspective. This is all the more true for explanatory efforts, which may easily fall into the trap of substituting the calculated social average for the reality that produced it. If we really want to explain social behaviour, we should not attempt to model how individuals come to display socially average behaviour (for they do not), but rather how they arrive at the behaviour they actually do display. This means we should incorporate variability as a fundamental notion in the conceptualization of social reality. Analogously, in modelling culture, we should take full account of the calculated character of average 'norms', and any explanatory principles should be able to capture the norm-compliant majority as well as any deviant minorities, since all of them together make up the reality of society.

5.3.2 Consensus

Bringing the individual and variability into focus affects the whole conceptualization of politeness, as it completely reorganizes the social model on which it is built. Incorporating empirical variability implies the acknowledgement that evaluations and notions of politeness can differ from individual to individual. Together with a view that empowers the hearer by focusing on the evaluative moment (see above, Chapter 3), and affirms the normativity of politeness by describing it in terms of social voices (see above, Chapter 4), this leads to a worldview that no longer requires a social consensus.

At least a 'real' consensus, where people all have the same norms and beliefs, is no longer a fundamental presupposition on which the proper functioning of the theoretical model depends. Although not totally excluded, its role is severely limited, and since it is no longer a presupposition, it now needs to be explained. Note how this entails a much more comfortable heuristic position: whereas in current theorizing observed empirical variability needs to be statistically processed to be brought in line with the theoretical presupposition of a consensus, consensus now becomes an observational fact, just like variability. Both need to be accounted for and explained, but only if they surface in empirical data.

A theoretical model that no longer takes socially shared norms for granted, by definition also challenges the commonsense association of politeness with such norms (see above, Chapter 4). Whereas the commonsense notion of objective norms is unproblematic for current conceptualizations of politeness because it is simply retained as a theoretical presupposition, it now needs to be confronted with empirical individual variability. Note that it is not the theoretical model itself that challenges the commonsense notion, but that this challenge is triggered by the discrepancy between two observational facts. Although in everyday evaluations and metapragmatic talk people act *as if* they are referring to absolute and objectively shared norms of behaviour, empirical observations point to the variability of those norms. Again, neither of these observations is taken for granted, and both phenomena need to be explained.

Instead of the more limited importance of a 'real' consensus, a variability-based social model accommodates the alternative notion of a 'working' consensus. A working consensus is an a posteriori rather than an a priori notion: it is not a *mental* consensus where identical beliefs are the *input* of interaction, but rather a *practical* consensus which is the *outcome* of interaction. As the combined result of variable (possibly even contradictory) beliefs-in-action, it consists of practices rather than beliefs. As such, it is a truly social phenomenon that exists only in and through interaction between people rather than in individual people's heads.[10]

Although based in variability, it is still a form of 'consensus' because it results in a consistent practice with some amount of unity and regularity. But even though in hindsight the actions that make up the practice may look like willing and conscious contributions to the achievement of that particular practice, in reality it is not the result of a teleological process. Each contributing action has its own socio-spatially and temporally 'local' purposes and motivations, which may be different from the role the action eventually winds up playing in the overall end result. So

---

[10] The only case when the mental reality inside an individual's head could be identical to the practical reality described here is when all the constituent actions of that practical reality would be carried out by that same individual, i.e. when that individual would live in complete isolation. But by definition the resulting practical reality would cease to be a 'social' reality.

although the resulting practice may display unity and regularity, it is regularity without conscious effort, external rules or common beliefs. The detailed implications of the notion of a working consensus for politeness will be discussed in a later section.

5.3.3 Social practice

The difference between a real and a working consensus can be characterized as the *"pass[age] from the* **opus operatum** *to the* **modus operandi**, *from statistical regularity or algebraic structure to the principle of the production of this order."* (Bourdieu 1977:72, original emphasis). The politeness theories' real consensus starts out from the statistically derived *opus operatum*, the 'end result' social reality, and constructs a suitable *modus operandi* (model of production) on its basis. As the latter takes the form of shared norms, the model of production becomes teleological: the end result is already present in the individuals' minds, and their behaviour is geared to produce exactly that particular end result. In the notion of a working consensus on the other hand, the *opus operatum* and *modus operandi* are not teleologically linked but separate phenomena which have to be studied separately. The *modus operandi* must be studied as a social practice rather than as mere execution of the *opus operatum*.

This can be exemplified by referring to Bourdieu's (1977: chapter 3) discussion of the Kabyle (Algeria) agrarian calendar.[11] This calendar is not fixed in written form, so it can only be approached by elicitation and reconstruction. However, informants produce information that is fragmented, equivocal and often (self-)contradictory, to the extent that no single unequivocal calendar can be produced either from the information given by one informant, or by the combined information given by them all. Because such a complete, unequivocal calendar does not exist in reality, attempting to construct one would be a purely theoretical endeavour, and would result in a purely analytical construction. The only place where the agrarian calendar really exists (and makes any sense) is in the practice of everyday living. It is, in other words, a *practical* calendar. As such, it does not abide by the cognitive, abstract laws of logical rigor, stability, completeness, temporal succession, etc., but rather by the exigencies and contingencies of everyday life.

---

[11] This calendar divides the year into different periods and defines significant moments, events, activities, festivities etc. that go with and mark the yearly agrarian activity cycle. The calendar is connected with values, beliefs, etc. from other spheres of life, such as religion, social structure, legal practices, etc.

In the practice of 'living' the calendar, decisions as to when a new period begins, or when a certain moment arrives, are based on local circumstances and local motivations – which may be different for different tribes, different villages and in some cases even different families – and often depend on events in other spheres of life. And the more important marking moments, for which it is important that they are experienced collectively (by all *and* simultaneously), are often declared or otherwise decided on, either by a person with social power or status appropriate to the occasion, or by some other form of collective decision-making. Such moments do not simply *arrive* (for the sake of the temporal sequencing of some abstract schematic calendar) but are *decided on*. The calendar thus depends on *practical* exigencies more than on the exigencies of some abstract schema.

The subject matter may be quite different, but it will be clear that a close parallel exists with politeness. Although the analytical temptation may be great to construct some sort of overall system of politeness from variable and often contradictory empirical information, politeness should first and foremost be regarded and studied as a *practice*. The question then becomes one of the characteristics or dimensions of the *modus operandi* of politeness as a social practice. Although this would of course be food for much further research, two prominent aspects will be discussed here. The first addresses issues of sharedness and temporal continuity, and draws on the Bourdieuan notion of 'habitus', while the second addresses issues of interpersonal power and argumentativity, two practical aspects of politeness largely lost in existing approaches.

Habitus
Bourdieu defines 'habitus' as:

> [...] systems of durable, transposable dispositions, structured structures predisposed to function as structuring structures, that is, as principles of the generation and structuring of practices and representations which can be objectively 'regulated' and 'regular' without in any way being the product of obedience to rules, objectively adapted to their goals without presupposing a conscious aiming at ends or an express mastery of the operations necessary to attain them and, being all this, collectively orchestrated without being the product of the orchestrating action of a conductor. (Bourdieu 1977:72)

The social and material conditions prevalent in individual and collective history create certain predispositions, which function both as enabling and constraining forces, defining a set of practical possibilities which actors unconsciously draw upon in structuring their behaviour. As such, habitus outlines a social mechanism that caters for regulated behaviour without the need for positing some external objective regulating force. It captures a process of structured creativity or collective individuality – in Bourdieu's words: "regulated improvisation"(1977 :78) – a halfway house between pure mechanistic collectivist objectivism and pure creative individualist subjectivism.

An important factor in accomplishing this middle position is historicity. In a radical interpretation, habitus even *is* historicity, as it describes how past experience mediates present action, creating a new experience which mediates both (the meaning and influence of) past experiences as well as further future action. In this way, present action becomes the intersection between present circumstances and past circumstances, or the transformation of present conditions by past experience, i.e. by past action, which itself was the mediation of past conditions by anterior experience, and so on. However, past experience does not *determine* present action. Present action is the creative transformation of present conditions from a position *based in* past experience. Action can thus never be reduced to past conditions, nor to present conditions, nor to the performing actor. It is relative to all three at the same time. The individual *creates* his or her own history, but not randomly: he or she is influenced by past conditions-turned-into-action as well as by present conditions. Note that the individual's own *action* also constitutes – part of – the present *conditions* for other actors, thus also influencing his or her choices of action. Habitus should not be interpreted as a weaker or less strict kind of rules or norms; it does not 'tell' people how to behave, it does not even 'make them do' anything at all. It merely defines a starting position from which people structure their actions, and describes the principle by which this position evolves through time, always renewing itself with every additional social act.

Although Bourdieu seems to be interested primarily in explaining – in a non-mechanistic, non-objectivist fashion – the mechanisms behind the generation of social continuity and regularity, habitus could just as well be used to capture variability. Owing to its focus on historicity, habitus is uniquely placed to account for the co-occurrence of regularity with individual variability. It enables a view where social reality is the 'coincidence' between consensus and variability or a 'variable consensus' – what was above referred to as a 'working consensus'. On the one hand, collective history creates a 'common' world in which each individual is embedded. On the other hand, each individual also has a unique individual history, and experiences the 'common' world from this unique position. The common world is thus never identical for everyone. It is essentially fragmented, distributed over a constellation of unique positions and unique perspectives. In this way habitus succeeds in specifying a single set of principles of production of social action that engenders a world of unique human beings, a dynamic world of variability and coordinated subjectivity.

In traditional politeness theory, continuity and consensus are secured by the process of socialization and the notion of a 'generalized Other'. From the perspective of habitus, socialization becomes a process in which both individual and collective historicity are manifest. It is at the same time unique for each individual – it involves a unique social trajectory – as well as a source for that individual's connection with the world around him or her. So it not only contributes to the individual's integration into the social world, it is just as much a source of his or her individuality, i.e. a cause of variability. Moreover, owing to the emphasis on historicity, where each new action and each new experience contribute to the starting position for the next action, socialization should be seen as an ongoing process, not confined to childhood, but continuously taking place throughout one's life.

The individual's concept of a generalized Other, which is formed on the basis of contacts with specific Others as well as through the media (TV, newspapers, books, movies, etc.) also combines commonality with individuality. It is formed from the perspective of a unique social position, but consists of information about other people and about the social world in general. Thus each individual has knowledge of many 'other' opinions and norms available in the world, which can engender abstractions about certain social 'facts' (genre 'when given something, it is generally considered polite to say thank you'). 'Generally' in this case can mean 'by many people', 'in many situations' or can simply refer to the commonplace nature of this fact – regardless of the individual's actual experience. It is this kind of knowledge that can be expected to surface when people are asked 'what politeness is', in rating experiments, or in parents' early socialization strategies when they intend to teach their children the basics of social interaction.

As the basis on which people form their opinions, this knowledge then functions as both a constraining and an enabling factor. On the one hand, it will limit the possible diversity of individuals' attitudes, as they will all largely be based on what 'other people' think, and there can be expected to be a large area of overlap between different individuals' knowledge – especially in our present era where mass-media have a prominent role. But on the other hand, it can also be an inspirational force, a laboratory for novel norms and opinions. People are always free to reject existing norms and values, or use them as a starting point for new ways of thinking. Apart from these creative possibilities, social knowledge also caters for individual variability through the fact that the specific knowledge of one individual will differ from that of another, not only in scope – in the amount or kind of social examples each individual encounters – but also because each individual interprets these examples from a unique position and socio-historical background.

Argumentativity

From the foregoing it will be clear that an approach based on variability quite naturally incorporates the argumentativity of politeness. In a social model based on habitus, notions of politeness are not simply the result of a passive learning process in which each individual internalizes 'the' societal/cultural politeness system, but are rather an active expression of that person's social positioning in relation to others and the social world in general. As such it becomes a social tool of identification and distinction on the basis of which the world is divided into 'normal', 'friendly', 'stuffy', 'well-mannered', 'uncouth', 'cool' and other kinds of people.

As a direct consequence of the role of argumentativity, the closely related issue of social power also fits in with a variability-based approach. In traditional approaches, social power is an 'independent' factor to which politeness is related in a passive, reflective way: people use politeness in a way that simply reflects their position in the social hierarchy. As an external, objective structural factor to which everyone pays tribute, power thus becomes an 'innocent' aspect of interaction. It is not something one person *does* to another, but an external factor applying equally to all individuals. On the contrary, in a view of politeness as social practice, power also becomes a practice and thus something people *do* to each other. The subordinate pays deference to the superordinate because the superordinate is in a position to *demand* deference from the subordinate. Although power is still associated with specific socio-structural positions, which convey power to their occupants, it is no longer an objective external force but becomes relative to how it is *used* by those occupants. So instead of determining behaviour, power becomes relative to behaviour – or better: is itself a form of behaviour.

For example, although a professor may insist on the use of deferential address terms by students, this is not an objective requirement: any professor might just as well insist on being addressed by first name, or may relinquish the power to decide on address forms altogether and accept whatever ToA a student wishes to use. Nevertheless, deferential address terms are always the *safest* way of proceeding for students – especially on initial contact – because they foreground the power difference between professor and student, and the acknowledgment of the student's subordinate position frames the interaction as non-threatening. So this practice of deferential ToA use can be expected to be widely used, and may even become a quantitative behavioural norm. But endowing that norm with moral force subject to a culture-wide consensus seems to miss the point of its how and why. Students may well find it a stupid practice and hold a norm for more informal student–professor interaction, but are simply not in a position to enforce it. In fact, any amount of variability among students as well as among professors may underlie such an empirical quantitative norm. Some may insist on deferential address forms, others may not care, find it convenient, alienating, regretful, think it is a downright stupid practice, etc.

The interplay between social power and politeness as an argumentative social tool of identification can be illustrated by means of an example from personal experience which also involves the use of ToAs in student–professor interaction. During my student days, one of the classes consisted of only a small number of students, so absentees were easily spotted. Because the subject matter – as well as the way it was presented – were not all that invigorating, most students practised a form of selective absenteeism, by not attending class just infrequently enough not to infuriate the professor. However, there were no internal consultations among the students in order to ensure minimal attendance, and so one time it happened that all female students were absent for a couple of consecutive weeks. The following week, only one (unfortunate) female student (re)appeared. The professor was obviously not satisfied with this low attendance, and so, barely able to mask his anger, he demanded an explanation from her. The student came up with a rather faint excuse (without using a ToA) that obviously did not satisfy the professor, so he replied:

(7)   That may well be the case, but you go and tell the other ladies that I will not tolerate this... *And you may call me professor, you know!*[12]

A traditional analysis of this exchange would refer to a cultural norm of

---

[12] As this happened a good number of years ago, I do not recall the exact wording. The second part is a free translation from Dutch *En u mag mij professor noemen, hoor!*

deferential ToA use by students *vis-à-vis* professors, which is violated by the student. The professor notices this violation, and reprimands the student accordingly. Such an analysis is rather sterile for two reasons. Besides losing sight of power as a social practice by confining it to the role-relationship between the actors – locating it only in social structure instead of in social structure *and* actors – it also loses sight of the argumentativity of the situation. The student's inappropriateness is seen as an objective cultural fact which the professor notices and points out. Any reasons or motives (social stakes) the professor may have do not enter the analysis.

However, much more is going on. On many previous occasions communication between students and this particular professor had proceeded smoothly without the use of explicit ToAs, so a cultural norm cannot provide a sufficient explanation for the professor's demand for one. A more fruitful interpretation can be reached by examining the argumentative nature of the situation. Absenteeism poses a double challenge to the professor's status: it marks (the subject of) his teaching as not interesting or at least not worth attending, and it challenges his position of power. After all, students are officially required to attend all classes, so blatantly violating this rule may convey the message that they do not fear his authority or respect his position – at least they do not pay him the respect of not showing their lack of interest. Moreover, the fact that the student's excuse was obviously made up on the fly (she probably didn't expect to be challenged like this) defies the professor's position even further: apparently students don't even bother to come up with a believable excuse.

The professor rectifies this awkward situation by giving the student a verbal spanking while ostensively displaying and thus reasserting his position of power. As a deferential ToA foregrounds the power aspect of social relationships, the professor's remark serves as a reminder of who is in charge and of the fact that (through his position) he deserves and expects to be treated with respect. The phrasing in terms of a permission ('you may') further enhances this effect, as it carries the double implication that its issuer occupies a position of power versus the person to whom the permission is issued, and that the action involved is something the latter wanted to do in the first place.

So an analysis based on variability and argumentativity acknowledges power as a practical factor co-determined by individual action, as something that can be asserted, maintained, claimed, and challenged. Power does not equally influence both interactants' behaviour, but allows one interactant to control the behaviour of another. And the combination of power and argumentativity also introduces the notion of social struggle[13] into the analysis (see also sections 2.1.2 and 3.4.2). Politeness becomes an argumentative social tool with which people ethically 'structure' or 'represent' the world that surrounds them. The terms in which this is done – 'well-(ill-)mannered', '(in)appropriate', '(im)polite' – are not objective referential, but practical argumentative classificatory terms. They are 'relational' (Bourdieu 1991:60): they only make sense in light of their counterparts, and the oppositions they carry are of the 'positive–negative' kind, referring not so much to the linguistic practices they denote, but rather to the people with whom these linguistic practices are associated.

5.3.4 Evolution and change

By introducing a dynamic conception of social reality and foregrounding the role of historicity, a notion of politeness based on habitus is also able to account more naturally for social change and evolution. Language production is no longer the reproduction of absolute, objective and thus static norms, but rather the active participation and (self-)positioning within a linguistic 'market' (Bourdieu 1991). Because they always involve a reaction to existing notions and evaluations, individual practices of politeness are not only determined by what exists – both historically and in the present – but also by the individual's own (perceived) place within the social structure and the linguistic market, and his or her subsequent reaction of self-positioning. For example, a woman who strongly identifies with feminist values may well object to a man's holding the door open for her, on the grounds that it is a demeaning expression of male chauvinism, and therefore constitutes 'impolite' behaviour towards women. This could only be interpreted in terms of shared cultural norms if one exploits to the full the fuzzy character of the notion of culture, and is willing to establish 'feminist culture', but then the example would actually become a cross-cultural misunderstanding, which rather seems to be missing the point of what is going on. So instead of simply 'expressing' their social positions by using 'appropriate' linguistic strategies, or merely 'recognizing' objective characteristics of Others' behaviours, actors are involved in a:

> [...] competitive struggle which leads each agent, through countless strategies of assimilation and dissimilation (vis-à-vis those who are

---

[13] Social struggle should be taken here as a very broad term, not only referring to large-scale phenomena such as political or class-struggle, but also to very small-scale phenomena, such as interpersonal differences of opinion – especially about moral issues of right or wrong, good or bad, etc.

ahead of and behind him in the social space and in time) constantly to
change his substantial properties [...] (Bourdieu 1991:64).

For example – to put it rather simplistically and at the risk of losing sight
of individual variability by overgeneralization – the lower strata in the
social structure may adopt behaviour associated with the higher classes in
their quest for social improvement. Not surprisingly, etiquette manuals
invariably promote behaviour associated with the higher circles of society, which is presented as constituting social competence. Traditionally
this process has been captured by the notion of social diffusion, in which
linguistic change originates in the higher classes and subsequently 'trick-
les down' to the rest of society. But this practice of *"locating the principle
of change in a determinate site in the linguistic field"* (ibid.:64) rather
misses the point, as the changes introduced by the higher classes are not
simply innovations, but themselves also argumentative actions of self-
positioning in reaction to the structure of the whole linguistic field. Burke
(1993) recounts how some writers of etiquette manuals advise against
certain forms of behaviour because they are 'common' and 'vulgar' (see
above, section 2.2.6). So once certain behaviours have trickled down to
the lower social strata, they will be countered by new behaviours promoted by the higher circles in order to preserve the social distinction
between themselves and the rest of society. On the other hand, social practices deprecated by the dominant groups of society may also be enhanced
and developed by non-dominant groups in a strategy of dissimilation (as
in the Hallidayan notion of 'antilanguages', Halliday 1978). Such a move,
which may be accompanied by a counter-deprecation of dominant group
behaviour – as 'posh', 'stuffy' or whatever – also establishes positive self-
identification (Martín Rojo 1994).

As the social mechanisms involved operate primarily on the individual
level, such macro-social phenomena are essentially a matter of individual
actors' perceptions and reactions. The adoption or deprecation of behavioural practices depends on individuals' perception of the linguistic field
and their current and aspired places in it, of the specific other agents they
are involved with, of their perceived relation to those others, of their interpretation of those others' actual practices and acts toward themselves,
of the specific situations they find themselves in, and so on and so forth.
So although in Lakoff's example (section 4.3.2), the fact that whether or
not you accept the adjectival use of 'fun' may well betray your age, (your
evaluation of) this practice involves a lot more than just age. Age does not
function as a determining factor of practice, but is only part of the game
on account of the possibilities it offers as a tool of social distinction. The
novel use of 'fun' may allow young people to assert their youth (their

being different from the 'old and stuffy' folks), their progressiveness or their self-determination (being able to define 'language' or decide more generally what is 'good' and 'proper'). But they may equally well evaluate it negatively to mark their distinction from whatever it is that they associate its use (or those who use it) with. On the other hand, older people may assimilate it to assert their own 'youth', or dismiss it to assert their being older and wiser and/or to distinguish themselves from the 'incompetence', 'lawlessness', or whatever, of the young folk. It all depends on individuals' self-perception, their perception of its use, their perception of the specific others whom they know use it or dislike it and whether they want to associate themselves with, or dissociate themselves from, those others.

So whereas in the Parsonian model, social change was an external force, it now becomes an inherent aspect of the social 'system' itself. It no longer needs to be located in a particular part of the system (in 'culture'), because it is inscribed in the very practices that make up the *modus operandi* of the system, and is thus continuously active throughout the whole linguistic/social field. As it is intrinsic to the actions and reactions that are constantly generated by the competitive relations within the social system in a never-ending process of assimilation and dissimilation, the centre of evolution and change is at the same time everywhere and nowhere (Bourdieu 1991:64).

Owing to this incorporation of change, the notion of 'creativity' can also be incorporated in the scientific model. In traditional accounts, creativity would be an equivocal aspect at best. Because of the cybernetic make-up of the model, it would either have to be a characteristic of culture (as the originator of cultural change) or it would have to be an idiosyncratic deviation from the cultural norm. So either its role would be quite limited (as an idiosyncratic and thus marginal factor), or its status would be fuzzy and intangible (as an element of the abstract supraindividual level). But since change is inherent in a variability-based framework, creativity becomes a central aspect of the social world and the processes of its evolution, as it is seen as one of the basic mechanisms through which the social world operates and evolves. In this light, creativity becomes important both in terms of the origination of new things (social evolution and change), as well as in capturing culture/society as the creation of human beings.

5.3.5 Norms and normativity
An approach that focuses on the mechanisms of social practice also influences the conceptualization of norms. Whereas in traditional accounts

norms are fairly straightforward – objective cultural entities as well as cognitive realities – a view based on variability, argumentativity and habitus leads to a more nuanced picture. Besides the fact that the commonsense normativity of politeness (involving shared objective norms) must be confronted with an empirically variable reality, the focus on politeness as a social practice also introduces a number of distinctions.

Precepts, evaluations and norms

On the operational level, politeness involves three analytically distinct notions that are closely interrelated: norms, precepts and evaluations. A *precept* refers to the actual statement that 'you should (not) do X', and is associated with a negative or positive *evaluation* of X as '(im)polite'. *Norms* are involved as explicit or implicit claims that those precepts and evaluations are to some measure 'universal' – in the broad sense of 'shared'. Their interrelationship has the appearance of being clear-cut and unidirectional, with precepts being based on evaluations, which in turn are based on shared norms, as in the following example:

(8)   'Don't do X'.
         'Why?'
         'Because it is impolite.'
         'Why is it impolite?'
         'Because it is something that is not done'.

However, in actual practice the differentiation between precepts, evaluations and norms cannot always clearly be made. The phrase 'X is impolite' can simultaneously function as an evaluation of X, the expression of a norm (through the impersonal syntactic construction) and as a way of saying 'Don't do that'. Norms and evaluations in particular seem to be interchangeable, or at least form a closed argumentative circle:

(9)   'X is impolite'
         'Why?'
         'Because it is not done'.

(10)   'X is not done'
         'Why not?'
         'Because it is impolite'.

Because norms can ground evaluations, and evaluations can ground norms, the two are not always clearly functionally distinguishable. As a result, norms can never be adequate explanatory concepts for politeness, as an explanation requires a simple unidirectional relationship where politeness evaluations are based on shared norms.

What remains is the fact that evaluations and norms form the grounds for behavioural precepts: they both provide a reason or argument for why behavioural precepts should be heeded – why 'you should (not) do X'. This argument is strengthened by reifying the norms/evaluations through a claim for universal validity – for example by phrasing them by means of an impersonal syntactic construction. This reification is a necessary component of (politeness) norms, for without it they would not be able to have their full effect: we would be forced to admit that our norms and evaluations are subjective and thus in no way 'better', more 'worthy' or more 'true' than those of other people. However, as empirical variability shows, the universality of politeness norms is not 'real', but rather an argumentative move, and one which is easily deconstructed by children – the ultimate devil's advocates, as parents will readily testify:

(11)   'Don't do X.'
         'Why?'
         'Because it is impolite.'
         'Why is it impolite?'
         'Because it is something that is not done.'
         'But Billy is allowed to do X.'
         'Well, maybe they do X over at Billy's house, but *we* sure
         don't do that *here*'.

So the distinction between norms and precepts reveals the functional nature of the commonsense notion that politeness operates through objectively valid socially shared norms: it is nothing but an intrinsic and functional ingredient of the argumentativity of politeness, the glue that holds precepts, evaluations and norms together and strengthens them into one firmly reified whole. As the argumentative backbone of evaluations and precepts, the idea of objective norms ensures that politeness actually works, by conveying to it the moral force of a social collectivity.

Multiple norms
The focus on politeness as a social practice also enables the distinction between different types of norms, according to how or by whom they are observed, or where, how and by whom they are used. As outlined in Chapter 4, observational norms must be carefully distinguished from operational norms. As a posteriori derivations from empirical reality, the former are part of the practice of observation, while the latter are a priori principles

structuring behaviour, and can never be directly observed. Observational norms can further be distinguished by type of observer: scientists have completely different techniques of observation than ordinary speakers, and their observations are differently motivated. These factors will profoundly influence observation: ordinary speakers' observations are usually more anecdotal and heavily informed by the observers' personal beliefs and values, while scientists mostly adhere to a more formal methodology, while their observations answer to well-defined goals of exhaustiveness or representativeness, and are usually informed by a specific scholarly purpose such as explanation. And when observational norms are not directly present in the data but are derived through statistical processes, calculation or typological classification, a further distinction needs to be made. Such derived norms are highly abstract entities pertaining to the level of the collective, and may be more or less remote from the actual operational norms that generated the data.

Operational norms are an equally mixed bag, a major distinction being between norms that are personally held versus norms of which one has knowledge (through the media, etiquette manuals or personal observation – see also section 5.3.3). The latter may influence the former to a greater or lesser extent, and this influence can be positive (assimilation) or negative (dissimilation). When norms are verbalized, further distinctions can be made according to situational context. In the practice of interaction, norms are never objective or innocent but always answer to the social stakes involved in the situation – as illustrated by the student–professor example (section 5.3.3) where a norm was invoked only on a specific occasion where it served a specific purpose. The same individual can be expected to express different norms in the socialization of his or her child, when socializing with a neighbour, or with a superior colleague, when advising a friend, when trying to get something done or when answering questions in a scientific experiment. And all of these norms may be more or less remote from norms that could be derived from that individual's own behaviour in various contexts.

All of these distinctions make clear that norms are never objective entities, but always purposive. Rather than informing practice in an objective way, they are themselves relative to the practice of which they are part. Consequently, they can never be safely mixed, or even directly compared. Data on parents' verbalizations of norms during socialization must not be taken to be equal to (or even comparable with) verbalizations of norms during a scientific interview. As each of these situations involves different social stakes, the verbalizations will have a different purpose, and norms expressed in one context may be irrelevant in another.

Comparison always needs to take account of such contextual factors. Likewise, those observed verbalized norms cannot simply be transposed to the operational level – especially when observation involves statistical or other derivational processes. Apart from the fact that it is not at all clear to what extent behaviour is norm-driven (if at all), individuals' metapragmatic comments about the importance of norms in a particular situational context may be quite different from their actual behaviour in that context.

So contrary to traditional accounts in which norms are simply taken for granted, a view that focuses on social practice reveals that norms are not straightforward entities, but rather highly versatile argumentative tools, and that their nature and operational aspects need to be examined more closely before they can be posited as explanatory concepts – and before they can be allocated any scientific role whatsoever.

Shared norms

Another thing we can learn from the discussion of habitus, is that politeness norms can be expected to involve a certain amount of sharedness, a certain amount of interpersonal variability, and may also be variable in time. While interpersonal variability derives from each individual's unique social history, temporal variability derives from the fact that each new experience contributes to and thus alters the basis on which future experiences will be interpreted and acted upon. Sharedness can take on a number of different forms.

A first form is that of 'real' sharedness, where two people hold or agree with the same personal norms. Such interpersonal similarities may be purely coincidental, as when two people do not know each other and neither have anything else in common, or it may be owing to a common social background. People may have common experiences to which they react similarly, or they may have common knowledge about the world, to which they either react similarly or which forms a pool of behavioural and ethical possibilities (as 'social examples') from which they make the same choices. Real sharedness is manifest in the fact that most if not all English-speaking people will confirm that 'it is polite to say thank you'; or the fact that there will be a clear tendency to say 'Could you pass the salt, please' rather than 'Give me the salt!' at dinner-table (at least in a formal setting), and to acknowledge that the former is the polite way to ask for the salt. However, a real consensus seems to be restricted in at least two ways. It can be expected to exist mainly for general commonplaces or cliché examples such as saying 'thank you' or the 'salt-asking' example, and probably does not hold for each and every kind of act or utterance. Although everyone might well agree that saying 'thank you' is the polite thing to do, the consensus would probably be a lot less widespread if one were to examine exactly when, in what situations, and towards which specific interactants people would consider it the polite thing to do in concrete everyday interaction – or when they would actually do it or expect it from others. And if more than one specific issue is considered, variability would probably increase even more. So when all of politeness is considered, a total, society-wide real consensus will most likely be non-existent, or at best highly limited in scope. Moreover, a real consensus would more readily be observed in verbalizations of norms than in actual interactional practice. Markedly frontstage settings such as scientific experiments, where social stakes are high, will elicit displays of social knowledge (consciously or unconsciously) and thus tend to provide a more consensual picture of social reality than actual social practice.

Also note that a common social background does not necessarily lead to shared personal norms. For example, children definitely share a close common background with their parents, not only in the form of a large body of common experiences, but also because the parents occupy an authoritative teaching role, both explicitly as well as implicitly – by setting a potentially powerful example. Nevertheless, adolescent children are often seen to adhere to different values from their parents – sometimes even diametrically opposed values, and equally often for the mere sake of opposition.

Besides real consensus, sharedness can take on the form of pure and simple knowledge. In general, three main sources of social knowledge can be identified. Every individual has a huge stock of personal interactional experience, with many different interactants and in many different situations, which yields information about others' reactions to one's own behaviour, and vice versa. Next, every individual also has a great number of examples of people interacting, evaluating each other's behaviour, etc., which he or she him- or herself has witnessed without being involved as a direct participant. Finally, every individual also has access to third-party information. This information is even further removed from the individual's personal experience, as it generally concerns others whom the individual does not know personally, and/or situations in which the individual is not present. Such information is gathered from the media (books, movies, etc., and including etiquette manuals). These three information sources contribute to the formation of a social knowledge-base which for different individuals may be more or less similar. The closer two individuals are, or the more time they spend together, the more similar their knowledge can be expected to be. On the other hand, events widely reported in the media can also be expected to be shared by many individuals.

However, sharedness in the form of knowledge is not real sharedness of norms *qua norms*. After all, similar knowledge of events does not mean similar interpretations of those events, let alone acceptance of any norms that might be derived from those interpretations.

The third form of sharedness is of an altogether different nature than the first two, which both were 'personal' in the sense of 'belonging to the individual'. Sharedness can also take on an interpersonal form, which is located in interaction between individuals rather than in the individuals themselves. This kind of sharedness comes in the form of *practice*, and arises out of the combination of the first and second forms together with other aspects of social interaction such as social power. This notion of a working consensus was already discussed in section 5.3.2, where it was shown how an essentially fragmented and distributed social reality could lead to a regulated social practice.

Such a practical notion could more appropriately be labelled a form of 'sharing' rather than 'sharedness'. It connects individuals through the practice of social interaction, where social reality is the outcome of social practice, and can be paraphrased as 'the process through which different subjectivities are behaviourally coordinated'. The practice of sharing comes in different forms. Frontstage behaviour is one of them, as well as different forms of interaction involving interpersonal power – such as student-professor ToA use (section 5.3.3), or any other power-related situation in which the subordinate acts according to the norms of the superordinate. Other variants of sharing can involve two interactants finding a 'common ground' (a practical arrangement involving aspects 'common' to both interactants' norms), or a 'middle ground' (a practical arrangement that does not correspond to either of the interactants' norms but is acceptable to both). Finally, sharing can also take on its commonsense form, of different people mutually conveying private interpretations and through that process influencing or altering each other's interpretations. Sharing then becomes a process of co-constructing (part of) social reality – jointly and coordinately 'signifying' reality – and may lead to real sharedness.

As sharing refers to the emergence of regulated practice without necessarily implying an underlying state of identity, it loses most of its connection with the traditional more commonsense meaning of 'sharedness', which refers exactly to such a state of identity. Also note that because of its emphasis on practice, 'sharing' can encompass the whole range of interpersonal variability, from the more passive 'real' sharedness (where 'practical' sharedness may be almost automatic and unnoticed) to complete non-sharedness, where sharing requires an adaptive effort by one or both of the interactants. So just as in the discussion of different types of norms, the focus on social practice once again reveals that sharedness is not the simple, straightforward datum it is taken to be when it is relegated to presuppositional status, but rather can take on many different forms which should be analytically distinguished.

5.3.6 Discursiveness

Bourdieu's sociological insights can be combined with insights from discursive psychology, which looks at psychological issues from the point of view of human behaviour (see, for example, Edwards 1997; Edwards & Potter 1992; Harré & Gillet 1994; Harré & Stearns 1995). Because it also concentrates on human practice, discursive psychology can complement Bourdieuan sociology in providing a psychological basis for a theory of politeness as social practice.

One of the main characteristics of discursive psychology is that it does not contrast thinking to acting, but rather regards thinking as a form of acting, in a view where *"[...] mental activity is not essentially a Cartesian or inner set of processes but a range of moves or techniques defined against a background of human activity"* (Harré & Gillet 1994:19). As mental processes cannot be isolated from behaviour, but must be understood as forms of human behaviour, phenomena such as norms are also seen as forms of behaviour rather than mental 'objects' or 'entities'. Their essence lies in what they *do*, in how they function *"[...] in the project of making sense of the world and our experience of it"* (ibid.:21).

This emphasis on the practice of human activity leads to the incorporation of social interaction and discourse into the subject matter of psychology, because *"[c]oncepts, the basis of thinking, are expressed by words, and words are located in languages, which are used to accomplish a huge variety of tasks"* (ibid.:21), and thus:

> [...] our delineation of the subject matter of psychology has to take account of discourses, significations, subjectivities, and positionings, for it is in these that psychological phenomena actually exist. For example, an attitude should not be seen as a semi-permanent mental entity, causing people to say and do certain things. Rather, it comes into existence in displays expressive of decisions and judgements and in the performance of actions. (ibid.: 22)

So the traditional view of norms is turned around: they are no longer (external) causes of human action, but rather themselves social practices, and as such they have social effects, purposes, and motivations. The discursive psychological view thus links up with the previous sections where norms were argued to be inherently argumentative. As discursive phenomena they cannot be isolated from the social practices in which they occur but only make sense in light of the modalities of these practices, in the light of what they (attempt to) accomplish. From this perspective the claim that norms verbalized in socialization are different from those verbalized in a scientific interview becomes tautological, as in each case they constitute different social practices, and accomplish different things. It also clarifies why metapragmatic talk in scientific interviews should not be taken as simple statements of fact: as social accounts of self-identification those verbalizations answer to various social and psychological motivations. Instead of being taken at face-value, such accounts should be studied *as accounts*, as social practices in their own right, with their own functional purposes.

So if politeness norms are discursive argumentative social tools, then what exactly do they *do* for people? The most obvious social effect of politeness is to condemn or approve of behaviour (and thus people). These acts of condemnation/approval establish a moral/social classification, separating the 'well-mannered' from the 'uncouth', the 'normal' from the 'deviant' and so on. As such, they structure the world in ethical terms, and in doing so also define the moral/social position of the speaker within that world. Through Other-identification politeness also provides Self-identification, and through general moral classification it outlines the relationship between the speaker and specific hearers. Norms thus allow people to position themselves in relation to others and in the world in general, and this process of positioning at the same time involves defining and structuring that world (both for the individuals themselves and for other people, for whom the individual's positioning is part of the social world they live in and to which they must react).

This practice of social positioning not only operates on the abstract philosophical and psychological level, but also in the concrete reality of everyday interaction, where, for example, the use of ToAs can establish, acknowledge, challenge, dismiss or dissimulate differences in social power – as when a professor who insists on being addressed by title vs. by first-name. Or behavioural norms can form the basis for group-formation, including some while excluding others (as in the case of 'sounding' – see above, sections 2.1.1 and 4.5.2 – or when explicitly defined behavioural rules and rituals regulate access to specific clubs, circles or occasions). And besides these direct effects, the social positionings of politeness can also be used for various other purposes, such as getting one's requests complied with, winning an argument, saving face (in the Goffmanian sense, as in the student–professor example in section 5.3.3), establishing behavioural control, etc.

5.3.7 Culture
Throughout all of these practices, the macro- and micro-, the individual and social levels are always intimately intertwined, as can be illustrated by referring back to the student–professor ToA example. On the micro-level, the professor's reaction gives meaning to the situation by establishing it as a breach of respect, and defends his position *vis-à-vis* the student by re-establishing his position of power. His implicit reference to a politeness norm allows him to win the momentary argumentative clash of interests and in general to gain control of the situation. On the other hand, the student may – and can be expected to – in turn also react to the professor's move (although advisably only privately), for example by defining him as 'stuffy' and in this way reclaiming her self-worth by tilting the ethical balance in her favour. On the macro-level, the professor draws from the power-relationship between professors and students in general, and the associated practice of acknowledging this relationship by using a for-mal ToA, while at the same time he also actively contributes to (the maintenance of) this relationship and practice, as well as to the norm that 'students should address professors by title'. Thus the macro-level does not simply determine what happens on the micro-level, and neither is the macro-level a mere function of the micro-level. The professor does not simply apply a learned social norm, nor does he instantaneously create such a norm out of the blue. The two levels cannot really consistently be separated, but are functionally intertwined, mutually and simultaneously influencing – even constituting – each other. Both levels are united in, and must thus be explained from within, the practice of human functioning.

In this light, the Parsonian claim that an individual cannot change a culture or society becomes a trivial truism. For individuals can be the creators of society without having to be able to single-handedly change it in its entirety. In fact, individuals *do* create and change society single-handedly, and they do so every day, but not at once and not entirely; rather on their own scale, by their own individual and unique contributions. In this way the current approach argues against the view of an 'external' society which determines human 'being', and for an 'internal' view of society *as* a process of human 'being' – of human beings 'being' human.

Secondly, just as in Bourdieu's notion of 'ethnic identity', 'culture' is also primarily a *discursive* notion, a tool for the (subjective) representa-tion of reality rather than itself an objective reality. Culture should not be treated as a given entity, but rather as an argumentative practice. Besides in other spheres of life (see, e.g. Blommaert 1991, Blommaert & Verschueren 1998, Hinnenkamp 1991), the argumentative nature of culture can also be witnessed in the scientific endeavour itself. In section 4.4.1 it was shown how current notions of culture in politeness research always and only involve positive aspects of behaviour. Because politeness is determined by cultural norms, polite behaviour is cultural, and conversely, cultures are made up of polite people. As those cultural norms make people behave 'properly' and cooperatively while avoiding conflict, cultures also become stable, harmonious, coherent entities where people are cooperative and conflicts are avoided. And through the association of politeness with 'good manners' and a 'good upbringing', cultures also consist of good-mannered, well-bred people. In short, belonging to a culture is truly something to be proud of. The Chinese, Japanese, American and whatever other culture are inherently 'good' entities where people are basically 'nice' to each other (since politeness is the norm). As such, the scientific analyses implicitly function as arguments for the ethical worth and righteousness of whatever specific culture they examine. At the same time, they also contribute to cultural self-identification: arguing for the 'special' characteristics of culture-specific notions of politeness establishes those cultures as separate, coherent entities, with their own clear-cut identities and their own notions of 'right' and 'wrong'.

This argumentative aspect can even be seen to play a role in the scientific debate itself, where culture has proven a useful concept in facilitating the peaceful cohabitation of scientific viewpoints through the notion of emic concepts and viewpoints: culture can be an argument for justifying the validity of a theoretical position (genre 'politeness is a matter of X... at least in culture A'). We saw how Ide uses this argument in positioning her theory in relation to Brown & Levinson's: both theories are correct and even compatible, as both are talking about culturally different notions of politeness; while in (American) English culture, it is foremost a matter of Volition, in Japan it is more a matter of Discernment. So in the end everybody can be right.

5.4 Summary

This chapter has brought together different arguments developed throughout the preceding chapters, and showed how various aspects of politeness theorizing cooperate in creating a specific social-psychological picture of human reality implicit to all the theoretical frameworks under investigation.

The social model bears close resemblance to the Parsonian worldview.

The main points of accord are the reification of the social/cultural into an objective entity that occupies the highest position in a cybernetic hierarchy, the presupposition of a social consensus that comes into being and is maintained through the mechanisms of socialization and the actor's gratification-deprivation balance and the functional role and conceptualization of social harmony, evolution and change.

The model of the individual is largely determined by the social model. Because of a strong preoccupation with the social level, the individual *qua* individual is more or less ignored, and largely defined in social terms – as a socio-structural location. In psychological terms the individual is characterized by a rationality of social conformity, with some aspects reminiscent of traditional Stimulus–Response psychology – especially where the hearer's evaluative behaviour is concerned.

A third section attempted to draw a few preliminary outlines for an approach in which the social and the individual are more in balance. It was argued that such a balanced approach can be attained by concentrating on the processes of social production (the *modus operandi*) rather than on the product of these processes (the *opus operatum*). The Bourdieuan notion of habitus was used as a guide in the development of such a theoretical framework where the social/cultural is the result of human (inter)action rather than vice versa. The main characteristics of politeness from such a perspective were argued to be variability, evaluativity, argumentativity, and discursiveness. The advantages of such a theory lie in its larger explanatory scope, where politeness and impoliteness are captured by the same concepts; the empowerment of the hearer and of individuals in general; a full(er) coverage of empirical data, since statistically marginal and contradictory data are also covered; a more adequate account of social change and evolution, which become internal productive processes rather than external destructive factors; a richer psychological and social picture, in which the individual and the social are (re)united; and a richer view on politeness itself, as more of its social and argumentative functional potential is revealed.

Chapter 6: Conclusion: politeness revis(it)ed

By means of a conclusion, I would like to do three things: summarize the major findings of the previous chapters, draw up a more coherent picture of the consequences of those findings for the conceptualization of politeness and make a few suggestions for possibly fruitful avenues of future research.

6.1 The arguments

First of all it was outlined how current theorizing does not engage in much explicit questioning of the politeness1–politeness2 distinction. Mostly, etic and emic concepts are assumed to more or less coincide. Even when the relevance of the distinction is acknowledged, attention is limited to the nominal recognition of its existence, and apart from an occasional general statement to the effect that politeness1 is about commonsense notions of politeness while politeness2 is about scientific notions, researchers tend to proceed with business as usual without examining the actual impact of this acknowledgement on the status or scope of theoretical concepts in any great detail.

However, the distinction is neither as straightforward nor as epistemologically innocent as current theorizing seems to presume. On the one hand, politeness1 comprises at least three different phenomena, depending on whether it involves an actor's evaluations, an actor's expressive behaviour or an actor's metapragmatic discourse. On the other hand, the relationship between politeness1 and politeness2 is not unequivocal either. While the theories heedlessly jump from one side of the distinction to the other, thereby presupposing a direct one-to-one relationship, it was claimed that this constitutes an unwarranted and potentially dangerous practice, as it fails to recognize the distinctive nature of everyday versus scientific reasoning, as well as the above-mentioned distinction between different practices within politeness1. Although both etics and emics always play a role in scientific accounts because of the simple fact that such accounts are both 'scientific' and 'about everyday reality', an acute awareness of the distinction can prevent the analysis from slipping into a trivial exercise of unidirectional *Hineininterpretation*, where the scientist's concepts are directly and thoughtlessly transposed into ordinary speakers' minds without any means of – or impetus for – questioning their everyday 'reality'.

Throughout the remainder of the discussion, it has subsequently been pointed out how the theories further disregard the distinction in that they more or less 'forget' their scientific role of outsiders by identifying with the viewpoint of the hearer, i.e. by 'looking through the hearer's eyes'. On the one hand they tend to mimic the hearer's evaluative behaviour (which implies taking an essentially emic standpoint) while on the other they attempt to capture that behaviour in scientific (and thus etic) terms. In this way the etic and emic standpoints are converged, and the distinction between the hearer and the scientist is blurred. Consequently the hearer is obscured from the scientific view and from the scientific conceptualization of politeness. The hearer's behaviour becomes that of the scientist and the scientist's behaviour becomes that of the hearer. And because in everyday politeness the hearer is involved in an evaluative practice, this has two immediate consequences: the evaluative nature of politeness is lost from the scientific view and it is transformed into – and lent the status and authority of – objective scientific analysis. Vice versa, this also leads the analysis itself to unwittingly become an evaluative practice, an aspect which it tries to substantiate by enlisting the notion of 'objective standards' and/or 'shared norms' for the evaluation of behaviour. This theoretical construction effects or enables – and thus seemingly also warrants, but in fact only extenuates – the coincidence of the hearer's and scientist's standpoints, because it provides a common point of reference for their evaluations. As politeness becomes relative to, and can thus be checked against a source that lies outside hearer and scientist, their positions become interchangeable. For the scientist this means that the hearer's disappearance from view is not such a bad thing, as it answers to the (presumed) nature of the phenomenon under investigation. For the hearer it means that the normativity of politeness1 is effectively 'reified' into scientific objectivity, and politeness now becomes a *characteristic* of behaviour instead of an evaluative *practice*.

In this way, the failure to adequately and consistently distinguish between politeness1 and politeness2 leads to – and can be seen from – the essentially normative nature of most theories, and their simultaneous denial of any such prescriptive intent. They are normative in that they confound their own position with that of the everyday hearer who is engaged in normative evaluations, and they deny prescriptivism because they are not aware of this confusion between the etic and emic viewpoints. The denial of prescriptivism is substantiated through a retreat onto the social level by reducing politeness to intersubjectively valid sociocultural norms. Some approaches prefer a retreat into the linguistic-technical corner by reducing politeness to a linguistic-technical principle, but this is only an intermediate position en route to a view based on shared social norms. As such principles derive their epistemological argumentative strength from being shared by speakers of a particular language, they can be regarded as just another kind of sociocultural norms.

Besides being a convenient means of justifying and/or dissimulating the overlap between the scientist's and the hearer's positions, shared norms also refer back to the politeness1–politeness2 distinction in the sense that they are the argumentative foundation on which politeness1 relies. Everyday evaluations are implicitly or explicitly justified and strengthened through references to socially shared norms. The fact that such norms – in various shapes – are the basis of the theoretical models, constitutes yet another instance of how scientific theories simply mimic everyday reality instead of questioning it. It thus becomes clear that the main points of the discussion – the conceptual bias on the speaker and the production of behaviour, politeness as a characteristic of language, the theories' normativity and the bias towards the social level of analysis – can all be related to the theories' (non-)positioning *vis-à-vis* the politeness1–politeness2 distinction.

The primary arguments also have a number of secondary effects on the scientific notion of politeness. For example, the theories' bias towards the polite end of the polite–impolite continuum can be related to the production bias, together with the choice for an explanatory scheme in terms of social norms. Since norms are geared to bring about positively rather than negatively evaluated behaviour, the notion of politeness as norm-guided behavioural production can handle politeness better than impoliteness. The latter needs to be captured in negative terms, as the lack or violation of social norms, and since norms *qua* norms cannot capture their own violation, the theoretical framework loses its explanatory grip on impoliteness. This negative definition of impoliteness – and the polite bias as a whole – is also found in emic notions of politeness, so again this represents a case of science mimicking commonsense notions.

The notion of 'variable competence', through which impoliteness can be captured as an instance of 'incompetence', provides a means of rectifying this limited explanatory scope, and can also be used – at least partly – to bridge the gap between the theoretical presupposition of sharedness and the empirical observation of variability. However, the notion eventually leads to a theoretical dead-end since it undermines the epistemological foundations on which the theories are built. Together, competence and sharedness lead to an implicit picture of culture as an 'ideal consensus' – at least as far as politeness is concerned. The requirement for a consensus derives from the assumption of socioculturally shared norms as the driving force behind the system of politeness –

without a consensus over the norms politeness would lose its regulative functionality. This consensus represents an 'ideal' because, although cultural members are differentially competent in the politeness system, they all strive to live up to the common standard of behaviour, and the ideal situation would be one in which every member has full competence in the system. As they only lead to conflict and communicative breakdown, incompetence and impoliteness are disrupting factors. Together with the functional association of politeness with 'smooth communication', 'normal interaction', 'conflict-avoidance' or 'equilibrium', this leads to the idea of politeness as a factor in the maintenance of social stability. Politeness is seen as a social regulatory force geared towards the establishment and maintenance of social order, so full competence in politeness matters leads to a stable social order.

The combination of all of these aspects leads to a Parsonian worldview, where the social/cultural level constitutes an independent reality residing on a cybernetically higher level than the individual, in the sense that social values and systems of social norms – which are internalized during socialization – are a priori regulative factors determining the individual's behaviour. As a result of this Parsonian worldview, the processes of evolution and historical change are necessarily conceptualized as external influences on a basically status quo-oriented social system. Evolution is not a direct and intrinsic characteristic of the social world, and is equally peripheral in the theoretical model. Just as in the Parsonian social world, the individual in politeness theory is relatively powerless in the sense that he or she plays only a severely limited role in the construction of social reality. Although in most approaches the individual is capable of using or even manipulating the politeness system to serve his or her own private needs (for example, in order to get the hearer to comply with a request), he or she cannot determine or even influence the rules of the system, or the definition of (im)politeness. This becomes particularly evident in the theories' (non-)conceptualization of the hearer, whose interpretation of speakers' behaviour is taken to be automatic and consistent. Because politeness is determined by a set of socially shared norms independent of speaker and hearer, any speaker behaviour is interpreted similarly by any hearer – within the limits of variable competence – and hearers become mutually interchangeable.

So the points raised in the present discussion do not constitute separate and unrelated theoretical choices, but all strongly depend on one another. A particular position on one issue almost automatically implies a particular position on another. They combine to establish a close-knit, coherent picture of the fundamental ontological characteristics, constituents and functions of politeness. This conceptualization hinges on a direct modelling on the basis of the surface-features of the commonsense notion of politeness, as well as on a strongly Parsonian social worldview. Its main characteristics are the notion of politeness as a form of (expressive) behaviour, driven by a system of culturally shared social norms, and constituting a socially regulative force in the maintenance of social order and stability.

So contrary to most overviews of politeness research which tend to emphasize the differences between the various theoretical approaches, from a metatheoretical perspective the field exhibits a definite coherence, as all the different theories share a common substratum of ontological, epistemological and methodological presuppositions. In the light of these common presuppositions their mutual differences become more or less superficial: rather than different genotypes, they are more like different phenotypes based on the same genetic material. This similarity is not limited to the core theories to which the bulk of the discussion was devoted, but extends to the periphery of the field. Besides research directly based on one or more of the core theories, most theoretical amendments, and even independent alternative approaches can be seen to share the basic notion of politeness as a form of behaviour related to some kind of 'shared norm' concept. So the vast majority of politeness research is also subject to many if not all the problematic issues identified throughout the preceding chapters. Only a radically different conceptualization, based on a more balanced social worldview and a more nuanced epistemological and heuristic position, can avoid the traditional pitfalls of mainstream sociolinguistic thinking and lead to a different – and deeper – understanding of the ontological and functional aspects of the social phenomenon of politeness.

6.2 The notion of politeness

On the basis of the metatheoretical analysis, Chapter 5 set out to sketch the main characteristics of such an alternative approach. As these characteristics must answer to the requirement of either solving or avoiding the problems engendered by the traditional conceptualization, those problems are a good starting point for the search for a more adequate model of politeness:

a) The inability to adequately account for impoliteness by the same concepts that explain politeness;

b) A complete disregard for the hearer's active position and the subsequent loss of the evaluative moment of politeness;

c) An ethically involved position resulting in a normative stance and the consequent loss of theoretical grasp on normativity;

d) The insistence on a consensus model which cannot adequately account for empirical variability, and the concurrent need for statistical data processing which leads to an epistemologically awkward position and a treacherous if not impossible road back from the model to the data on which it is based;

e) An 'a priori' notion of culture where the social level is causally prior to the individual, which leads to the unidirectional determination of the individual by the social level and the disappearance of the former from the cybernetic picture;

f) A static view of social reality resulting from the functionality of politeness as a social stabilizing and normalizing force;

g) A social world devoid of human individuality, human creativity and historicity which lacks the dynamic that has made human evolution from the Stone Age to modern times possible.

By taking many aspects of politeness1 at face value, generally mimicking its procedures and unquestioningly accepting its representation of reality, politeness theory becomes largely based on the very commonsense commonplaces it sets out to examine, and thus fails to provide any original insights beyond those already available on the intuitive level. As such it presents a good example of *"how linguists merely incorporate into their theory a pre-constructed object, ignoring its **social laws of construction** and masking its social genesis"* (Bourdieu 1991:44, original emphasis), where 'social' should not be taken to mean 'on the level of society/culture', but rather as a reference to what goes on *between human beings*, between individuals, in the construction of social reality. Bourdieu's statement encourages us to look beyond the commonsense social 'object' of politeness (as a unique and shared objective system), to the social mechanisms of its construction, to examine how it is intersubjectively created and maintained between *and thus also by* (individual) human beings.

This is not an argument for an extreme constructivist viewpoint where social reality is constantly (re)invented anew, on the spot and out of the blue, with society being a mere epiphenomenon to individual reality. However, it does promote a view where society is (re)created in and through everyday individual interaction, but *is seen in its full historical context*, with a bi-directional and dynamic relationship between culture and the individual, where culture is the large-scale outcome of people interacting over time. Rather than taking it for granted, such a view attempts to *explain* culture by looking at the mechanisms behind its ongoing construction.

Within a view that focuses on the processes of construction of social reality, politeness should be seen as such a constructional process, with evaluations of politeness as particular 'representations of reality' instead of as factual references to an objective reality. In any division of the world into polite and impolite people, the act of division is primary in respect of the social reality it creates, and both should be studied in terms of what such a division accomplishes for the person who makes it, and for human functioning in general – issues which are totally beyond the grasp of current theoretical approaches. And this line of thinking can be expanded beyond the evaluations themselves to include the means by which they are effected. Notions such as 'norms', 'sharedness', 'competence' or even 'culture' can also be regarded as representations rather than realities, as 'arguments' instead of 'givens'.

On this basis section 5.3 attempted to lay the foundations for an alternative view of politeness. Inspired by Bourdieu's notion of 'habitus', its main tenets are argumentativity (which incorporates evaluativity), historicity and discursiveness. The incorporation of these characteristics leads to a notion that takes full account of the hearer's position and the evaluative moment; is able to capture both politeness and impoliteness; provides a more dynamic, bi-directional view of the social-individual relationship; and thus acknowledges the individual (in terms of both variability and creativity) as well as evolution and change as intrinsic to the very nature of politeness. But rather than repeating what was already outlined more in detail, I will concentrate here on tracing some further consequences of this alternative conceptualization for our general understanding of and theorizing about the notion of politeness.

The discursive nature of politeness points out that politeness is first and foremost a *word*, and should therefore be treated as such. Words are made up by human beings, and allow us to structure and give meaning to the world and to coordinate behaviour. As such, they are not objective referential signs in the sense that if a word exists, something 'out there' in reality must also exist to which that word refers. On the contrary, words are used for everyday (inter)action, and as such can be regarded as actions in their own right, with their own particular purposes and effects on the world. In examining politeness we must therefore look for these purposes and effects. The question is not 'Who is (im)polite when, where and why?', but rather 'What does the evaluator do, how does he or she do it and why?'. Needless to say, this leads to an entirely different conceptualization and model, and even to an entirely different kind of knowledge about politeness. The traditional approach is paraphrased nicely by Ehlich (1992:76), when he claims one of the central concerns of politeness theorizing is the *"[...]need to know what constitutes the standard S"* that is involved in politeness evaluations. The search is for the 'content' of the norms of politeness, for a scientific description of 'what is polite and what impolite'. This has led to the identification of politeness with linguistic forms or formulae, or to a general outline of the rules of behaviour that lead to politeness (of the type 'Do this, but don't do that'). In short, the attempt has generally been to make explicit the evaluative rules applied by the hearer – under the implicit assumption that these will be the same for all hearers.

In the present approach such a model no longer makes sense, as the assumption of consensus is no longer valid, and a content-oriented description necessarily ends up becoming morally involved in the ethical struggle of everyday life. And as even the assumption of temporal and situational consistency of evaluations by one and the same hearer is no longer made, content-oriented descriptions could at best have highly locally restricted descriptive validity. They would only be valid for the particular evaluator involved, at that particular time, in that particular situation, and in relation to that particular interactant. Even in instances in which a definite amount of real consensus can be identified – for example in the notion that 'It is polite to say thank you' – such a content-descriptive account does not make much sense, as it merely reproduces a commonsense commonplace, giving no indication or clue as to how this commonplace works, when and for what purposes it is applied and so on. Because a description of a norm says nothing about its actual *use* or about the processes behind its production (what it actually *does* or what people *can do with it*), traditional content-oriented approaches seem rather to miss the point in their analyses of politeness, and have no more real explanatory power than the etiquette manuals they so often dismiss as 'popular' and 'unscientific'.

Although of a different nature than the traditional approaches, the present perspective can nevertheless still be called a 'model' of politeness, in which politeness is still seen as a 'system', although these terms now receive a different interpretation. The model no longer concentrates on how politeness influences behaviour, but on how behaviour influences politeness, while its systematic nature is sought not in the content of politeness norms, but in the processes of production and use of the notion. And although the traditional theories can also be regarded as models of production of politeness, with norms, scripts and rules as concepts capturing the process of production, and notions such as conflict-avoidance, equilibrium or smooth communication as the purposes behind that production, the difference lies in that the traditional focus is on the *production of (im)polite behaviour*, while the present perspective focuses on the *production of (im)politeness evaluations*: the traditional research question of 'why are people (im)polite?' is rephrased as 'why do people evaluate each other as (im)polite?'.

That this approach results in an entirely different kind of knowledge about politeness can be seen from the notion of scientific predictability. Whereas scientific prediction is crucial to the traditional theories, whose validity hinges on their ability to foretell what evaluations people will make in specific situations, it is no longer an issue in the present approach. On the contrary, the emphasis on variability and individual creativity even implies that prediction will no longer be possible. When politeness is seen as an argumentative social tool with which the individual can accomplish things, and morality is no longer regarded as a fixed higher-order set of rules that determines the individual's behaviour, but as something that people do to – or with – each other, it no longer makes sense to try to predict which evaluations a specific individual will make.

At the same time, the pitfall of prediction slipping into prescription is avoided. The recognition that in producing a politeness evaluation the hearer is acting prescriptively – is 'doing' morality – immediately reveals that any scientific attempt to (re)produce such evaluations would also become a prescriptive effort. In fact, when morality is placed in the hands and power of the hearer, the dividing line between prediction and prescription simply disappears. Owing to the very nature of the subject matter, any scientific attempt at prediction in politeness matters immediately and unavoidably becomes a case of prescription, as the scientist assumes a morally involved role. So the scientific account can effectively avoid prescriptivism by relinquishing the need for prediction.

When politeness is seen as a moral argumentative social tool it also becomes an "essentially contested concept" (Shotter 1993:169ff). As such it is on a par with, for example, aesthetic notions such as 'beauty', political notions such as 'democracy' or religious and philosophical notions. Essentially contested concepts have a number of characteristics that fully concur with what was said above about politeness. They are intrinsically vague, in the sense that their content or referent cannot be determined by a fixed and/or objective set of criteria; they are often appraisive, i.e. can be used to establish a hierarchy of relative worth; they are internally complex, in the sense that they can receive a variety of descriptions *"[...] in which [their] different aspects can be graded in order of importance"* (ibid.:171); and in their discussion, people try to make their meaning clear by the use of exemplars.

Vagueness and appraisiveness have been observed in the amount of empirical variability and in the moral involvement of politeness respectively. Internal complexity can be gleaned from the different aspects of politeness emphasized by both commonsense and scientific accounts: the strategic-utilitarian aspect, the conflict-avoidance aspect, the strategic-deceptive aspect (the proverbial 'iron fist in a velvet glove'), the moral-obligatory aspect and the argumentative aspect adduced in the present discussion. But it is also attested to by more detailed aspects of the traditional accounts: supportiveness, equilibrium, cost-benefit, FTA-mitigation, moral worth, power, distance, etc. all go to show that politeness can be related to a whole range of different notions. Finally, the fact that ordinary people use exemplars to clarify their notions of politeness has been observed by, for example Blum-Kulka (1992), but is also prominent in the fact that many empirical investigations use exemplar-based elicitation techniques such as DCTs and role-plays.

On a more general level, the essentially contested nature of politeness overlaps with its argumentativity. For essentially contested notions are said to elicit a social debate in which there can never be real winners or losers, because there is no objective way to decide on the relative worth of different viewpoints (Shotter 1993:171). In fact, the relative worth of any particular position is entirely a function of the other existing positions within the debate, and lies precisely in the claim for the alternative position it proposes. In other words, taking a specific position itself already comprises a claim for its relative worth, and vice versa, the relative worth of any position is argued for by its positioning in relation to other positions. So the debate is not a matter of right or wrong, true or false, etc., but rather one of social worth based on occupying a specific position in relation to other positions.

This is exactly what goes on in politeness1, where any definition or delimitation of what is (im)polite, and any practical *in situ* evaluation, itself already constitutes a claim for its own (and the evaluator's) social worth, both on a large and on a small scale. On a large scale, it is exemplified by politeness as a socially distinctive tool or force, where, for example, particular forms of behaviour are markers of a higher social standing or of a particular social class. On a small scale, it is evident in any application of this general principle, as well as in the positive and negative judgements attached to the 'polite' and 'impolite' evaluations respectively. As such, the essentially contested nature of politeness underlines once more the moral/ethical involvement of any content-oriented scientific approach, as any attempt to outline what is (im)polite inescapably involves taking a specific position within the ongoing social moral debate. (In this sense, the 'scientific' nature of the endeavour constitutes a further authoritative argument for the social worth of the position defended. For even though the scientific approach may claim to be 'merely descriptive', the statistical abstractions involved indicate that it is only one position among many others that is promoted to the status of either 'objective validity' – as when politeness is connected to linguistic-technical principles – or of 'society-wide validity' – where any other positions are socially marginalized.) As such, the essentially contested nature of politeness points out that a morally non-involved account is only made possible by focusing on the structure and processes of the social debate (by studying politeness *as* a social debate) rather than taking a position within it.

As the discussion of politeness as an essentially contested concept has profound repercussions on the epistemological status of the traditional theoretical approaches, it indicates the need to equally examine the epistemological status of the present perspective. An obvious remark to be made here is that although it may avoid a normatively involved position, it cannot escape the everyday argumentative struggle entirely. Because science is also part of the everyday world, its position in relation to everyday social reality must be taken into account. It would seem that any scientific account necessarily constitutes an argumentative stance because it presents only a particular perspective rather than some objective truth about politeness. It differs from commonsense notions in that it does not cater for the use of politeness – it is not geared to enabling actual evaluations of (im)politeness – but rather for its understanding as a social phenomenon. Its viewpoint is that of social science, which aims for the social examination of morality rather than for claiming the relative worth of any particular moral position – and even examines the why and how of the notion of 'relative social worth' itself. As such it presents a particular picture of politeness and of social reality, from a particular, analytical viewpoint. This viewpoint is also 'involved', because it answers to particular motivations and purposes: to provide a view from which a deeper (or perhaps simply a 'different') insight into the nature of social reality can be gained. Its aim is to broaden our view of social reality, to expand it with a different-from-everyday-commonsense perspective. So whereas the commonsense notion of politeness might be called a notion 'from within the practice of everyday life', the scientific notion constitutes an analytical perspective on the commonsense notion and its relationship to the practice of everyday life.

This brings us back to the starting point of the analysis: the position of the scientific approach in relation to the politeness1-politeness2 distinction. From the way I have been discussing politeness, it will be clear that in my view politeness1 should be the object of investigation, the input, and thus the starting point of the scientific analysis. A 'theory of politeness' should first and foremost be an 'examination of politeness1', of the everyday phenomenon of politeness. After all, it seems obvious that our scientific efforts should be aimed primarily at understanding the (social and linguistic) world we live in, so it is to this real world that our attention should be directed. In this respect, any framework that starts off with an artificial notion of politeness as input for the analytical process – as when Brown & Levinson qualify their subject matter as politeness 'very broadly and specially defined' – would seem to be in an uncomfortable starting position for such an understanding of real-world politeness. It may of course be a valid procedure and lead to an understanding of some aspect of the world, but to call that aspect 'politeness' would seem unwarranted, as confusion with politeness1 is then only to be expected. As we have seen, this is indeed one way in which the politeness1-politeness2 confusion manifests itself: the researchers provide their own special definition of politeness around which a theoretical model is elaborated, and subsequently apply this model to 'real-world' politeness1. Watts and Arndt & Janney deal with this aspect in a more consistent way, in using the terms 'politic' and 'emotive' behaviour instead of 'politeness', but the question then arises as to what extent their theories are still theories of politeness. It seems safest therefore to define the subject matter of any theory of politeness as politeness1, however vague, contradictory or generally elusive this subject may seem at first (empirical) sight. As I have indicated, if such characteristics are encountered, they deserve to be examined more closely rather than in some way or other be removed from the picture – they may prove to be essential characteristics of the social world we live in.

However, because a scientific account will always to a certain degree represent an etic viewpoint (if only because of its analytic purpose and motivation), an examination of politeness1 may well end up using notions or terminology that do not directly derive from politeness1. In fact, throughout the discussion, a case was made for avoiding mimicking politeness1 notions in our scientific accounts, so an understanding in non-commonsense terms is only to be expected. For example, if ordinary speakers invoke norms in their explications of politeness, then we should not simply do the same, but rather zoom in on that activity of norm-invoking and examine it more closely, as it is likely to give us an insight into what politeness actually involves. As such, any analysis will at some point necessarily depart from the insider viewpoint, but this is different from the above-mentioned artificial accounts which already *start out* with a 'special' (etic) notion of politeness. Since emics and etics will both always be present, they must at all times be clearly distinguished and their relationship clarified. If we use the notion of 'habitus' in capturing politeness, it must be made clear how this notion manifests itself in social reality, and how it relates to, for example, the commonsense notion of shared norms. Thus etics and emics must not simply be different and separate systems of thought without any real interface, but rather must interlock to form a coherent picture. A situation in which the scientific account contradicts informants' claims and dismisses them as being 'wrong' does not represent a healthy situation. Such a practice immediately leads to a rupture between scientific and commonsense notions, causing the theory to lose its grasp of the object of analysis. In an investigation of everyday social reality informants can never be 'wrong', for the simple reason that it is their behaviour and notions we set out to examine in the first place.[1] Contradictions should not be ignored but examined, treated as data rather than as noise, and obviously theories should be made to fit data rather than vice versa.

6.3 Further research

A number of points emphasized by the discussion also occur to some extent in the traditional approaches. As illustrated throughout the analysis, researchers often manifest a definite awareness of the importance or problematic nature of particular aspects of the traditional conceptualization of politeness (witness the arguments against prescriptivism) or the notion of competence as a means of accommodating the individual. However, as I have attempted to show, owing to the nature of the fundamental ontological, epistemological and methodological premises on which the theories are jointly based, this awareness mostly remains nominal or superficial, and the solutions proposed are hardly up to their task, often complicating matters more than they solve them. The present account has tried to show how their adequate solution would involve a radical change of premises, discarding the old fundamentals and starting anew from an entirely different basis.

---

[1] It must be kept in mind that we are talking here of ethical, i.e. 'essentially contested' phenomena such as politeness. Of course, a contradiction between informants on, for example, the exact date of an event in a historical examination would have different implications, and would also need to be treated differently.

The question then arises as to how this alternative view can be explored further. What avenues of research are opened up by the new perspective introduced here? The answer seems to be twofold. On the one hand, the emphasis here has been on a critique of existing theories, while the alternative view has not been the subject of much elaboration. As only its fundamental underpinnings were outlined in any detail, the present discussion has provided an alternative starting point rather than a fully-fledged alternative theory. So a lot remains to be done in the theoretical department. Most of the theoretical superstructure still remains to be developed, with questions relating to the kinds of interactional purposes politeness evaluations can serve, the factors influencing their occurrence, their interactional and psychological effects, and so on. But some of the fundamentals also need more elaboration. Norms, obviously a central aspect of politeness, should be further examined: what is their precise nature, how exactly do they function? Likewise for the notion of sharedness: what is its precise scope and depth? How is it established? What is the extent of variability – both interpersonally and intrapersonally? Or more generally, the import and implications of the discursive psychological view could be explored further.

On the other hand, we are also faced with the question of what empirical research on the basis of the alternative view would look like. After all, the details of the theoretical framework need to be filled in on the basis of empirical analyses, and it is only in empirical reality that theoretical claims can prove their worth. Two general remarks can be made about empirical research. First, it must be emphasized that empirical analyses are always and necessarily theoretically informed. One cannot search for 'what is there' unless one has at least a general idea of what one is looking for. The elaboration of the theoretical perspective is therefore always primordial, while in later stages empirical research may be used to illustrate and examine theoretical premises. Secondly, it was argued that traditional content-descriptive accounts of politeness are of limited value within the present approach. At best such descriptive accounts would have to describe all possible moral-political positions, but then the analysis would become a rather trivial exercise. A more fruitful avenue might lie in the investigation of actual debates about politeness issues, but in the light of the moral-political value of politeness, such debates would then have to be analysed *as debates*.

On a more concrete level, the emphasis on politeness1 as the input for the theoretical model points towards the kind of research that has up till now been most scarce: actual investigations of ordinary people's concepts of politeness, along the lines of Blum-Kulka (1992) and Ide et al. (1992).

What kind of situations do they associate with politeness? Which inter-actional events elicit politeness evaluations? When is politeness deemed irrelevant? What are perceived as the most important characteristics of politeness? What are its most closely associated notions and what is their precise relationship *vis-à-vis* politeness? What form can politeness evalua-tions take on – in terms of the terminology used? and so on. Apart from the notion of politeness itself, such investigations could also provide some indication of the amount of sharedness/variability involved, the kind of aspects that are most susceptible to being shared, etc. For this kind of research the informal interview format such as that used by Blum-Kulka (1992) seems most appropriate, although more structured investigations (such as in Ide's study) might also work well.

On the other hand, one would also want examples of actual (im)-politeness evaluations, but due to the situational embeddedness and argumentativity of politeness, they would have to derive from natural settings and occur spontaneously, as elicited evaluations and/or an experi-mental setting introduce particular social aspects and motivations that warrant their classification as separate social practices. This points towards the need for real-life spontaneous conversational data, but these could prove difficult to obtain, because in everyday interaction people only sel-dom verbalize evaluations of (im)politeness – except perhaps for parents to their children. So if those data are deemed necessary for the analysis, some kind of elicitation procedure would probably need to be used. At first sight, the most suitable method might again be the informal interview structure, in which the researcher and informant jointly discuss real-life examples. But whatever technique is used, the specific argumentative el-ements it introduces should be taken into account and brought to bear on the interpretation of the data.

Because of the discursive nature of politeness, the data would also need to receive a different analytical treatment from traditional investiga-tions. Instead of cataloguing the behaviours evaluated as (im)polite, the focus would be more on the discursive role and functionality of the evalu-ations themselves. Possible analytical questions are, for example, 'What is the argumentative/discursive structure of the situation, and how does the evaluation contribute to it?', 'What is the interactional effect of the evaluation?', 'If the argumentative/discursive structure were changed, would the same evaluation still be made?', and so on. The discursive structure of a situation refers to its description in terms of the kind of interactional practices or tasks that are being accomplished. The argu-mentative structure is much narrower in its definition, and refers to the purely argumentative stakes at hand. It is not limited to antagonistic situations, but can also involve, for example, aspects of interactional face.[2] The search would thus be for the processes or circumstances that bring about an evaluation, as well as for the interactional purposes it serves. Traditional cataloguing of evaluated behaviours may of course also be undertaken, although it is of lesser importance and must equally be related to the discursive nature of the situation.

As already mentioned, the discursive and argumentative structure of the experimental situation itself also needs to be accounted for. This not only applies to highly artificial settings such as DCTs or rating experiments, but also to informal interviews and even to the recording techniques used in gathering real-life spontaneous data. Whatever the setting, it always needs to be examined in terms of its effects on the involvement, sincerity, frontstage behaviour, self-identification, etc. on the part of the informants. In interviews or questionnaires, informants are obviously not involved in real-life interaction but in producing accounts of real-life interaction, which influences the status of the information derived from those settings as well as the possible interpretations it may receive. Although such aspects are not easily retrieved from unidirectional and impersonal formats such as questionnaire forms, the situation is quite different in informal interviews, where the whole interview text can serve as 'data'. The information provided by the informant can be examined in the light of its functionality in the flow of the interaction, in light of its relationship to the researcher's input (questions, hints), as a means of self-positioning towards the researcher, etc. The data of such an analysis would no longer simply be the content of the information provided by the informant, but rather the interactional text of the interview as a whole, and the analysis would become a discursive analysis of the interview itself.

Obviously, the characteristics of each investigation will differ for any specific empirical design. In principle, any research technique may be useful, provided that careful attention is devoted to its discursive and argumentative aspects and their influence on the nature and interpretation of the resulting data. As such, methodological issues are a field of study in their own right, and they themselves constitute an additional area in which there is room for much further study.

---

[2] In its Goffmanian rather than its Brown & Levinsonian interpretation, i.e. having to do with the – highly individual – image an interactant claims for him- or herself, rather than with – interpersonally shared – wants for independence and social acceptance.

6.4 Epilogue

The revision of the notion of politeness proposed here also has broader implications. I believe that in essence it constitutes a turn towards a firmer embedding of politeness within the dynamics of social reality. The combination of discursive psychological thinking with Bourdieuan sociology provides an example of how the social and the individual, the macro and micro, may be integrated into one coherent view of human reality as a spatio-temporally and intersubjectively dynamic process. As such, not only our view of politeness may be enhanced, but the study of politeness may also contribute to a deeper understanding of social reality in general, because it would lead to the examination of fundamental notions such as social norms or the nature of culture and society, and more generally to a contemplation of the processes involved in the day-to-day constitution of the social world by individual human beings, i.e. the processes of everyday life. And because politeness is only one of a number of social phenomena that play a role in how we relate to others around us and how, through those relations, we actively contribute to the (re)creation of culture and society, its study may also enhance our understanding of other aspects of social life.

Owing to the incorporation of individual variability and social change, this perspective may well lead to a notion of politeness that is more vague and less tangible – less 'systematic' – than the traditional notions, which to some may seem a deplorable evolution. After all, the idea of cultures as systems of shared norms leads to a clear and sharp division between 'polite' and 'impolite' – and right and wrong – and thus to an equally clear-cut (notion of) social order, while the emphasis on social equilibrium and status quo entertains the idea of society as a basically stable system and thus a safe haven to dwell in. Admittedly these elements are lost in a view that centres on variability, change, and social struggle – all potential sources of social instability – and which thus introduces a definite amount of uncertainty and harshness into social reality and human existence.

But it is my conviction that this represents a truer picture of reality, as it emphasizes that certainty, understanding, stability and equilibrium are not natural states that simply happen to us, but can only arise when people want them to happen and actively strive for their production. And there is much to be gained by such a view. Individuals are put back in charge of their own lives and thoughts, while culture and society are relegated to their proper ontological status of creations rather than creators. And the empowerment of the individual opens up the road to social change and evolution, allowing human beings to progress through time and through life, with discursive interaction as the pivotal point between the individual and the social, and between past and future. As such it implies a vision of discourse as the dynamic, living realm of social life, where human beings can determine their proper destinations and enjoy the full richness of human 'being'.

References

Adegbija, Efurosibina (1989) 'A comparative study of politeness phenomena in Nigerian English, Yoruba and Ogori', *Multilingua* 8/1:57-80.

Ajiboye, Tunde (1992) 'Politeness marking in Yoruba and Yoruba learners of French', *Language Learning Journal* 6:83-86.

Arndt, Horst and R.W.Janney (1979) 'Interactional and linguistic models for the analysis of speech data: An integrative approach', *Sociologia Internationalis* 17/1-2:3-45.

------ (1980) 'The clanger phenomenon: The non-deviant nature of deviant utterances', *International Review of Applied Linguistics* 18/1:41-57.

------ (1981a) 'Intuitive linguistic knowledge as a problem of non-autonomous linguistic research: The verbal coordination of group role identities', *Forum Linguisticum* 6/2:95-116.

------ (1981b) 'An interactional linguistic model of everyday conversational behavior', *Die Neueren Sprachen* 80/5:435-451.

------ (1983) 'Towards an interactional grammar of spoken English', in John Morreal (ed) *The Ninth LACUS Forum 1982*, Columbia, SC: Hornbeam.

------ (1985a) 'Politeness revisited: Cross-modal supportive strategies', *International Review of Applied Linguistics in Language Teaching* 23/4:281-300.

------ (1985b) 'Improving emotive communication: Verbal, prosodic, and kinesic conflict avoidance techniques', *Per Linguam* 1:21-33.

------ (1987) 'The biological and cultural evolution of human communication', in Wolfgang Lörscher and R.Schulze (eds) *Perspectives on language in performance: Studies in linguistics, literary criticism, and language teaching and learning*, Tübingen: Gunter Narr.

------ (1991) 'Verbal, prosodic, and kinesic emotive contrasts in speech', *Journal of Pragmatics* 15:521-549.

Aronsson, Karin and U.Sätterlund-Larsson (1987) 'Politeness strategies and doctor-patient communication: On the social choreography of collaborative thinking', *Journal of Language and Social Psychology* 6/1:1-27.

Austin, J.L. (1962) *How to do things with words*, Oxford: Clarendon.

Axia, Giovanna and M.R.Baroni (1985) 'Linguistic politeness at different age levels', *Child Development* 56:918-928.

Barnlund, Dean C. and S.Araki (1985) 'Intercultural encounters: The management of compliments by Japanese and Americans', *Journal of Crosscultural Psychology* 16/1:9-26.

------ and M.Yoshioka (1990) 'Apologies: Japanese and American styles', *International Journal of Intercultural Relations* 14:193-206.

Baroni, Maria Rosa and G.Axia (1989) 'Children's metapragmatic abilities and the identification of polite and impolite requests', *First Language* 9:285-297.

Bates, Elizabeth and L.Silvern (1977) 'Social adjustment and politeness in preschoolers', *Journal of Communication* 27:104-111.

Bayraktaroglu, Arin (1991) 'Politeness and interactional imbalance', *International Journal of the Sociology of Language* 92:5-34.

Becker, Judith A. (1982) 'Children's strategic use of requests to mark and manipulate social status', in Stan A. Kuczaj (ed) *Language development. Volume 2: Language, thought and culture*, Hillsdale: Lawrence Erlbaum.

------ (1988) 'The success of parents' indirect techniques for teaching their preschoolers pragmatic skills', *First Language* 8:173-182.

------ and H.D.Kimmel, M.J.Bevill (1989) 'The interactive effects of request form and speaker status on judgments of requests', *Journal of Psycholinguistic Research* 18/5:521-531.

------ and P.C.Smenner (1986) 'The spontaneous use of *thank you* by preschoolers as a function of sex, socioeconomic status, and listener status', *Language in Society* 15:537-546.

Berk-Seligson, Susan (1988) 'The impact of politeness in witness testimony: The influence of the court interpreter', *Multilingua* 7/4:441-439.

Bernstein, Basil (1971) *Class, codes, and control*, London: Routledge & Kegan Paul.

Besnier, Niko (1990) 'Language and affect', *Annual Review of Anthropology* 19:419-451.

Bilbow, Grahame (1995) 'Requesting strategies in the cross-cultural business meeting', *Pragmatics* 5/1:45-55.

Blommaert, Jan (1991) 'How much culture is there in intercultural communication?', in Jan Blommaert and J.Verschueren (eds) *The Pragmatics of international and intercultural communication*, Amsterdam/Philadelphia: John Benjamins.

------ (1997) 'Workshopping: Notes on professional vision in discourse analysis', *Antwerp Papers in Linguistics* 91.

------ and J.Verschueren (1998) *Debating diversity: Analysing the discourse of tolerance*, London: Routledge.

Blum-Kulka, Shoshana (1982) 'Learning to say what you mean in a second language: A study of the speech act performance of learners of Hebrew as a second language', *Applied Linguistics* 3/1:29-59.

------ (1985) 'Modifiers as indicating devices: The case of requests', *Theoretical Linguistics* 12/2-3:213-229.

------ (1987) 'Indirectness and politeness in requests: Same or different?', *Journal of Pragmatics* 11:131-146.

------ (1989) 'Playing it safe: The role of conventionality in indirectness', in Shoshana Blum-Kulka, J.House, G.Kasper (eds) *Cross-cultural pragmatics: Requests and apologies*, Norwood: Ablex.

------ (1990) 'You don't touch lettuce with your fingers: Parental politeness in family discourse', *Journal of Pragmatics* 14:259-288.

------ (1992) 'The metapragmatics of politeness in Israeli society', in Richard Watts, S.Ide, K.Ehlich (eds) *Politeness in language: Studies in its history, theory and practice*, Berlin: Mouton de Gruyter.

------ and J.House (1989a) 'Investigating cross-cultural pragmatics: An introductory overview', in Shoshana Blum-Kulka, J.House, G.Kasper (eds) *Cross-cultural pragmatics: Requests and apologies*, Norwood: Ablex.

------ and J.House (1989b) 'Cross-cultural and situational variation in requesting behavior', in Shoshana Blum-Kulka, J.House, G.Kasper (eds) *Cross-cultural pragmatics: Requests and apologies*, Norwood: Ablex.

------ and J.House, G.Kasper (eds) (1989) *Cross-cultural pragmatics: Requests and apologies*, Norwood: Ablex.

------ and E.Olshtain (1984) 'Requests and apologies: A cross-cultural study of speech act realization patterns (CCSARP)', *Applied Linguistics* 5/5:196-213.

------ and H.Sheffer (1993) 'The metapragmatic discourse of American-Israeli families at dinner', in G.Kasper and S.Blum-Kulka (eds) *Interlanguage pragmatics*, New York, Oxford: Oxford University Press.

------ and E.Weizman (1988) 'The inevitability of misunderstandings: Discourse ambiguities', *Text* 8/3:219-241.

Bourdieu, Pierre (1977) *Outline of a theory of practice*, Cambridge: CUP.

------ (1991) *Language and symbolic power*, Cambridge: Polity Press.

Braun, Friederike (1988) *Terms of address: Problems of patterns and usage in various languages and cultures*, Berlin: Mouton de Gruyter.

------ and Klaus Schubert (1988) 'When polite forms are impolite, or what politeness actually is', in F.Braun *Terms of address: Problems of patterns and usage in various languages and cultures*, Berlin: Mouton de Gruyter.

Briggs, Charles L. (1997) 'Introduction: From the ideal, the ordinary, and the or-derly to conflict and violence in pragmatic research' *Pragmatics* 7/4:451-459.

Brown, Penelope (1990) 'Gender, politeness, and confrontation in Tenejapa', *Discourse Processes* 13:123-141.

------ and S.C.Levinson (1978) 'Universals in language usage: Politeness phenomena', in E.Goody *Questions and Politeness*, Cambridge: Cambridge University Press.

------ and S.C.Levinson (1987) *Politeness: Some universals in language usage*, Cambridge: Cambridge University Press.

Brown, Roger (1965) *Social psychology*, London: Collier-Macmillan.

------ and Albert Gilman (1960) 'The pronouns of power and solidarity', in Thomas A.Sebeok (ed) *Style in language*, New York: Wiley.

Burke, Peter (1993) *The art of conversation*, Cambridge: Polity Press.

Cameron, Deborah (1995) *Verbal hygiene*, London/New York: Routledge.

Chen, Rong (1993) 'Responding to compliments: A contrastive study of politeness strategies between American English and Chinese speakers', *Journal of Pragmatics* 20:49-75.

Chen, Victoria (1991) '*Mien Tze* at the Chinese dinner table: A study of the interactional accomplishment of face', *Research on Language and Social Interaction* 24:109-140.

Chilton, Paul (1990) 'Politeness, politics and diplomacy', *Discourse & Society* 1/2:201-224.

Clancy, Patricia M. (1986) 'The acquisition of communicative style in Japanese', in Bambi B. Schieffelin and Elinor Ochs (eds) *Language socialization across cultures*, Cambridge: Cambridge University Press.

Coulmas, Florian (ed) (1981) *Conversational routine: Explorations in standardized communication situations and prepatterned speech*, The Hague: Mouton.

------ (1992) 'Linguistic etiquette in Japanese society', in Richard Watts, S.Ide, K.Ehlich (eds) *Politeness in language: Studies in its history, theory and practice*, Berlin: Mouton de Gruyter.

Coupland, Nikolas, K.Grainger, J.Coupland (1988) 'Politeness in context: Intergenerational issues (Review article)' *Language in Society* 17:253-262.

Culpeper, Jonathan (1996) 'Towards an anatomy of impoliteness', *Journal of Pragmatics* 25:349-367.

Demuth, Katherine (1986) 'Prompting routines in the language socialization of Basotho children', in Bambi B. Schieffelin and Elinor Ochs (eds) *Language socialization across cultures*, Cambridge: Cambridge University Press.

Du Bois, John W. (1987) 'Meaning without intention: Lessons from divination', *IPrA Papers in Pragmatics* 1:80-122.

Dufon, Margaret A., G.Kasper, S.Takahashi, N.Yoshinaga (1994) 'Bibliography on linguistic politeness', *Journal of Pragmatics* 21:527-578.

Duranti, Alessandro (1988) 'Intentions, language, and social action in a Samoan context', *Journal of Pragmatics* 12:13-33.

Edwards, Derek (1997) *Discourse and cognition*, London: Sage.

------ and J.Potter (1992) *Discursive psychology*, London: Sage.

Ehlich, Konrad (1992) 'On the historicity of politeness', in Richard Watts, S.Ide, K.Ehlich (eds) *Politeness in language: Studies in its history, theory and practice*, Berlin: Mouton de Gruyter.

Elias, Norbert (1978) *The civilizing process: The history of manners*, Oxford: Basil Blackwell, translation of Norbert Elias (1939) *Uber den Prozess der Zivilisation*, Basel: Haus zum Falken.

El-Sayed, Ali M. (1989) 'Politeness formulas in English and Arabic: A contrastive study', *Indian Journal of Applied linguistics* 15/2:96-113.

Ervin-Tripp, Susan (1982) 'Ask and it shall be given unto you: Children's requests', in Heidi Byrnes (ed) (1982) *Contemporary perceptions of language: Interdisciplinary dimensions*, Georgetown University Round Table on Languages and Linguistics 1982, Washington D.C.: Georgetown University Press.

------ and Jiansheng Guo, Martin Lampert (1990) 'Politeness and persuasion in children's control acts', *Journal of Pragmatics* 14:307-331.

Figeroa, Esther (1994) *Sociolinguistic metatheory*, Oxford: Pergamon.

Fraser, Bruce (1980) 'Conversational mitigation', *Journal of Pragmatics* 4:341-350.

------ (1990) 'Perspectives on politeness', *Journal of Pragmatics* 14:219-236.

------ and William Nolen (1981) 'The association of deference with linguistic form', *International Journal of the Sociology of Language* 27:93-109.

Garcia, Carmen (1993) 'Making a request and responding to it: A case study of Peruvian Spanish speakers', *Journal of Pragmatics* 19:127-152.

Garfinkel, Harold (1972) 'Studies of the routine grounds of everyday activities', in D.Sudnow (1972) *Studies in social interaction*, New York: The Free Press.

Garton, Alison F. and C.Pratt (1990) 'Children's pragmatic judgements of direct and indirect requests', *First Language* 10:51-59.

Glass, L. (1991) *Confident conversation: How to talk in any business or social situation*, London: Piatkus.

Gleason, Jean Berko (1980) 'The acquisition of social speech: Routines and politeness formula', in Howard Giles, W.P.Robinson, P.M.Smith (eds) *Language: Social psychological perspectives*, Oxford: Pergamon.

------ and Rivka Perlmann, Esther Greif (1984) 'What's the magic word: Learning language through politeness routines', *Discourse Processes* 7:493-502.

Goffman, Erving (1956) 'The nature of deference and demeanor', *American Anthropologist* 58:473-502.

------ (1959) *The presentation of self in everyday life*, New York: Doubleday.

------ (1967) *Interaction ritual: Essays on face-to-face behavior*, New York: Doubleday.

Gordon, David, S.Ervin-Tripp (1984) 'The structure of children's requests', in Richard L. Schiefelbusch and J.Pickar (eds) *The acquisition of communicative competence*, Baltimore: University Park Press.

Grice, H.P. (1975) 'Logic and conversation', in Peter Cole and J.L.Morgan (eds) *Syntax and semantics, Vol.3: Speech acts*, New York: Academic Press.

Gu, Yueguo (1990) 'Politeness phenomena in modern Chinese', *Journal of Pragmatics* 14:237-257.

------ (1993) 'The impasse of perlocution', *Journal of Pragmatics* 20:405-432.

------ (1994) 'Pragmatics and rhetoric: A collaborative approach to conversation', in Herman Parret (ed) *Pretending to communicate*, Berlin/New York: Walter de Gruyter.

Gumperz, John, T.C.Jupp, Celia Roberts (1979) *Crosstalk: A study of cross-cultural communication*, London: The National Centre for Industrial Language Training.

Halliday, M.A.K. (1978) *Language as social semiotic*, London: Arnold.

Harré, Rom (1993) *Social being*, Oxford: Blackwell.

------ and G.Gillet (1994) *The discursive mind*, Thousand Oaks: Sage.

------ and P.Stearns (eds) (1995) *Discursive psychology in practice*, London: Sage.

Harris, Marvin (1979) *Cultural materialism: The struggle for a science of culture*, New York: Random House.

Haverkate, Henk (1988) 'Toward a typology of politeness strategies in communicative interaction', *Multilingua* 7/4:385-409.

Headland, Thomas N. (1990) 'Introduction: A dialogue between Kenneth Pike and Marvin Harris on emics and etics', in Thomas N. Headland, K.L.Pike, M.Harris (eds) *Emics and etics: The insider/outsider debate*, London: Sage.

Held, Gudrun (1989) 'On the role of maximization in verbal politeness', *Multilingua* 8/2-3:167-206.

------ (1992) 'Politeness in linguistic research', in Richard Watts, S.Ide, K.Ehlich (eds) *Politeness in language: Studies in its history, theory and practice*, Berlin: Mouton de Gruyter.

------ (1994) *Verbale Höflichkeit: Studien zur linguistischen Theoriebildung und empirische Untersuchung zum Sprachverhalten französischer und italienischer Jugendlicher in Bitt- und Dankessituationen*, Tübingen: Gunter Narr.

Hill, Beverly, S.Ide, S.Ikuta, A.Kawasaki, T.Ogino (1986) 'Universals of linguistic politeness: Quantitative evidence from Japanese and American English', *Journal of Pragmatics* 10:347-371.

Hinnenkamp, Volker (1991) 'Talking a person into interethnic distinction: A discourse-analytic case study', in Jan Blommaert and J.Verschueren (eds) *The Pragmatics of international and intercultural communication*, Amsterdam/Philadelphia: John Benjamins.

Hymes, Dell (1974) *Foundations in sociolinguistics: An ethnographic approach*, Philadelphia: University of Pennsylvania Press.

------ (1986) 'Discourse: Scope without depth', *International Journal of the Sociology of Language* 57:49-89.

Ide, Sachiko (1982) 'Japanese sociolinguistics: Politeness and women's language', *Lingua* 57:357-385.

------ (1989) 'Formal forms and discernment: Two neglected aspects of universals of linguistic politeness', *Multilingua* 8/2-3:223-248.

------ (1993) 'Preface: The search for integrated universals of linguistic politeness', *Multilingua* 12/1:7-11.

------ and B.Hill, Y.M.Carnes, T.Ogino, A.Kawasaki (1992) 'The concept of politeness: An empirical study of American English and Japanese', in Richard Watts, S.Ide, K.Ehlich (eds) *Politeness in language: Studies in its history, theory and practice*, Berlin: Mouton de Gruyter.

------ and M.Hori, A.Kawasaki, S.Ikuta, H.Haga (1986) 'Sex difference and politeness in Japanese', *International Journal of the Sociology of Language* 58:25-36.

Janney, Richard W. and H.Arndt (1992) 'Intracultural tact versus intercultural tact', in Richard Watts, S.Ide, K.Ehlich (eds) *Politeness in language: Studies in its history, theory and practice*, Berlin: Mouton de Gruyter.

------ (1993) 'Universality and relativity in cross-cultural research: A historical perspective', *Multilingua* 12/1:13-50.

Kandiah, Thiru (1991) 'Extenuatory sociolinguistics: Diverting attention from issues to symptoms in cross-cultural communication studies', *Multilingua* 10/4:345-379.

Kasher, Asa (1986) 'Politeness and rationality', in J.D. Johansen, H.Sonne, H.Haberland (eds) *Pragmatics and linguistics. Festschrift for J.L.Mey*, Odense: Odense University Press.

Kasper, Gabriele (1990) 'Linguistic politeness: Current research issues', *Journal of Pragmatics* 14:193-218.

------ (1996) 'Politeness', in Jef Verschueren, J.-O.Östman, J.Blommaert, C.Bulcaen (eds) *Handbook of pragmatics 1996*, Amsterdam/Philadelphia: John Benjamins.

------ and S.Blum-Kulka (1993a) 'Interlanguage pragmatics: An introduction', in Gabriele Kasper and S.Blum-Kulka (eds) *Interlanguage pragmatics*, New York, Oxford: Oxford University Press.

------ and S.Blum-Kulka (eds) (1993b) *Interlanguage pragmatics*, New York, Oxford: Oxford University Press.

Kelley, William R. (1987) 'How to get along with language: A theory of politeness phenomena', *Papers from the 23rd Annual Regional Meeting of the Chicago Linguistics Society*: 181-195.

Kerbrat-Orecchioni, Catherine (1992) *Les interactions verbales, Tome II*, Paris: Colin.

------ (1997) 'A multilevel approach in the study of talk-in-interaction', *Pragmatics* 7/1:1-20.

Keshavarz, Mohammad Hossein (1988) 'Forms of address in post-revolutionary Iranian Persian: A sociolinguistic analysis', *Language in Society* 17:565-575.

Kienpointner, Manfred (1997) 'Varieties of rudeness: Types and functions of impolite utterances', *Functions of Language* 4/2:251-287.

Knapp-Potthoff, Annelie (1992) 'Secondhand politeness', in Richard Watts, S.Ide, K.Ehlich (eds) *Politeness in language: Studies in its history, theory and practice*, Berlin: Mouton de Gruyter.

Koike, Dale April (1989) 'Requests and the role of deixis in politeness', *Journal of Pragmatics* 13:187-202.

Krummer, Manfred (1992) 'Politeness in Thai', in Richard Watts, S.Ide, K.Ehlich (eds) *Politeness in language: Studies in its history, theory and practice*, Berlin: Mouton de Gruyter.

Kuhn, Thomas S. (1962) *The structure of scientific revolutions*, Chicago: University of Chicago Press.

Kwarciak, Boguslaw Jan (1993) 'The acquisition of linguistic politeness and Brown and Levinson's theory', *Multilingua* 12/1:51-68.

Labov, William (1972) *Language in the inner city: Studies in the black English vernacular*, Oxford: Blackwell.

Lakoff, Robin Tolmach (1973) 'The logic of politeness; or, minding your p's and q's', *Papers from the Ninth Regional Meeting of the Chicago Linguistic Society (1973)*: 292-305.

------ (1977) 'What you can do with words: Politeness, pragmatics, and performatives', in A. Rogers, B.Wall, J.P.Murphy (eds) *Proceedings of the Texas conference on performatives, presuppositions, and implicatures*, Arlington: Center of Applied Linguistics.

------ (1979) 'Stylistic strategies within a grammar of style', in Judith Orasanu, M.K.Slater, L.L.Adler (eds) *Language, sex and gender: Does la différence make a difference?*, New York: New York Academy of Sciences.

------ (1984) 'The pragmatics of subordination', *Proceedings of the Tenth Annual Meeting of the Berkeley Linguistics Society*: 481-492.

------ (1989a) 'The limits of politeness: Therapeutic and courtroom discourse', *Multilingua* 8/2-3:101-129.

------ (1989b) 'The way we were; or; The real actual truth about generative semantics: A memoir', *Journal of Pragmatics* 13:939-988.

------ (1990) *Talking power: The politics of language in our lives*, Glasgow: HarperCollins.

------ (1995) 'Conversational logic', in Jef Verschueren, J.-O.Östman, J.Blommaert (eds) *Handbook of pragmatics: Manual*. Amsterdam/Philadelphia: John Benjamins.

------ and Deborah Tannen (1979) 'Communicative strategies in conversation: The case of *scenes from a marriage*,' *Proceedings of the Fifth Annual Meeting of the Berkeley Linguistics Society*: 581-592.

Lee-Wong, Song Mei (1998) 'Face support - Chinese particles as mitigators: A study of BA A/YA and NE', *Pragmatics* 8/3:387-404.

Leech, Geoffrey N. (1977) 'Language and tact', *Linguistic Agency University of Trier (L.A.U.T.)* A/46.

------ (1980) *Explorations in Semantics and Pragmatics*, Amsterdam: John Benjamins.

------ (1981) 'Pragmatics and conversational rhetoric', in Herman Parret, M.Sbisà, J.Verschueren (eds) *Possibilities and limitations of pragmatics: Proceedings of the conference on pragmatics, Urbino, July 8-14, 1979*, Amsterdam: John Benjamins.

------ (1983) *Principles of pragmatics*, London/New York: Longman.

Macauley, Marcia (1996) 'Asking to ask: The strategic function of indirect requests for information in interviews', *Pragmatics* 6/4:491-509.

Mao, LuMing Robert (1994) 'Beyond politeness theory: "Face" revisited and renewed', *Journal of Pragmatics* 21:451-486.

Martín Rojo, Luisa (1994) 'The jargon of delinquents and the study of conversational dynamics', *Journal of Pragmatics* 21:243-289.

Matsumoto, Yoshiko (1988) 'Reexamination of the universality of face: Politeness phenomena in Japanese', *Journal of Pragmatics* 12:403-426.

------ (1989) 'Politeness and conversational universals: Observations from Japanese', *Multilingua* 8/2-3:207-221.

Meier, A.J. (1995) 'Passages of politeness', *Journal of Pragmatics* 24:381-392.

Mertz, Elisabeth (1993) 'Learning what to ask: Metapragmatic factors and methodological reification', in John A. Lucy *Reflexive language: Reported speech and metapragmatics*, Cambridge: Cambridge University Press.

Nakamura, Keiko (1996) 'The use of polite language by Japanese preschool children', in Dan Isaac Slobin, J.Gerhardt, A.Kyratzis, J.Guo (eds) *Social interaction, social context, and language: Essays in honor of Susan Ervin-Tripp*, Mahwah: Lawrence Erlbaum.

Neuendorf, Dagmar (1987) 'Indicating politeness: A study into historical aspects of complex behavioral strategies', in Kari Sajavaara (ed) *Discourse analysis: Openings*, University of Jyväskylä: Department of English.

Nippold, Marilyn A., L.B.Leonard, A.Anastopoulos (1982) 'Development in the use and understanding of polite forms in children', *Journal of Speech and Hearing Research* 25:193-202.

Nwoye, Onuigbo G. (1989) 'Linguistic politeness in Igbo', *Multilingua* 8/2-3:259-275.

Ochs, Elinor (1993) 'Constructing social identity: A language socialization perspective', *Research on Language and Social Interaction* 26/3:287-306.

O'Driscoll, Jim (1996) 'About face: A defence and elaboration of universal dualism', *Journal of Pragmatics* 25:1-32.

Okamoto, Shigeko (1995) 'Tasteless Japanese: Less "feminine" speech among Japanese women', in Kira Hall and Mary Bucholtz (eds) (1995) *Gender articulated: Language and the socially constructed self*, New York/London: Routledge.

------ (1998) 'The use and non-use of honorifics in sales talk in Kyoto and Osaka. Are they rude or friendly?', in Noriko Akatsuka, Hajime Hoji, Shoichi Iwasaki, Sung-Ock Sohn, Susan Strauss (eds) (1998) *Japanese/Korean linguistics*, Stanford: Center for the Study of Language and Information.

Olshtain, Elite (1989) 'Apologies across cultures', in Shoshana Blum-Kulka, J.House, G.Kasper (eds) *Cross-cultural pragmatics: Requests and apologies*, Norwood: Ablex.

Ortigue de Vaumorière, Pierre D' (1688) *L'art de plaire dans la conversation*, Paris.

Oxford Advanced Learner's Dictionary of Current English, 6th ed. (1989), Oxford: Oxford University Press.

Parsons, Talcott (1966) *Societies: Evolutionary and comparative perspectives*, Englewood Cliffs: Prentice Hall.

------ (1967) *Sociological theory and modern society*, New York: The Free Press.

------ (1968 [1937]) *The structure of social action*, New York: The Free Press.

------ (1968 [1951]) *The social system*, New York: The Free Press.

------ (1970) *Social structure and personality*, New York: The Free Press.

------ (1971) *The system of modern societies*, Englewood Cliffs: Prentice-Hall.

Pike, Kenneth L. [1954, 1955, 1960] (1967) *Language in relation to a unified theory of the structure of human behavior (2nd edition)*, The Hague: Mouton.

------ (1990) 'On the emics and etics of Pike and Harris', in Thomas N. Headland, K.L.Pike, M.Harris (eds) (1990) *Emics and etics: The insider/outsider debate*, London: Sage.

Rhodes, Richard A. (1989) 'We are going to go there: Positive politeness in Ojibwa', *Multilingua* 8/2-3:249-258.

Rickford, John R. (1986) 'The need for new approaches to social class analysis in sociolinguistics', *Language & Communication* 6/3:215-221.

Rosaldo, Michelle Z. (1982) 'The things we do with words: Ilongot speech acts and speech act theory in philosophy', *Language in Society* 11:203-237.

Sarangi, Srikant and Stefaan Slembrouck (1992) 'Non-cooperation in communication: A reassessment of Gricean pragmatics', *Journal of Pragmatics* 17:117-154.

Schiffrin, D. (1984) 'Jewish argument as sociability', *Language and Society* 13/3:311-335.

Searle, John (1969) *Speech acts*, Cambridge: Cambridge University Press.

Sell, Roger D. (1992) 'Literary texts and diachronic aspects of politeness', in Richard Watts, S.Ide, K.Ehlich (eds) *Politeness in language: Studies in its history, theory and practice*, Berlin: Mouton de Gruyter.

Shotter, John (1975) *Images of man in psychological research*, London: Methuen.

------ (1993) *Conversational realities: Constructing life through language*, London: Sage.

Sifianou, Maria (1992a) *Politeness phenomena in England and Greece: A cross-cultural perspective*, Oxford: Clarendon.

------ (1992b) 'The use of diminutives in expressing politeness: Modern Greek versus English', *Journal of Pragmatics* 17:155-173.

------ (1993) 'Off-record indirectness and the notion of imposition', *Multilingua* 12/1:69-79.

Smith-Hefner, Nancy J. (1988) 'Women and politeness: The Javanese example', *Language in Society* 17:535-554.

Snow, Catherine E., Rivka Y.Perlman, Jean Berko Gleason, Nahid Hooshyar (1990) 'Developmental perspectives on politeness: Sources of children's knowledge', *Journal of Pragmatics* 14:289-305.

Spencer-Oatey, Helen (1996) 'Reconsidering power and distance', *Journal of*

Pragmatics 26:1-24.

Stalpers, Judith (1992) 'Between matter-of-factness and politeness', in Richard Watts, S.Ide, K.Ehlich (eds) *Politeness in language: Studies in its history, theory and practice*, Berlin: Mouton de Gruyter.

Srivastava, R.N. and I.Pandit (1988) 'The pragmatic basis of syntactic structures and the politeness hierarchy in Hindi', *Journal of Pragmatics* 12:185-205.

Takahashi, Tomoko and L.M.Beebe (1993) 'Cross-linguistic influence in the speech act of correction', in Gabriele Kasper and S.Blum-Kulka (eds) *Interlanguage pragmatics*, New York, Oxford: Oxford University Press.

Taylor, Talbot J. and Deborah Cameron (1987) *Analysing conversation: Rules and units in the structure of talk*, Oxford: Pergamon.

Vanderbilt, Amy and L.Baldridge (1978) *The Amy Vanderbilt complete book of etiquette: A guide to contemporary living*, New York: Doubleday.

Verschueren, Jef (1981) 'The semantics of forgotten routines', in Florian Coulmas (ed) (1981) *Conversational routine: Explorations in standardized communication situations and prepatterned speech*, The Hague: Mouton.

------ and J.-O.Östman, J.Blommaert (eds) (1995) *Handbook of pragmatics: Manual*, Amsterdam/Philadelphia: John Benjamins.

------ and J.-O.Östman, J.Blommaert, C.Bulcaen (eds) (1996) *Handbook of pragmatics 1996*, Amsterdam/Philadelphia: John Benjamins.

Vollmer, Helmut J. and E.Olshtain (1989) 'The language of apologies in German', in Shoshana Blum-Kulka, J.House, G.Kasper (eds) *Cross-cultural pragmatics: Requests and apologies*, Norwood: Ablex.

Vygotsky, L.S. (1986) *Thought and language*, Edited and newly revised version of the original 1934 publication, Cambridge, Massachusetts: M.I.T. Press.

Walper, Sabine and R.Valtin (1992) 'Children's understanding of white lies', in Richard Watts, S.Ide, K.Ehlich (eds) *Politeness in language: Studies in its history, theory and practice*, Berlin: Mouton de Gruyter.

Watts, Richard (1989a) 'Relevance and relational work: Linguistic politeness as politic behavior', *Multilingua* 8/2-3:131-166.

------ (1989b) 'Taking the pitcher to the 'well': Native speakers' perception of their use of discourse markers in conversation', *Journal of Pragmatics* 13:203-237.

------ (1991) *Power in family discourse*, Berlin/New York: Mouton de Gruyter.

------ (1992a) 'Linguistic politeness and politic verbal behaviour: Reconsidering claims for universality', in Richard Watts, S.Ide, K.Ehlich (eds) *Politeness in language: Studies in its history, theory and practice*, Berlin: Mouton de Gruyter.

------ (1992b) 'Acquiring status in conversation: 'Male' and 'female' discourse strategies', *Journal of Pragmatics* 18:467-503.

------ and Sachiko Ide, Konrad Ehlich (1992a) 'Introduction', in Richard Watts, S.Ide, K.Ehlich (eds) *Politeness in language: Studies in its history, theory and practice*, Berlin: Mouton de Gruyter.

------ and Sachiko Ide, Konrad Ehlich (eds) (1992b) *Politeness in language: Studies in its history, theory and practice*, Berlin: Mouton de Gruyter.

Werkhofer, Konrad T. (1992) 'Traditional and modern views: the social constitution and the power of politeness', in Richard Watts, S.Ide, K.Ehlich (eds) *Politeness in language: Studies in its history, theory and practice*, Berlin: Mouton de Gruyter.

Wierzbicka, Anna (1985) 'Different cultures, different languages, different speech acts', *Journal of Pragmatics* 9:145-178.

Williams, Glyn (1992) *Sociolinguistics: A sociological critique*, London/New York: Routledge.

Wolfson, Nessa, T.Marmor, S.Jones (1989) 'Problems in the comparison of speech acts across cultures', in Shoshana Blum-Kulka, J.House, G.Kasper (eds) *Cross-cultural pragmatics: Requests and apologies*, Norwood: Ablex.

Wood, B.S., R.Gardner (1980) 'How children "get their way": Directives in communication', *Communication Education* 29:264-272.

Woolard, Kathryn A. (1985) 'Language variation and cultural hegemony: Toward an integration of sociolinguistic and social theory', *American Ethnologist* 12/4:738-748.

Young, Linda W.L. (1994) *Crosstalk and culture in Sino-American communication*, Cambridge: Cambridge University Press.

Yahya-Othman, Saida (1994) 'Covering one's social back: Politeness among the Swahili', *Text* 14/1:141-161.

Index

Made in the USA
Lexington, KY
26 January 2017